Designing Information Literacy Instruction

Designing Information Literacy Instruction

The Teaching Tripod Approach

JOAN R. KAPLOWITZ

ROWMAN & LITTLEFIELD
Lanham • Boulder • New York • Toronto • Plymouth, UK

Published by Rowman & Littlefield
4501 Forbes Boulevard, Suite 200, Lanham, Maryland 20706
www.rowman.com

10 Thornbury Road, Plymouth PL6 7PP, United Kingdom

British Library Cataloguing in Publication Information Available

Library of Congress Cataloging-in-Publication Data

Kaplowitz, Joan R.
  Designing information literacy instruction : the teaching tripod approach / Joan R. Kaplowitz.
     pages cm
  Includes bibliographical references and index.
  ISBN 978-0-8108-8584-4 (pbk. : alk. paper)—ISBN 978-0-8108-8585-1 (electronic)
  1. Information literacy—Study and teaching. 2. Curriculum planning. I. Title.
  ZA3075.K367 2014
  028.7071—dc23   2013051099

♾️™ The paper used in this publication meets the minimum requirements of American National Standard for Information Sciences—Permanence of Paper for Printed Library Materials, ANSI/NISO Z39.48-1992.

Printed in the United States of America

Dedication

This book is dedicated to all my information literacy instruction (ILI) colleagues who have so generously shared their knowledge, experiences, and expertise with me over the years. Thank you all for helping me become a better library instructor. I also dedicate this book to my children, Hillary and Greg, both of whom have chosen somewhat nontraditional career paths and have demonstrated the value of following one's own passions. I want to be just like them when I grow up.

After being a librarian and teacher for close to thirty years, I have now reached that wonderful point in my career where those with whom I have shared my expertise are now taking leadership roles in the profession. I take great pleasure in watching as they go on to shape future generations of instructional librarians. And so this book is also for all those librarians who not only dedicated themselves to educating their own users, but who have also chosen to share their ideas about effective information literacy instruction with their colleagues. And so we can be assured that the ILI beat goes on.

Contents

List of Figures and Tables

FIGURES

TABLES

Preface—or Why Should You Read This Book

I know what you are thinking. Not another book on information literacy instruction (ILI)! And you are wondering—given all the other things you have to do, why would you add reading this book to your "to-do" list? In other words, you are asking yourself, "What's in it for me?" So let me try to answer that question for you by sharing how I came to writing *Designing Information Literacy Instruction: The Teaching Tripod Approach.*

As is probably true for many of you, I had no formal training in teaching before entering the library profession—despite the fact that I had already obtained a doctorate in psychology and had previously taught on the college level for a few years after obtaining that degree. My doctorate meant I had a certain level of subject expertise, but it did not guarantee that I knew how to share that expertise with my students. I pretty much was making it up as I went along during those college teaching years.

However, my psychology background did instill in me a keen interest in teaching and learning, and this interest only grew more intense when I entered the library profession. It is probably why I dedicated much of my library career to ILI. Lacking formal teacher training, I made it my business (as many of you probably did as well) to educate myself about effective teaching through my readings and by attending relevant workshops and conferences—both within librarianship and in other relevant disciplines—most notably education, pedagogy, psychology, and teaching, as well as various aspects of instructional technology. My goal was to learn how to become the most effective teacher I could be.

As the years went by, I felt I had gotten a pretty good grounding in the art and craft of teaching. But I continued to feel as if I was missing some critical elements. I had always been a firm believer that careful planning was vital to creating "good" ILI, but it was not until my daughter Hillary began to pursue a career in instructional design (ID) that I came to realize what was missing from my own knowledge base. Here was an entire discipline dedicated to ensuring that instruction was effective and engaging. I knew I had to find out more about the field of ID.

As I began my explorations, I found a lot of common ground between the basic fundamentals of ID and what I had come to consider was important when developing my own ILI. ID's emphasis on starting with outcomes and looking at the interrelationships between outcomes, learning activities, and assessment particularly resonated with me. ID encourages us to "think before we teach." It endorses and promotes a systematic and methodical approach to planning for and developing instruction—all with the goal of improving instructional effectiveness. The more I read, the more I realized that I needed to formalize my somewhat casual approach to designing my instruction, and this lead to the development of the Teaching Tripod.

The Tripod formed the basis of my own instructional planning process during the latter part of my time as a "frontline" library instructor, and as well as for the development of the continuing education workshops I began to offer once I retired from my "day job." While I had included brief mentions of the ideas that underlie the Tripod approach to planning in my writings, when I taught my library school students over the years, I thought the time had come to put a more fully fleshed out version of these ideas down on paper, and so this book was born.

The format for the book is based on the one-shot workshops I have been offering and is intended to be a kind of "teach yourself" workbook. In order to accomplish that, I have laid out each chapter in the same way I would if I were teaching this material in person. So each chapter starts with some kind of hook or attention-getting (I hope) paragraph, followed by a series of questions to keep in mind as you read that particular chapter. These questions were my way of sharing the outcomes I set for each chapter. Next you will see a brief "sales pitch" paragraph that is intended to answer the "What's in it for me if I read this chapter?" question.

Each chapter is interspersed with worksheets intended to help you check for comprehension and review the information as you go, thus offering you the opportunity to actively engage with the material. And each chapter ends with a "What Stuck?" section—a reflection opportunity that asks you to review the material with an eye toward sharing what you have learned with your colleagues. So you can read the book to teach yourself about ID for ILI, and also use it as the basis for teaching others about the concepts and methods presented.

The book begins with a discussion of why instruction librarians should care about ID (chapter 1). Chapter 2 is an attempt to introduce the reader to the field of ID. It is, of course, just a brief glimpse into the history and theory of the field, but hopefully there is enough in there to help you get a feel for ID, learn some of the jargon, and introduce you to some major figures and landmarks in the development of the field. Chapter 3 offers a first look at the Teaching Tripod as a potentially useful way for instruction librarians to incorporate ID into their own practice. In a sense, the Tripod is directed at selecting the content and how you will go about sharing that content with your learners. However, before you can decide on what and how to teach, you must find out what your learners need to know as well as what is feasible in your environment. So chapter 4 addresses how to gather the necessary background information needed to help you make appropriate instructional decisions. In other words, chapter 4 discusses the concept of needs assessments.

The basic tenet of the Teaching Tripod approach is the interrelationship between expected learning outcomes (ELOs), learning activities, and assessments. These three elements comprise the heart of the Tripod and are discussed in chapters 5, 6, and 7, respectively. Once you have decided what you will be teaching and how you will be teaching it, one further task still remains—that is, how to present the material in a logical and coherent fashion that will support your learners' attainment of the ELOs you set for the instruction. Chapter 8, therefore, deals with various ways to sequence your instruction to create the most effective and engaging ILI.

But your ID does not end there. You still are faced with the task of getting your ILI to your learners. So chapter 9 deals with the issues related to marketing, implementation, logistics, and delivery. And finally, chapter 10 is my attempt to provide you with some kind of closure. It includes several worksheets and checklists that can be used as you plan your ILI in the future. The chapter ends with a challenge. In it I ask you to take a few minutes to reflect on the entire book and how you might use the material you have read in your own practice, and then complete one final "What Stuck?" exercise.

If the ideas presented in this book have intrigued you and you wish to find out more about the topics that have been discussed, please see the "Moving On" reading list in the appendix. The items on this list represent my explorations that led me to write *Designing Information Literacy Instruction: The Teaching Tripod Approach*. I have also included some of my previous works in which I began to develop some of the ideas presented here.

So that is why I wrote this book and why I hope you will consider reading it. As instruction librarians, we all endeavor to create instruction that enables our learners to deal appropriately with the massive amounts of information that bombards them at every turn. I believe that following the Teaching Tripod approach to ID for ILI can help you design the kind of engaging and effective instruction that will empower your learners to be thoughtful and responsible users and creators of information. Developing an information-literate society is one of the most fundamental aims of our profession. I hope you find this book helpful as you work toward that noble and laudable goal.

Acknowledgments

We who choose to write books need constant nurturing, support, and encouragement to allow us to survive (and remain sane) through the long, lonely road from idea to manuscript completion. My biggest booster, sounding board, colleague, and constructive critic as I worked my weary way through all my writing endeavors has been and continues to be my daughter, Hillary. Her unquenchable thirst for learning inspires me to challenge myself to learn new things, keep an open mind, and always be on the lookout for new experiences that will enhance my own skills, knowledge, and abilities. Hillary's instructional design expertise and input was invaluable as I began to explore this new-to-me field, and tried to develop a way to present the concepts associated with it to my instruction librarian colleagues. Her thoughtful and honest review of my ideas made this a much better book than it would have been if I had written it totally on my own.

I would also like to thank the members of my yoga community who offered unconditional love and encouragement as I developed the ideas for this book, put it together piece by piece by piece, and finally brought it into the light of day. Through it all they helped to keep me sound in mind, body, and spirit.

Finally a special shout-out to Aidan, Kieran, and Ronan, my wonderful feline companions who joined my household as I was just starting this writing project. They were with me every step of the way—monitoring my progress by sitting on my keyboard, purring at my feet, and generally helping to create a home where good things can happen. I am so glad my three boys picked me to be their kitty guardian.

1

Why Do I Need to Know about Instructional Design?

So much to know—so little time. Bad enough I had to learn how to teach on my own. Now you are asking me to add one more thing to the mix—instructional design. Why should I care?

If you are reading this book, you must be curious about how instructional design (ID) might help you in your information literacy instruction (ILI) endeavors. However, part of you is sighing, "Not another book about ILI. And if that is not bad enough, this one is asking me to learn one more complicated and complex topic. Why on earth would I want to do that? I already know what I want to teach about in my ILI sessions. Can't I just go do it?"

The biggest reason to care is that ID will help you become a better teacher. As a dedicated instruction librarian, you are already committed to providing ILI for your user population. But whether you are working alone or will be collaborating with other librarians or members of your community, the task of creating appropriate ILI for everyone is an overwhelming task. Furthermore, you often have very little lead time between an instructional request and the time you must provide the instruction. So you feel rushed and pressured and often have to create the instruction more or less on the fly.

But down deep you wonder if you are doing the best job you could be doing. You wonder if there might be a better way to plan, develop, create, and implement ILI in your environment. That is where ID comes in. This book will both introduce you the principles and practice of ID and offer you some pointers on how to incorporate ID into your ILI endeavors. Let's start with a discussion of how ID can help you reach your instructional goals and become a more effective provider of ILI.

QUESTIONS TO CONSIDER
➤ Why should ILI librarians care about ID?
➤ What will ID do to help instruction librarians reach and teach their learners?
➤ What is the relationship between ID and learner-centered teaching?
➤ How do changes in technology impact ILI and ID?

WHAT DOES INSTRUCTIONAL DESIGN HAVE TO OFFER?
You are not alone in thinking that learning about instructional design (ID) might be an unnecessary burden. Teachers at all levels—whether they are familiar with the principles, concepts, and theories of ID or not—often pay only minimal attention to ID when they are getting ready to teach, and they vary greatly about how much ID methodology they incorporate into their planning. At the extreme are those who just concentrate on content.

They decide what topics they will address, make brief notes about the concepts they will cover and the resources they will share, and then more or less wing it with their learners. But without giving more attention to the ID details, these offerings often end up being more along the lines of information sharing. Although important and potentially useful, information sharing may not be the best way for learners to gain the skills they need to address their information needs.

Most ILI librarians do some kind of preliminary planning—often concentrating their efforts on designing the demonstrations, activities, and exercises that will be included in the instruction. They might also give some thought to including ways to measure or assess what learners attained from the instruction. But more often than not, instruction librarians do not engage in any thoughtful and systematic development process. In neglecting to do so, they are shortchanging themselves and their learners (Bell and Shank 2007). Adopting an ID mind-set improves your ability to design effective, engaging, and efficient ILI. So how does ID supports our teaching roles, and align with the goals of ILI?

INFORMATION LITERACY INSTRUCTION IN TODAY'S WORLD

As an information literacy librarian, you are already fully committed to the idea that people in all walks of life need to be empowered to find the best, most trustworthy information in order to succeed in just about everything they do. Governments and educational leaders worldwide support the idea that we live in an information society—one in which information has replaced material goods as the chief factor in socioeconomics (Grassian and Kaplowitz 2009). Furthermore, new information is being generated every minute of every day. So people must not only be able to deal with the here and now, but they also must be prepared to deal with whatever is on the horizon (Farmer 2011). Adopting a lifelong learning mind-set has never been more important than it is today.

We are all faced with the need to make multiple decisions on a daily basis—whether it is about what product to buy, where to live, health care options, or which candidates to vote for in an upcoming election. All these decisions require that we have the ability to find information to support our choices. And that is where ILI enters the picture. From school to public to academic to special libraries, librarians are working hard to provide instruction that prepares the members of their communities to find the best information available in order to successfully navigate a highly complex and information-dependent world (Goodman 2009; Grassian and Kaplowitz 2009).

However, while instruction librarians endorse the idea of providing ILI, there is an enormous amount of material that can be included in any ILI endeavor. Not only are there concepts to share and resources to highlight, today's learners need to be encouraged to examine and think critically about the information they find, and the social, economic, and political context for the production and consumption of information (Goodman 2009; Luke and Kapitzke 1999; Simmons 2005), as well as the ethical use of the information they gather (ALA Presidential Committee on Information Literacy 1998, 1989). With this vast amount of potential content, and the often-limited contact you might have with your learners (in person or online), you need to be even more careful that you are making the best pedagogical decisions you can. Adopting an ID approach can help you make these decisions and create the most effective and efficient instruction possible. Let's take a quick look at how ID relates to teaching in general.

INSTRUCTIONAL DESIGN—THE FOUNDATION OF EFFECTIVE TEACHING

Chapter 2 will discuss the principles of ID in more detail, but the overall value of ID is that it encourages a thoughtful and systematic approach to teaching (Branch and Merrill 2012; Morrison et al. 2011). Pedagogical decisions are based on sound educational and psychological theories that have been vetted and tested in practice (Bell and Shank 2007). ID asks instructors to take a step back before jumping into the development process, to take the time to really get to know who their learners are and to identify the information needs of that population. It promotes the creation of expected learning outcomes (ELOs) based on this knowledge, and ties these outcomes to both instructional activities and teaching strategies. And finally, ID suggests that the instruction must be assessed in some manner in order to determine how well learners have attained the ELOs set for the instruction (Chao, Saj, and Tessier 2006; Grassian and Kaplowitz 2009; Miller and Bratton 1988).

ID has been around for a long time. However, the growth of technology and the increased reliance on distance education has renewed interest in this area. While ID is important regardless of the delivery mode (face-to-face, online, or blended), the online environment seems to require a bit more thoughtful planning. While teachers in the face-to-face situation can (and often do) make on-the-spot changes based on feedback from their students, online learning environments are often set up in advance and are less subject to instantaneous modification. That is not to say that online instruction is set in stone. If anything, online resources can often be updated quickly and easily. However, the distance aspects of online instruction can mean that learners and teachers are not in the same place and/or interacting with the material at the same time (asynchronous), and so a certain immediacy and responsiveness to learners' questions and concerns can be lost (Kaplowitz 2012). Even if the instruction is synchronous with instructor and learners interacting in real time, changes to the online material suffer a time delay as the instructor must make the changes and then upload them to the site. So ironically, distance education has encouraged teachers to spend more time planning their instruction in advance, and to rely more heavily on ID ideas.

As more and more teachers have become involved in online instruction and conversant with the ID process, they have also come to realize the benefits of adopting this more systematic approach for their face-to-face instruction as well. In short, teachers have found that ID leads to better-organized and effective instruction regardless of the delivery mode—face-to-face, online, or blended.

WHY LIBRARIANS SHOULD LEARN ABOUT INSTRUCTIONAL DESIGN

Although the vast majority of librarians today seem to be involved in some aspect of ILI, many of us have not had the benefit of any kind of formal training. If you are anything like me, you learned a lot of your teaching skills as you went along—from mentors, workshops, books, articles and websites, conferences, and just by observing other instructional librarians. Some of you might have been fortunate enough to attend a library program that included a course in ILI. But those courses are not offered in all programs, and when they are, they are often electives available maybe once a year or once every other year. So if you do the math, you will see that a very small percentage of librarians will enter the profession having had this educational experience.

And even if you were among the lucky few, these courses are generally only one term long. So the ILI course instructor has anywhere from ten to maybe fifteen weeks to address a wide range of topics including what is ILI and where did it come from, the pedagogical and psychological theory that underlies effective teaching, teaching methods, assessment, and so forth. With all that to cover it is not surprising that the planning or the ID process does not get as much attention as one would like. When I teach my ILI courses, I spend part of one class meeting talking about ID concepts such as needs assessment, defining ELOs, designing and developing instruction and materials, delivery, and assessment. So students get a quick glimpse into the ID process and are then encouraged to continue to learn more about it (as well as other ILI topics) as they progress in their careers. The net result is that whether you have taken an ILI course or not, much of what you know about ID (and teaching in general) is probably self-taught. And though you may have acquired bits and pieces that assist you in improving your instruction, you may not have experienced the big ID picture.

Because of this less-than-thorough ID grounding, when instruction librarians do their planning they often tend to focus on some aspect of ID—outcomes, teaching methods, types of activities, assessment techniques—and may even become very proficient at that aspect. But in taking this segmented approach, these librarians can miss the ways that all these aspects interrelate and affect each other. ID allows anyone who is engaged in teaching to put the pieces together in a systematic way in order to provide the best educational experience they can for their learners.

As a first step in your journey to learning about ID, you need to think about how much (or little) ID principles you already use when you are designing your ILI. So what do you do when you are getting ready to teach? What preliminary steps do you regularly go through as you plan your instructional endeavors? Take a moment to do a little self-reflection and then complete the following rating scale in figure 1.1. Be as honest with yourself as possible. Reflecting on your own process may help you discover steps in the ID process you might be neglecting and that you might wish to explore more deeply.

LIBRARIANS AS TEACHERS

Reflecting on your current process is a good place to begin an exploration of ID as it relates to ILI. The importance of teaching in most librarians' working lives is clearly reflected by the interest in ILI being taken by our own professional associations. Competency standards developed by associations representing libraries of all types further support the centrality of our teaching roles. ALA's (American Library Association) 2009 list of core competencies include several teaching-related elements as does those of the Association of Library Service to Children and the Young Adult Library Services Association directed at librarians who work in a public library setting (American Library Association 2009; Association of Library Service to Children 2009; Young Adult Library Services Association 2010). ACRL's Standards (Association of College and Research Libraries 2007) address the teaching of academic librarians listing forty-one core proficiencies for instruction librarians and twenty-eight additional proficiencies for coordinators. Librarians who work in school library settings are expected to have a firm grasp of teaching and learning and to be able to integrate information literacy concepts into the curriculum (National Board for Professional Teaching Standards 2001). And those who work in special library settings are also expected to help their clients attain the capabilities to integrate and apply information in their work (Special Library Association 2003).

Clearly, teaching is viewed as a professional responsibility regardless of where we work. In short, teaching matters. Whether we are interacting with the members of our communities over a reference desk, meeting with them one-on-one in private consultation appointments, running one-shot workshops, or teaching more formal classes and courses, there is no denying our teaching role. And being dedicated professionals, we want to do the best job we can for our learners. So developing an ID mind-set just makes good sense. Although reference desk interactions and consultations are valuable ways to assist learners in the short term, they are not enough to prepare people to become lifelong learners (Farmer 2011). Our instructional efforts need to be carefully and thoughtfully planned in order to accomplish this goal. Understanding basic ID principles helps ensure that our efforts are purposeful, meet the needs of our learners, are engaging and well organized, are delivered effectively, and are continually reviewed, assessed, and improved. It provides us with a framework and a structure for our instructional planning (Goodman 2009; Morrison et al. 2011). We are encouraged to teach intentionally, based on a thorough understanding of our audience and learners' needs. Building on this knowledge, we identify the knowledge gaps—the discrepancy between what our learners currently know and what they need to know (Goodman 2009). And as a result, we avoid the temptation to include everything about ILI in our instruction, but instead concentrate on the "more is less" rule and focus on just those things that will empower our learners and help them address their specific information needs (Grassian and Kaplowitz 2009; Kaplowitz 2012; Miller and Bratton 1988).

ID helps us make the most of our instructional efforts. It helps us create independent, self-sufficient, lifelong learners. ID instills an intentionality into our teaching, and encourages an attitude of thoughtfulness, adaptability,

FIGURE 1.1

How Do You Prepare for Instruction?

Think about what you typically do when you are planning your ILI endeavors. What are some of things you generally do, and what are some of the things you don't do very often? On a scale of 1 to 5 with 5 being "always" and 1 being "never," rate the following statements about your planning process.

When I am developing my ILI, I . . .

Find out as much about my learner as possible.	1	2	3	4	5
Identify gaps between what they know and what they need to know.	1	2	3	4	5
Write observable and measurable learner-centered ELOs.	1	2	3	4	5
Select methods that will best support the attainment of the ELOs set.	1	2	3	4	5
Develop at least one activity/exercise for each ELO.	1	2	3	4	5
Include formal or informal assessment for each ELO.	1	2	3	4	5

flexibility, reflection, and continuous improvement (Booth 2011). So ID definitely relates to our teaching role. Now let's turn to how advances in technology have affected both ID and ILI.

INSTRUCTIONAL DESIGN, INFORMATION LITERACY INSTRUCTION, AND TECHNOLOGY

There is no denying that technology has had a major impact on just about every aspect of our daily lives, and ILI is no exception. Changes in technology have affected how we locate and access information, how we share it, and how we interact with it in the world at large. Furthermore, new technologies have increased our ability to reach our learners in innovative and exciting ways. As mentioned above, technology has also influenced how educators think about ID. In fact, ID and technology are often viewed as very much intertwined. As technology advanced, so too did interest in ID. Educators, overwhelmed by the instructional choices offered by technology, turned to ID as a way to make decisions about which technologies to use in support of their teaching.

However, ID goes beyond merely dealing with technology. Technology is just one aspect of the bigger picture, and should be viewed as a tool, not a necessity. In other words, just as we select teaching methods based on their efficacy in helping our learners attain ELOs, we evaluate technology in terms of whether or not it supports our instructional effort. We don't become so enamored of a particular technology that we feel we have to try and shoe-horn it into our instruction. We start with our ELOs and look for the best methods and modes to create the most effective learning situation possible—whether it uses technology or not (Kaplowitz 2012).

Admittedly, as technology becomes more and more integral to our lives, many of our learners expect us to integrate technology into our libraries and into our instruction (Campbell and Oblinger 2007; Farmer 2011). But we must be cautious in our adoption of new technology as a means of both outreach and instruction. When considering the potential value of a new technology, we must ask ourselves these questions:

➢ Is this technology the best way to address the content?
➢ Will the technology be around for a while or is it just a passing fad?
➢ How hard is it to learn how to use this technology—both from the instructor and the learners' perspective?
➢ What are the software and hardware requirements for this technology?
➢ Will learners have the necessary equipment to access material based on this technology?
➢ What if any accessibility issues exist regarding the use of this technology for people with special needs and/or disabilities?

Once again, concentrating on ID helps us restrain ourselves and make thoughtful and appropriate decisions. If we follow ID mandates and start with our learners and their needs, look at the instruction from their perspective, and focus on creating instruction that helps our learners attain ELOs, we will make the best decisions we can both for our learners and ourselves (Grassian and Kaplowitz 2009; Goodman 2009; Kaplowitz 2012). That brings us to the concept of learner-centered teaching.

INSTRUCTIONAL DESIGN AND LEARNER-CENTERED TEACHING

Learner-centered teaching (LCT) has gained popularity in all educational settings. Based on sound research from education, psychology, and the neurosciences, it helps tie learning theory to teaching practice in order to enhance instructional effectiveness that focus on the learner and his or her actual information needs (Bransford et al. 2006; Kaplowitz 2012). Because ID also focuses on the learner, it helps us achieve a more LCT approach in our practice (Morrison et al. 2011).

Being learner centered means changing our teaching role from leader to facilitator. We abandon the idea of being the "sage on the stage" and become the "guide on the side" (King 1993). Rather than starting with what we think is important content to address, we examine what learners need to know. And we create a learning environment in which they can actively work with the material. The LCT approach is very much activities driven and as such requires even more thoughtful planning than ever before. While preparing a teacher-centered lecture on a subject does take some thought and organization, lecturing creates a much more structured type of instruction. Delivering a lecture can be fairly straightforward since it is very much under instructor control. Adopting a learner-centered perspective requires that we are willing to allow more chaos into our teaching. Much of the learning that goes on is in the hands of the learners as they interact with the content and each other, often engaging in problem-solving activities in which learners can learn about and construct their own personal meaning of the topics being addressed. Learner-centered instructional settings, therefore, are a bit more free form than lecture-based types, with specific groups of learners interacting with the material in individual and often unique ways (Doyle 2011; Kaplowitz 2012; McCombs and Miller 2007).

However, this more open-structure type of teaching requires very careful planning. So following an ID mind-set becomes even more important to the learner-centered teacher. Each activity must be weighed for its "bang for the buck" quotient. Since learner-centered activities often tend to take more time than lecturing on the topic, instructors must consider if the time spent is worthwhile in terms of ELOs. Does the activity support the attainment of one or more ELOs? If so, then the extra time might be worth it given that learner-centered approaches have been shown to enhance retention, transfer of learning, motivation, and the creation of a lifelong learning mind-set (Kaplowitz 2012, Weimer 2002). Learner-centered teachers benefit greatly from following ID principles and practices. ID helps the learner-centered teacher to focus on what matters—the creation of an effective, engaging, and valuable instructional experience.

Adhering to ID principles also helps us address diversity issues in our ILI. Our instruction must be both culturally responsive and sensitive to accessibility needs. ID, with its focus on knowing our learners, keeps us honest on both fronts. When we take the time to gather relevant data about our learners, we become more familiar with their values, backgrounds, and educational experiences, as well as any accessibility issues that they might have (Cifuentes and Ozel 2006; Goodman 2009; Pliner and Johnson 2004). Although originally focused on technology issues, the principles of Universal Design for Learning (UDL) are an excellent resource to help us design our ILI so it meets the needs of all learners (CAST 2011). UDL's three guiding principles (providing multiple means of representation, action and expression, and engagement) line up nicely with the LCT approach to ILI. If we follow these ideas, we will ensure that our ILI materials are presented in multiple modes to accommodate the various ways that people perceive and process information—both in terms of modalities and providing alternatives for those with sensory or learning disabilities. It also means using language that is understandable and appropriate for the audience, and offering learners options, whenever possible, for how they will interact with the material to be learned (Kaplowitz 2012).

Figure 1.1 asked you to reflect on your own practice in terms of how often you include various steps in the ID process. To deepen that reflection, please complete the worksheet in figure 1.2 and describe how you address the various elements in the ID process.

FIGURE 1.2

What's Your Process?

Chapter 2 will introduce you to a variety of ID models in more detail. To help you reflect on your own practice as it relates to ID, here are some elements that are generally included in most ID models:

➢ Gathering data about your learners
➢ Determining what learners need to be able to do to address their information needs
➢ Developing appropriate instructional endeavors
➢ Implementing instruction
➢ Determining the effectiveness of the instructional endeavors (i.e., assessing what learners gained from the instruction)

Think about how you personally get ready to teach, and complete the following worksheet.

1. How do you find out about your learners?

2. What are some of the things you want to know about your learners?

3. How do you decide what you will include in the instruction?

4. What factors do you take into account when you organize your instruction?

5. How do you select the methods, modes, activities, and/or exercises you include in the instruction?

6. How do you determine what your learners have attained from the instruction?

WRAP-UP

So why should you care about ID? You should care because your goal is to empower your learners. And you want to be equipped to do this in the best possible way. To do so you need to be methodical, systematic, and thoughtful in your instructional planning. You would not embark on a journey or cook a meal without some kind of plan or idea of the end result. So you should not set foot into a classroom or create online instruction without doing some preparation. ID gives you the tools to be organized as you plan your ILI, and so helps you to develop the best, most effective and efficient ways to reach and teach your learners.

Hopefully I have won you over or at least intrigued you enough to want to know more about ID. Chapter 2 will give you a general overview of the field of ID, as well as introduce you to some ILI-focused ID ideas. While the chapter will not go into great depth, it should provide you with enough background to be able to pursue more on your own should you wish to do so. Furthermore, it will equip you to "talk the talk" with ID professionals with whom you might wish to collaborate as you design your instruction. But before you go on to the next chapter, take a few minutes to wrap up this chapter by taking the following comprehension check self-test.

WHAT STUCK?

You want to share the idea of ID for ILI with your fellow instruction librarians. So you come up with the idea of a continuing education workshop on the topic. With their busy schedules and heavy workload, you first need to sell them on the idea that spending several hours learning about ID will be worth their while. Complete the worksheet in figure 1.3 to help you come up with ideas for "marketing" this workshop to your ILI librarian colleagues.

FIGURE 1.3

Planning My Sales Pitch

You really want your ILI librarian colleagues to buy into the idea of ID for ILI. So you decide to develop a continuing education workshop on the topic. But first you need to get them there. Create a marketing flyer, poster, or brief presentation that includes the following:

➢   Why ILI librarians should care about ID.

➢   How ID supports ILI standards.

➢   How ID will help them create more effective ILI and support them in their efforts to empower their learners in today's information dependent and technologically complex world.

REFERENCES

ALA Presidential Committee on Information Literacy. 1989. *Final Report*. Chicago: American Library Association.

———. 1998. *A Progress Report on Information Literacy: An Update on the American Library Association Presidential Committee on Information Literacy: Final Report*. Chicago: American Library Association.

American Library Association. 2009. "Core Competencies of Librarianship." American Library Association. Accessed June 15, 2012. http://www.ala.org/educationcareers/careers/corecomp.

Association of College and Research Libraries. 2007. "Standards for Proficiencies for Instruction Librarians and Coordinators: A Practical Guide." American Library Association. Accessed June 15, 2012. http://www.ala.org/acrl/standards/profstandards.

Association of Library Service to Children. 2009. "Competencies for Librarians Serving Children in Public Libraries." American Library Association. Accessed June 15, 2012. http://www.ala.org/alsc/edcareeers/alsccorecomps.

Bell, Stephen, and John D. Shank. 2007. *Academic Librarianship by Design*. Chicago: American Library Association.

Booth, Char. 2011. *Reflective Teaching, Effective Learning*. Chicago: American Library Association.

Branch, Robert M., and M. David Merrill. 2012. "Characteristics of Instructional Design Models." In *Trends and Issues in Instructional Design and Technology*, edited by Robert A. Reiser and John V. Dempsey, 8–16. Boston: Pearson.

Bransford, John D., Reed Stevens, Dan Schwartz, Andy Meltzoff, Roy Pea, Jeremey Roscelle, Nancy Vye, Phillip Bell, Brigid Barron, Byron Reeves, and Nora Sabelli. 2006. "Learning Theories and Education: Toward a Decade of Synergy." In *Handbook of Educational Psychology*, edited by Patricia A. Alexander and Philip H. Winne, 209–44. Mahwah, NJ: Erlbaum.

Campbell, John, and Diana Oblinger. 2007. "Top-Ten Teaching and Learning Issues." *Educause Quarterly* 30 (3).

CAST. 2011. "Universal Design for Learning Guidelines—Version 2.0." National Center on Universal Design for Learning. Accessed May 29. http://www.udlcenter.org/aboutudl/udlguidelines.

Chao, Tracy, Tami Saj, and Felicity Tessier. 2006. "Establishing a Quality Review for Online Courses." *Educause Quarterly* 3: 32–39.

Cifuentes, Lauren, and Serkan Ozel. 2006. "Resources for Attending to the Needs of Multicultural Learners." *Knowledge Quest* 35 (2): 14–21.

Doyle, Terry. 2011. *Learner-Centered Teaching: Putting the Research into Practice*. Sterling, VA: Stylus.

Farmer, Lesley S. J. 2011. *Instructional Design for Librarians and Information Professionals*. New York: Neal-Schuman.

Goodman, Valeda Dent. 2009. *Keeping the User in Mind: Instructional Design and the Modern Library*. Oxford: Chandos.

Grassian, Esther, and Joan Kaplowitz. 2009. *Information Literacy Instruction: Theory and Practice*. 2nd ed. New York: Neal-Schuman.

Kaplowitz, Joan R. 2012. *Transforming Your Information Literacy Instruction Using Learner-Centered Teaching*. New York: Neal-Schuman.

King, Alison. 1993. "From Sage on the Stage to Guide on the Side." *College Teaching* 41 (1): 30–35.

Luke, Allan, and Cushla Kapitzke. 1999. "Literacy and Libraries: Archives and Cybraries." *Pedagogy, Culture and Society* 7 (3): 467–91.

McCombs, Barbara L., and Lynda Miller. 2007. *Learner-Centered Classroom Practices and Assessments: Maximizing Student Motivation, Learning, and Achievement.* Thousand Oaks, CA: Corwin.

Miller, Marian I., and Barry D. Bratton. 1988. "Instructional Design: Increasing the Effectiveness of Bibliographic Instruction." *College and Research Libraries* 49 (6): 545–49.

Morrison, Gary R., Steven M. Ross, Howard K. Kalman, and Jerrold E. Kemp. 2011. *Designing Effective Instruction.* 6th ed. Hoboken, NJ: Wiley.

National Board for Professional Teaching Standards. 2001. *Library Media Standards.* Arlington, VA: National Board for Professional Teaching Standards.

Pliner, Susan, and Julia Johnson. 2004. "Historical, Theoretical, and Foundational Principles of Universal Design in Higher Education." *Equity and Excellence in Education* 37: 105–13.

Simmons, Michelle. 2005. "Librarians as Disciplinary Discourse Mediators: Using Genre Theory to Move toward Critical Information Literacy." *Portal: Libraries and the Academy* 5 (3): 297–311.

Special Library Association. 2003. *Competencies for Information Professionals.* Alexandria, VA: Special Libraries Association.

Weimer, Mary Ellen. 2002. *Learner-Centered Teaching: Five Key Changes to Practice.* San Francisco: Jossey-Bass.

Young Adult Library Services Association. 2010. *Young Adults Deserve the Best.* Chicago: American Library Association.

2

What Do I Need to Know about Instructional Design?

OK. You have convinced me that using instructional design (ID) practices will help me create more effective information literacy instruction (ILI). But I really don't want to become an expert in ID. I just want to know enough to apply it to my teaching. So why do I need to read about the history of ID and the various ID approaches that have evolved over time?

You may be tempted to skip this background chapter and move on to the step-by-step descriptions of the Teaching Tripod ID approach for ILI that comprise the rest of this book. After all, you really just want to know "how to do it" in regard to ID for ILI. However, I urge you to resist that temptation and take a look at where ID came from, what has influenced it over the years, and how ID relates to teaching in general and ILI in particular.

ID has a rich and fascinating history, which is in many ways similar to the history of ILI. Both fields have grown immensely over the last forty to fifty years and have been significantly influenced by various psychological learning theories, by theories of instruction that have grown out of those learning theories, by changes in technology, and by the increased interest in providing online and distance educational opportunities.

Understanding where ID ideas and principles originated will help you integrate these concepts into your teaching practices. Obviously this chapter can only give you a glimpse into this large and complex field. My goal for the chapter is to provide you with enough of an overview of the field so you will be able to understand why ID developed as a field, and what parts of that field may be relevant to your ILI. In addition, I hope this foray into ID will provide a sufficient foundation in the basic vocabulary and concepts, as well as the names of important theories and people in the field to assist you if you choose to pursue ID in more depth and detail later on. Furthermore, instructional designers themselves are a valuable resource for you. If you are fortunate enough to have access to these excellent and knowledgeable professionals, this chapter will help you be able to "talk the talk" with them when you collaborate on ILI design and development.

QUESTIONS TO CONSIDER
- ➤ What are the basic characteristics of ID?
- ➤ Where did ID come from?
- ➤ What are some of the major ID models?
- ➤ What are some elements common to most ID models?
- ➤ What ID models have been developed specifically for ILI?
- ➤ How can I apply ID to my ILI practice?

SO WHAT IS INSTRUCTIONAL DESIGN ANYWAY?

The goal of ID is to increase the effectiveness of instruction by applying principles of research-based learning theory. It is about focusing on the needs of the learner and creating instruction that has a practical impact on the situation in question. Instruction developed following ID principles is more than just information sharing. Well-designed instruction results in learners being able to apply new skills and knowledge (Reiser 2012a). ID begins with knowing your learners and identifying any learning gaps that may exist—that is, highlighting the difference between existing knowledge and abilities, and the skills and subject matter learners need in order to succeed. In many ways, the focus of ID is problem solving—the problems in question being:

1. What do learners need to know and/or be able to do?
2. How can I create opportunities for my learners to acquire the requisite skills, knowledge, and abilities (Bell and Shank 2007; Goodman 2009; Morrison et al. 2011)?

ID is both thoughtful and systematic. It is primarily about identifying the instructional problem and then looking for the best solutions to that problem. So designers look beyond specific methods and/or technology to select the best approach to address the situation. In fact sometimes, the best solution may not be instruction at all (Bell 2008; Morrison et al. 2011; Reiser 2012a). Instruction is just one of many options. For example, changes in procedures, business practices, and/or modes of communication may be recommended as ways to deal with the problem. Creating handouts, updating signage, and/or online help screens are also possible ways to address the situation under review. ID utilizes what we know about learning from many fields—education, psychology, and instructional technology—to formulate these solutions. The instructional designer, therefore, takes theoretical principles and puts them into practice (Booth 2011; Goodman 2009; Morrison et al. 2011).

Instruction librarians teaching from the learner-centered perspective should find a lot that is appealing about ID. The goal of both ID and learner-centered teaching (LCT) is to improve learning. Success is measured in terms of the effect instruction has on learners' skills, abilities, and knowledge. While traditional teacher-centered approaches tend to start with content—"What should I include in this instruction?"—ID and LCT look for factors that could influence learning outcomes and include ways to measure if those outcomes have been achieved (Booth 2011; Miller and Bratton 1988; Morrison et al. 2011).

Furthermore, starting with the learner and his or her learning needs ensures that instruction is appropriate for the audience for which it is being designed. Although a basic tenet of ID is that it is systematic, that does not mean ID needs to be overly proscriptive. While many people criticize ID for being inflexible, adhering to ID principles does not mean rigidly or mindlessly following a specific sequence of steps or stages. ID can be and often is a reflective and iterative process. It encourages us to analyze how our instructional interventions and materials are actually used and experienced (Booth 2011; Morrison et al. 2011; Reiser 2012a) and to improve our instruction as needed. As such, ID is a way to create effective and targeted instruction that addresses the learners' needs and the identified content, and takes advantage of subject matter experts and/or instructors' expertise, so that instruction is delivered in a creative and engaging fashion.

Another way to look at the systematic nature of ID is that it helps us to align learners' needs, learning outcomes, subject content, teaching methods, and instructional assessment in such a way that they are all working toward the common goal of learner success. The various elements are interrelated, working together in a systematic way, so that changes in any element may, and often does lead to the need to modify other elements (Farmer 2011, Miller and Bratton 1988; Smith and Ragan 2005). While the various models that will be discussed later in this chapter do have specific steps or stages, there is nothing to prevent you from retracing your steps and returning to a previously completed step if and when new information arises. So for example, if more information is discovered about your learners after you have completed the learner analysis stage, you may wish to revisit and rethink the outcomes you have identified, and/or the methods you have chosen to deliver the instruction. At the very least, you should always be looking at completed instruction to gauge how effective it was, and to identify places where changes may increase the effectiveness in the future.

By creating instruction based on what is known about the learner, the designer ensures that the instructional content focuses on what is important for the learner to know and be able to do to solve the identified instructional problem. By eliminating extraneous material the resultant instruction is not only more effective, it is often more efficient and cost-effective as well (Morrison et al. 2011). Instruction designed in this fashion tends to be less prone to the bandwagon effect—that is, being enticed by a particular new teaching method or instructional technology and trying to shoehorn that approach into the instruction.

Although ID is often associated with instructional technology, the two are not synonymous. The instructional designer views technology as just another possible tool for the delivery of effective instruction. Advances in instructional technology have vastly increased our teaching arsenal. But the ID mantra remains the same. Start with the learner and the instructional problem and select the best approaches (technological or not) to help the learner attain the learning outcomes you have identified to solve that problem. So that is a brief overview of how ID professionals view their field. But before you go on to read about the field's historical roots and some of the more prominent ID models, it might be a good idea for you to consider what you think ID actually is. Take a moment to decide how you would define ID for yourself. Then complete the worksheet in figure 2.1.

WHERE DID INSTRUCTIONAL DESIGN COME FROM?

Hopefully you have been able to use that brief overview to begin formulating your own definition of ID. As we begin to examine the roots of ID, it is important to note that one of ID's main tenets is that it utilizes what is known about how people learn based on research being done in education, psychology, and related fields. So let's take a look at how those theories and the research behind them have influenced the growth of the ID field.

ID is often said to have its origins in the WWII era as the need arose to train large numbers of people quickly and effectively—both in the military and in industry. These early ID approaches drew heavily on the cognitive, educational, and behavioral psychological principles that were favored at the time. The 1950s and 1960s saw the rise in prominence of such psychologists as B. F. Skinner and Benjamin Bloom, and ID models developed in these decades relied heavily on principles supported by these theorists, for example, behavioral objectives, formative evaluation, and criterion-referenced testing, and were very much focused on what the instructor did to teach the learner (Goodman 2009; Reiser 2012a; Wilson 2012). That is, they were extremely teacher-centric.

Two very influential texts were published during these two decades. Bloom's *Taxonomy of Educational Objectives* (1956) offered educators a hierarchy of cognitive objectives arranged from concrete to abstract. Each level (knowledge, comprehension, application, analysis, synthesis, and evaluation) is described along with suggestions on how to write objectives for each. Bloom's work continues to be influential and was revised in 2001. The levels in this later version are known as remembering, understanding, applying, analyzing, evaluating, and creating, and so include the idea of knowledge creation as an important component of knowledge comprehension (Anderson and Krathwohl 2001). Bloom's work had an enormous effect on both education and ID, as did the publication of Robert Mager's *Preparing Objectives for Programmed Instruction* (1962). Mager's work advised educators to write instructional objectives that included not only a description of desired learner behaviors but also the conditions under which these behaviors are to be performed and the criteria with which to judge learner success in attaining these objectives—elements that are still considered important parts of writing objectives to to this day (Goodman 2009, Reiser 2012b).

FIGURE 2.1

My Personal Definition of ID

Your colleagues have noticed that you have been spending some of your time and energy learning about instructional design (ID). They are curious about what has drawn you to this area and wonder what you mean when you use the phrase "ID." Use the following worksheet to help you formulate your answer to your colleagues' question, "What is ID?"

➤ Think about what you know so far about ID and come up with a brief definition of ID that emphasized what you find most relevant about the field.

  ○ My definition of ID is:

➤ Now highlight three to five key elements that seem to underlie how those in the field view ID. The first one has already been filled in for you.

  ○ ID is a systematic approach to developing instruction.

➤ Next, list a few ways you think ID might help you enhance your ILI.

Psychological learning theories of the 1980s shifted away from the purely behavioral approach, moving into a more cognitive outlook. The emphasis here was how people process and store information, and the ID models formulated in this decade mirrored this change in viewpoint. The advent of a constructivist approach to learning in the 1990s with its emphasis on authentic practice and community participation moved ID approaches away from stressing the acquisition of knowledge and toward the aim of empowering learners with new skills and abilities. It was no longer enough to tell learners what you wanted them to know. Instructors were encouraged to incorporate opportunities for learners to show that they could use that information appropriately to solve real problems (Goodman 2009). Currently advances in technology, especially in terms of web-based instruction and educational games, offered designers new opportunities to create engaging and participatory instruction (Reiser 2012b, Wilson 2012). We will return to a discussion of the impact of technology later in this chapter.

While psychological learning theories greatly influenced the evolution of ID, so too did developments in the field of instructional theory. Robert Gagne's work, starting with his *Conditions of Learning and the Theory of Instruction* (1965), was and continues to be highly influential in the ID field. Gagne refined and expanded his instructional theory over the years and in 1992 published *Principles of Instructional Design* which is now in its fifth edition (Gagne 1992; Gagne et al. 2004). Gagne's views, as expressed in his *Principles*, include the idea that ID should focus on the learner, and that it should be based on knowledge of how people learn (Driscoll 2012; Gagne et al. 2004; Goodman 2009). To Gagne, the essential parts of teaching are as follows:

➢ How we present knowledge or demonstrate a skill to learners;
➢ The practice opportunities (with feedback) we offer to our learners; and
➢ The guidance we provide to our learners along the way.

Furthermore, Gagne posited what he called the nine events of instruction, which were meant to assist educators in organizing their instructional offerings (Driscoll 2012; Gagne et al. 2004; Walster 1995). These events are intended to inform the designer/instructor as he or she organizes the actual delivery of the instruction and include both affective and cognitive components.

1. Gain attention
   Start with something that will gain learners' interest such as a thought-provoking quote, a video that illustrates the points to come, a common problem that they might need to solve, or some intriguing questions.
2. Describe the instructional goal
   Let students know what they will gain from this instruction. Tell them "what's in it for them."
3. Stimulate recall of prior knowledge
   Help learners connect what they already know to what will be learned in this instruction. Provide them with a framework for understanding the new material.
4. Present the material to be learned
   Regardless of delivery format (text, lecture, graphics, media, etc.), chunk the information into easily digestible segments to avoid overload and to promote recall.
5. Provide guidance for learning
   Supply appropriate scaffolding as needed to promote learning.
6. Elicit performance (practice)
   Give learners the opportunity to practice newly acquired knowledge/skills and to apply what they have just learned.

7. Provide informative feedback

   Let learners know what the correct response is, where they went wrong, how to successfully respond, and how to get help with performing the task.

8. Assess task performance

   Give score or grade if appropriate.

9. Enhance retention and transfer

   Give examples of similar problem situations. Offer additional practice opportunities that ask learners to apply what was learned in different scenarios. Allow learners to review and reflect on what was learned.

As you can see, Gagne's approach is quite behavioral in nature—emphasizing the teacher's role in the delivery of information. However, it does show the influence of cognitive and constructivist learning theories in its attention to connecting new information to old, supplying frameworks, offering constructive feedback, and allowing for review and reflection. Gagne's instructional events provide an effective way to think about how to organize any instructional effort and as such can be incorporated into most ID approaches. Underlying Gagne's work is the idea that when you are designing instruction you have identified what the learner knows and what he or she needs to know, have articulated those learning goals (outcomes) and shared them with your learners, and have developed some way of measuring the attainment of those goals—all common elements in ID practice.

Gagne's ideas also reflect research findings in human memory and information processing. Retention and transfer requires that learners are given time to process new information so that it moves from short-term to long-term memory storage. So we must be careful not only in how much we try to teach, but also how we chunk that teaching into appropriately sized segments. It is vitally important that we do not overload our learners with too much information during instruction. Research into cognitive load theory (Paas, Renkl, and Sweller 2003; Sweller, van Merrienboer, and Paas 1998) has led to practical recommendations about how to design instruction that takes these issues into account, and helps to improve the effectiveness of instruction by encouraging us to focus on the most important aspects of the material being addressed, and by enhancing the organization, chunking, and presentation techniques of to-be-learned information. Furthermore, we want to ensure that learners have correctly learned the material in a particular segment before moving on to the next. That is where constructive feedback comes into play. Supportive feedback shows learners where they need to modify behavior and correct misconceptions or other performance errors. Learners can use this information to continually modify what is stored in long-term memory, and utilize that modified information to guide future performance (Driscoll 2012). These are important ideas to keep in mind as we decide how much content can be addressed in a given instructional endeavor, the types of activities to include, and the sequencing of these activities into a logical order as we engage in the ID process. We will return to these concepts as we examine how to select activities for our instruction (chapter 6) and how to sequence our instruction (chapter 8).

While the Gagne approach has had a major impact on instruction, it is not the only instructional theory to have been developed over the years. Other significant ones include Reigeluth's elaboration theory (Reigeluth and Stein 1983) and Collins and Stevens's cognitive theory of inquiry teaching (1983). Reigeluth's theory is a top-down approach starting with an overview of the material that identifies the major concepts, principles, and/or strategies involved in the material to be learned. This is followed by further elaboration providing more depth and detail on each individual element. The Collins and Stevens theory focuses on eliciting learning through a series of questions. So in contrast to the elaboration theory, learners in this approach are building up to the big picture through a kind of discovery process (Walster 1995).

Finally, a discussion of the evolution of ID cannot be complete without a look at how advances in instructional technology have influenced the field. In many ways, the field of ID began when educational technology became a significant part of teaching and training (Farmer 2011). In fact, the field is often referred to as instructional design and technology (ID&T) reflecting the major impact technology has had on the way we teach. Early technologies such as film, radio, and TV were each viewed as a magic bullet that would change the way we teach forever after. However, although these all have had instructional uses, none of them lived up to the hopes educators had for them. Even though teacher resistance and cost concerns for purchasing and maintaining these technologies are often cited as reasons for this lack of promise, the often poor instructional quality of the materials being produced as well as the lack of attention given to helping teachers learn how to effectively use them in their practice are probably even more important factors (Reiser 2012a, 2012b). While not changing the overall face of teaching, these alternative ways to reach learners continue to be utilized in some way.

The rise of affordable computers and mobile devices with user-friendly interfaces and Internet access makes it easy to access large amounts of information from anywhere and at any time. As people gain more access to information, it becomes even more crucial to arm them with the skills and strategies that allow them to make thoughtful decisions about where to look for information, and to encourage them to critically evaluate the material they find. Technological advances have also had a huge impact on how we view our teaching. Each new type of instructional technology that is developed offers teachers the opportunity to vary the ways in which they present information and interact with their learners. Of even more importance is the possibilities technology offers for learners themselves to create and share their knowledge, and be more active participants in the learning process (Anderson 2012; Reiser 2012b). When instructors look to advances in instructional technology for new ways to work with and engage their learners, they first need to understand what each new technology has to offer and the best way to incorporate that technology into their instruction. It is not surprising that instructors turned to the field of ID for support in transitioning to ways of teaching that were less dependent upon the "sage on the stage" lecture-type delivery of information to a more interactive and participatory learner-centered approach.

WHAT ARE SOME INSTRUCTIONAL DESIGN MODELS/APPROACHES?

As we can see from the brief historical review above, the principles that underlie ID have been influenced by changes in the prevalent theories of learning at various points in time, research studies that examined the way people learn and retain information, and the rise of instructional technology as a central part of teaching. A variety of models have been developed over the years based on these theories and research. Before we begin a discussion of these models it is important to note that there is a hierarchical relationship between learning theory, instructional theory, and ID models. At the top are the various theories of learning that address the question of how people learn. These theories inform instructional theories such as Gagne's, which look at how to make sure learners attain the desired learning outcomes. The instructional designer then takes what he or she knows about learning and instruction to develop models for creating effective instructional interactions (Booth 2011; Driscoll 2012; Morrison et al. 2011).

➤ Theories of learning—How people learn
➤ Theories of instruction—Strategies of teaching to achieve specific goals and outcomes based on various theories of learning
➤ ID models—The application of instructional theories to the development of effective instructional endeavors (Morrison et al. 2011)

The models described below were all based on learning and instructional theories. The professionals who developed these models did so as a way to help practitioners apply these theories to their own instructional practice. This brief overview of ID models is not intended to be comprehensive, but should give you a better idea of some of the threads that run through most ID models being used today. Each one is an attempt to provide a systematic approach to the development of instruction that includes some kind of analysis of the instructional problem and the design, development, implementation, and evaluation of instructional methods and materials intended to solve that problem. Furthermore, all the models focus on designing instruction with well-defined goals and outcomes. The ultimate aim of ID is to create instruction that helps learners to attain these goals and outcomes in order to solve real problems, and to offer them opportunities to demonstrate the attainment of these stated aims (Branch and Merrill 2012, Goodman 2009, Reiser 2012b). All ID models identify the elements that go into creating effective instruction and provide guidelines for both implementing instruction and evaluating and reflecting on the effectiveness of that instruction (Booth 2011). How you use those guidelines is entirely up to you.

Let's start with what is probably the most recognizable acronym in ID—ADDIE—which stands for

- ➢ Analysis
- ➢ Design
- ➢ Development
- ➢ Implementation
- ➢ Evaluation

It is important to note that although ADDIE represents a very common view of ID, ADDIE itself is not a model. Rather, ADDIE is shorthand for the various elements that comprise the ID process. Although ADDIE is an extremely well-known view of ID, extensive research into its origins shows no original attribution. ADDIE, therefore, seems to be something that evolved informally through oral tradition among instructional designers in the 1980s (Booth 2011; Goodman 2009; Morrison et al. 2011). It is a label used to describe the elements in systematic ID and represents a generic or general conceptual framework developed to guide designers, and to promote a systematic approach to ID (Bichelmeyer 2005; Molenda 2008, 2003). ADDIE, therefore, seems to be an umbrella term used to describe the basic elements favored by trainers in the U.S. Armed Forces in the 1970s, that is, those individuals who were tasked to create training modules for military personnel (Branson 1978; Goodman 2009; Morrison et al. 2011). Regardless of the confusion surrounding its origins, the ADDIE acronym does help us to remember the basic components of the ID process.

Although the five elements tend to appear in a numerical list, this does not mean that the steps must be followed in this exact order, or that once a step is completed the designer cannot return to an earlier step. A thorough reading of the material associated with ADDIE shows an emphasis on interdependency of the steps and promotes an iterative and self-correcting approach to design (Branch and Merrill 2012). When/if designers discover more about the learners and the instructional problem as data are collected and analyzed, and prototypes are tested, they often must return to a previous step. Review, reflection, and revision are all crucial parts of ADDIE.

ADDIE and the ID models that will be described below are based on the concept of a "backward" approach to ID, that is, the idea that we start with where we want to learners to be at the end of instruction. We formalize that end point by writing learning objectives (what we expect them to know how to do), and identifying how we will know they have attained those objectives (assessment). It is only after determining our objectives and assessments that we can go on to develop the instructional activities that will get our learners to the desired end point (Farmer 2011; Wiggins and McTighe 2006).

While ADDIE may be a very common way of describing ID, those in the field often refer to the Dick and Carey model as another very influential and foundational ID framework. This model, which originated in the late 1970s, describes a total of ten key elements (Dick, Carey, and Carey 2011):

➢ Identify an instructional goal.
➢ Conduct an instructional analysis.
➢ Identify entry behaviors and characteristics.
➢ Write performance objectives.
➢ Development assessment instruments.
➢ Develop instructional strategy.
➢ Develop and select instruction.
➢ Design and conduct formative assessments.
➢ Revise instruction based on formative evaluations.
➢ Develop summative assessments.

Dick and Carey's model starts with identifying goals and a thorough analysis of what type of learning is required to get learners to those goals. The next step is to write objectives and the development of ways to measure the attainment of those objectives before moving on to the selection of actual instructional methods and materials. The model also includes a feedback loop that includes both formative assessment to inform the instructor about potential trouble points along the way, and summative assessment that is intended to measure the effectiveness of the instruction once it has been completed.

Now let's take a look at the ASSURE model, a six-step process for designing instruction that seems reminiscent of both the ADDIE and the Dick and Carey model (Heinrich et al. 2001, Lowther and Ross 2012). ASSURE steps are as follows:

➢ Analyze learners.
➢ State standards and objectives.
➢ Select strategies, technology, media, and materials.
➢ Utilize materials.
➢ Require learner participation.
➢ Evaluate and revise.

ASSURE specifically mentions the use of technology and media, and is a more active learning model that gives learners opportunities to practice with and apply new knowledge and skills, and receive feedback on their progress. The authors also offer a very useful way for dealing with technology. Termed the five Ps (prepare and preview the technology, prepare the environment, prepare the learners, and provide the learning experience) that is an excellent approach for making sure that any technology selected is not only appropriate, but that it is suited to the environment in which it will be used, and perhaps even more importantly, that learners will be able to successfully interact with it. ASSURE expands on the objectives step by suggesting that objectives should include intended audience, target behavior, conditions for performance, and degree to which new knowledge or skill has been mastered (Lowther and Ross 2012).

Another major contributor to the ID field is Gary Morrison, whose ID textbook is now in its seventh edition. Morrison and his colleagues Steven Ross and Jerrold Kemp break down the ID process into four basic questions:

➢   For whom are you designing this instruction?—Learner Characteristics.

➢   What do you want the learners to learn and/or demonstrate?—Objectives.

➢   What is the best way for learners to learn this material?—Instructional Strategies.

➢   How will you determine that learning has been achieved?—Assessment (Morrison et al. 2011).

The nine elements in the Morrison, Ross, and Kemp model (Morrison, Ross, Kalman, and Kemp 2011) are as follows:

➢   Identify instructional problems and specify instructional goals to address those problems.

➢   Examine learner characteristics that will impact the planning process.

➢   Identify content and analyze task components to determine what you need to include in the instruction.

➢   Share instructional objectives with the learner.

➢   Sequence content to promote logical learning.

➢   Design instructional strategies that will empower learners to master the objectives.

➢   Plan the instructional message and delivery.

➢   Develop evaluation instruments to assess objectives.

➢   Select resources to support instruction and learning activities.

As with all ID models, Morrison and colleagues emphasize a real "start with the learner" mind-set. That is, they urge designers not only to identify learning gaps in their target population, but also to delve into learners' backgrounds and readiness levels so designers can be better able to select the most appropriate instructional strategies. This information is used not only to identify instructional goals and objectives, but also as a way to both select the most appropriate instruction methods and materials (including possible media and technology), and also the order in which to present that instruction (Morrison et al. 2011).

Other notable models include several referred to as "whole-task approaches" (Branch and Merrill 2012). Examples of these are the "pebble in the pond" model and the "ten steps to complex learning" model, both of which promote the idea that learners should be presented with progressively more difficult task problems of the type that they will be expected to solve at the end of instruction with the expectation that learners will then be more likely to perform the complex whole task upon completion of the entire sequence (Merrill 2002; van Merrienboer and Kirschner 2007). The ISD4 model adds the idea of risk analysis to the basic, core ID elements as a way to decide which of a variety of alternatives for meeting identified learners' needs is the best choice based on a cost-benefit-risk analysis (Tennyson 1999).

HOW DID INSTRUCTION LIBRARIANS RESPOND?

As you can see, many ID models have been developed for use by educators at all levels, and by trainers working in business and industry. While any of the ones described above could certainly be applied to ILI, it is interesting to note that several specific approaches have been developed by and for instruction librarians. Probably one of the earliest attempts to introduce ID to ILI was in the work of Cottam and Dowell (1981). So over thirty years ago, these authors were urging instruction librarians to consider what learners need to know to successfully find the information they need, to identify appropriate instructional goals, and to select instructional methods that would best help learners attain those goals and to utilize ID principles to do so. The seven phases of Cottam and Dowell's model are the following:

1. Identify instructional need.
2. Analyze and describe need.
3. Formulate objectives, and select instructional strategies, methods, materials, and evaluation measures.
4. Develop or locate appropriate methods, materials, and resources.
5. Deliver instruction.
6. Analyze evaluation data.
7. Review and revise as needed.

Although this model is reminiscent of ADDIE, its value to instruction librarians is that it includes examples that apply directly to what was then called bibliographic instruction. It is an early attempt to encourage instruction librarians to consider the principles of ID as they developed their instructional endeavors.

In 1988, Miller and Bratton (1988) published an overview of ID aimed at the teaching librarian audience. Drawing upon Cottam and Dowell's work described above, as well as standard concepts from the ID field itself, Miller and Bratton identified five key elements librarians should consider when designing their instruction. These are the learners, the objectives, subject content, teaching methods, and evaluation. While Miller and Bratton do not present a systematic model of their own, they do recommend that instruction librarians refer to the earlier Cottam and Dowell work.

Not much happened regarding adapting ID models for ILI in the 1990s. But the same changes in technology and rising interest in distance education that prompted a renewed look at ID in education caused librarians, especially those interested in technology, to return to the ideas promoted by ID as we entered the twenty-first century. An updated look at ID for librarians appeared in the library literature in 2007 when Bell and Shank (2007) presented the ILI world with BLAAM, which stands for "blended librarians' adapted ADDIE model." BLAAM gained a bit more attention than the earlier ones, as it built on the impact educational technology was having both in education in general and ILI in particular. The term "blended librarian" is defined as someone who not only has information literacy knowledge, but who also understands and effectively uses technology to support ILI. Furthermore, the skill set recommended for the blended librarian includes a thorough familiarity with the concepts and principles of ID. As its name implies, the phases in BLAAM seem to be derived from ADDIE. BLAAM phases are as follows:

➢ Assess (analysis of population and environment)
➢ Design objectives (development)
➢ Develop (implementation plans as well as materials, methods, media)
➢ Deliver the instruction
➢ Measure effectiveness

BLAAM was instrumental to librarianship's renewed focus on ID. But its ties to blended librarianship and the emphasis on including technology in instruction led many librarians to feel that BLAAM was only applicable to those teaching with technology. Though this was not Bell and Shank's intention, and they quite specifically included discussions of the appropriate use of technology, BLAAM seems to have had only a limited influence on ILI practice. However, as more and more instructional librarians begin to incorporate elements of educational technology into their practice, it is very possible that BLAAM will gain some additional momentum. It is a rare ILI librarian these days who does not use some kind of technology to support and/or extend contact with his or her learners. So this may be a good time for all of us to reexamine Bell and Shank's ideas.

Another attempt to apply ID ideas to ILI comes from Char Booth (2011). Her USER method for ID consists of four elements:

➢ Understand
➢ Structure
➢ Engage
➢ Reflect

The parallels to models already discussed are clear. In the first phase (Understand) librarians gather data about the learners, the learners' needs, and the situation. During Structure the librarian identifies what he or she wants learners to accomplish (goals and outcomes) and outlines methodologies that will get help learners to accomplish those goals and outcomes as well as identifying methods that will involve the learners. It is also in this stage that Booth encourages strategic thinking about how to engage with learners before, during, and after the instructional encounter—whether it is face-to-face or in an online environment. The Engage phase is when instructional products are created and the instruction is actually delivered. And finally, in Reflect librarians are tasked to assess the impact of instruction, and to revise and reuse as appropriate (Booth 2011). While most of the elements of USER are similar to many of the traditional ID models, the added value of Booth's ideas is that it is written for instruction librarians, by someone who herself is an ILI professional. So the issues that face ILI librarians are directly addressed as Booth describes her USER method. For example, the challenges of the one-shot (which is a fairly unique phenomenon to ILI) are discussed and ways to deal with those challenges are illustrated. This makes the USER method a bit more accessible than some of those that appear in ID textbooks and articles.

Now that we have reviewed both general and ILI-specific ID, please reflect on your own ILI practice, and complete the worksheet in figure 2.2.

A Note about Objectives and Outcomes

As you read through this chapter, especially in the sections on theories and models, you may have noticed the use of both the terms "objectives" (what learners will be able to do following instruction) and "outcomes" (how you will observe and measure that they can do it). While educational, instructional, and ID professionals often distinguish between the two terms, I have found it easier to combine the two concepts into one and refer to this combined concept as "outcomes." Therefore, when I refer to outcomes I will be talking about both what learners will be able to do and also how the instructor will know they can do it (Grassian and Kaplowitz 2009; Kaplowitz 2012). Thus "outcomes" is one of the three major elements in my "Teaching Tripod" approach to ILI design and planning.

WHAT DOES ALL THIS MEAN TO YOU?

So what have we gotten from this brief, but perhaps intense stroll through the field of ID? First of all, I think we can see that we are not alone in our struggles to come up with the best ways of reaching and teaching our learners. As instruction librarians we are tasked to empower the members of our communities to be able to address their information needs. In order to do that we should aim to develop the best instructional endeavors we can so that our learners get the most out of our instruction. Following an ID approach can offer us a framework that not only addresses instructional planning systematically, but also provides guidance during the process.

As you read through the historical and conceptual frameworks of ID, you probably noticed common themes and elements. And some of the ideas presented may have resonated with you better than others. So perhaps now is the time to step back, reflect on what you read, and decide for yourself which approach and/or design elements make the most sense to you and begin to build your own, personal "ID for ILI" approach. Use the worksheet in figure 2.3 to help you along.

FIGURE 2.2

ID Elements in My Own ILI Practice

There are many different ID models and approaches. Now that you know a bit more about ID, reflect on your own ILI design process and then answer the following questions:

➢   Think about how you design your own ILI endeavors. Do you use any of the elements from the models/approaches described in this chapter when you are designing your instruction? If so, which ones do you use?

➢   Why do you use those particular elements?

➢   Do you think using these elements in your ILI design process contribute to the effectiveness of your final instructional product? If so, how?

FIGURE 2.3

What's Your ID Approach?

What do you know about the field of ID? Complete this worksheet as a way to review what you read in chapter 2 regarding the history of the fields and the various models/approaches associated with it over the years.

➤ List some of the common threads or design elements you noticed as you read about the various ID theories, approaches, and models. For example, an important common step is the identification and analysis of the instructional need/problem.

    ○ Identify instructional need/problem.

➤ Now identify any elements or concepts that seem to appear in only certain, specific models. For example, risk analysis is only in ISD4.

    ○ Risk analysis (ISD4)

➤ Drawing on what you have described in the previous two steps, choose the elements that you would consider in your own personal ID approach.

WRAP-UP

The moral of this chapter is that we should THINK BEFORE WE TEACH—about who we are teaching, where and in what context we are teaching, and what would best address our learners' needs. That is what all the ID professionals discussed in this chapter are telling us. The underlying thread is that those of us who teach (regardless of the environment in which we do so) should not jump into any instructional situation without first doing our homework, finding out as much as we can about our learners and the instructional situation, and only then develop a studied, thoughtful, and systematic approach that will engage, motivate, and empower our learners. We need to select learning outcomes that will address any knowledge gaps we have identified and provide learning opportunities or activities that allow our learners to attain those outcomes. Furthermore, we must incorporate assessing the attainment of these outcomes into our ILI so that learners can demonstrate they have attained the learning outcomes we set for the instructional experience.

I am hopeful that you have come away from this chapter even more inspired about creating the best instructional offerings you can. Furthermore, I hope that you also have gained a better understanding of what ID as a field can offer us as we go about creating those offerings. My own readings in both ID, which I have tried to summarize here, as well as my interest in LCT inspired me to examine how I go about designing my own instruction. Drawing on established ID principles, I came up with a methodology I call the "Teaching Tripod." The Tripod is grounded in ID theory and uses the various models as a framework, but as it is my personal methodology, it is also heavily influenced by my views on ILI and LCT. The chapters that follow this introduction will take you through the elements of my approach and will include worksheets and exercises that you can use to design your own instruction.

WHAT STUCK?

Now that you have created the publicity for your continuing education (CE) workshop on ID (see chapter 1), it is time to start thinking about what you will include in your instruction. Use the worksheet in figure 2.4 to help you create an outline for your instructional endeavor.

FIGURE 2.4

Worksheet for Developing a CE Offering on ID for ILI Librarians

Answer the following questions in order to develop a draft outline for your CE workshop on ID for ILI.

➤ What do you think your colleagues need to know or be able to do regarding ID to assist them in their ILI planning? That is, what is the knowledge gap you wish to address?

➤ How did you identify that gap?

➤ Having identified the knowledge or skill gap, what elements and/or concepts do you think you need to include in your CE offering?

➤ Draft an outline of your CE instructional session.

REFERENCES

Anderson, Lorin W., and David R. Krathwohl. 2001. *A Taxonomy of Learning, Teaching and Assessing: A Revision of Bloom's Educational Objectives*. Boston: Allyn & Bacon.

Anderson, Terry. 2012. "Networks, Web 2.0, and the Connected Learner." In *Trends and Issues in Instructional Design and Technology*, edited by Robert A. Reiser and John V. Dempsey, 299–308. Boston: Pearson.

Bell, Stephen. 2008. "Design Thinking." *American Libraries* 39 (1/2): 44–49.

Bell, Stephen, and John D. Shank. 2007. *Academic Librarianship by Design*. Chicago: American Library Association.

Bichelmeyer, Barbara A. 2005. "The ADDIE Method: A Metaphor for the Lack of Clarity in the Field of IDT." IDT Record. Accessed June 6, 2012. www.unco.edu/cetl/sir/clt/documents/IDTf_Bic.pdf.

Bloom, Benjamin Samuel. 1956. *Taxonomy of Educational Objectives: The Classification of Educational Goals. Handbook 1: Cognitive Domain. Handbook 2: Affective Domain*. 2 vols. New York: McKay.

Booth, Char. 2011. *Reflective Teaching, Effective Learning*. Chicago: American Library Association.

Branch, Robert M., and M. David Merrill. 2012. "Characteristics of Instructional Design Models." In *Trends and Issues in Instructional Design and Technology*, edited by Robert A. Reiser and John V. Dempsey, 8–16. Boston: Pearson.

Branson, Robert K. 1978. "The Interservice Procedures for Instructional Systems Development." *Educational Technology* 18 (3): 11–14.

Collins, Allan, and Albert Stevens. 1983. "A Cognitive Theory of Inquiry Teaching." In *Instructional Design Theories and Models*, edited by Charles M. Reigeluth, 247–77. Hillsdale, NJ: Erlbaum.

Cottam, Keith M., and Connie V. Dowell. 1981. "A Conceptual Planning Method for Developing Bibliographic Instruction Programs." *Journal of Academic Librarianship* 7 (4): 22–28.

Dick, Walter, Lou Carey, and James Carey. 2011. *Systematic Design of Instruction*. 7th ed. Boston: Allyn & Bacon.

Driscoll, Marcy P. 2012. "Psychological Foundations of Instructional Design." In *Trends and Issues in Instructional Design and Technology*, edited by Robert A. Reiser and John V. Dempsey, 35–44. Boston: Pearson.

Farmer, Lesley S. J. 2011. *Instructional Design for Librarians and Information Professionals*. New York: Neal-Schuman.

Gagne, Robert. 1965. *The Conditions of Learning and the Theory of Instruction*. Fort Worth, TX: Harcourt Brace College.

———. 1992. *Principles of Instructional Design*. Fort Worth, TX: Harcourt Brace Jovanovich.

Gagne, Robert, Walter Wager, Katharine Golas, and John M. Keller. 2004. *Principles of Instructional Design*. 5th ed. Belmont, CA: Wadsworth/Thomson Learning.

Goodman, Valeda Dent. 2009. *Keeping the User in Mind: Instructional Design and the Modern Library*. Oxford: Chandos.

Grassian, Esther, and Joan Kaplowitz. 2009. *Information Literacy Instruction: Theory and Practice*. 2nd ed. New York: Neal-Schuman.

Heinrich, Robert, Michael Molenda, James D. Russell, and Sharon E. Smaldino. 2001. *Instructional Media and Technologies for Learning*. 7th ed. Upper Saddle River, NJ: Prentice Hall.

Kaplowitz, Joan R. 2012. *Transforming Your Information Literacy Instruction Using Learner-Centered Teaching*. New York: Neal-Schuman.

Lowther, Deborah, and Steven M. Ross. 2012. "Instructional Designers and P-12 Technology Integration." In *Trends and Issues in Instructional Design and Technology*, edited by Robert A. Reiser and John V. Dempsey, 208–17. Boston: Pearson.

Mager, Robert. 1962. *Preparing Objectives for Programmed Instruction*. Belmont, CA: Fearon.

Merrill, M. David. 2002. "A Pebble-in-the-Pond Model for Instructional Design." *Performance Improvement* 41 (7): 39–44.

Miller, Marian I., and Barry D. Bratton. 1988. "Instructional Design: Increasing the Effectiveness of Bibliographic Instruction." *College and Research Libraries* 49 (6): 545–49.

Molenda, Michael. 2003. "In Search of the Elusive ADDIE Model." *Performance Improvement* 42 (5): 34–36.

———. 2008. "Historical Foundations." In *Handbook of Research on Educational Communications and Technology*, edited by J. Michael Spector, M. David Merrill, Jeroen van Merrienboer, and Marcy P. Driscoll, 5–20. New York: Erlbaum.

Morrison, Gary R., Steven M. Ross, Howard K. Kalman, and Jerrold E. Kemp. 2011. *Designing Effective Instruction*. 6th ed. Hoboken, NJ: Wiley.

Paas, Fred, Alexander Renkl, and John Sweller. 2003. "Cognitive Load Theory and Instructional Design: Recent Developments." *Educational Psychologist* 38 (1): 1–4.

Reigeluth, Charles M., and Albert Stein. 1983. "The Elaboration Theory of Instruction." In *Instructional Design Theories and Models*, edited by Charles M. Reigeluth, 335–81. Hillsdale, NJ: Erlbaum.

Reiser, Robert A. 2012a. "A History of Instructional Design and Technology." In *Trends and Issues in Instructional Design and Technology*, edited by Robert A. Reiser and John V. Dempsey, 17–34. Boston: Pearson.

———. 2012b. "What Field Did You Say You Were in? Defining and Naming Our Field." In *Trends and Issues in Instructional Design and Technology*, edited by Robert A. Reiser and John V. Dempsey, 1–7. Boston: Pearson.

Smith, Patricia L., and Tillman J. Ragan. 2005. *Instructional Design*. 3rd ed. Hoboken, NJ: Wiley.

Sweller, John, Jeroen van Merrienboer, and Fred Paas. 1998. "Cognitive Architecture and Instructional Design." *Educational Psychology Review* 10 (3): 251–96.

Tennyson, Robert D. 1999. "Instructional Development and ISD4 Methodology." *Performance Improvement* 38 (6): 19–27.

van Merrienboer, Jeroen, and Paul Kirschner. 2007. *Ten Steps to Complex Learning: A Systematic Approach to Four-Component Instructional Design*. Mahwah, NJ: Erlbaum.

Walster, Dian. 1995. "Using Instructional Design Theories in Library and Information Science Education." *Journal of Education for Library and Information Science* 36 (3): 239–48.

Wiggins, Grant, and Jay McTighe. 2006. *Understanding by Design*. Upper Saddle River, NJ: Prentice Hall.

Wilson, Brent. 2012. "Constructivism in Practical and Historical Context." In *Trends and Issues in Instructional Design and Technology*, edited by Robert A. Reiser and John V. Dempsey, 45–52. Boston: Pearson.

What Is the Teaching Tripod?

An Overview

It seems like instructional design (ID) has been around for a while and there are lots of approaches for designing instruction already in practice. So why can't I just use one of these already developed ideas to design my information literacy instruction (ILI) endeavors?

Life for instruction librarians can be hectic. We often have limited lead time for planning and preparing our instruction. Plus, teaching may only be a part of our job responsibilities. So as much as we might like to spend unlimited amounts of time and effort on our instructional planning, we often are unable to do so. What we need is an ID approach that allows us to create effective instruction regardless of the preparation time we have. And we need a methodology that emphasizes learning (identifying skills and knowledge that will help people address their information needs), engagement (creating ways for people to learn the identified skills and knowledge), and effectiveness (checking that people have gained the requisite skills and knowledge from the instructional experience).

QUESTIONS TO CONSIDER
➢ Why would the Teaching Tripod approach be more useful for my ILI planning than more traditional ID approaches?
➢ What are the three elements of the Teaching Tripod?
➢ What other elements of the ID process should I consider?
➢ How do these other elements relate to the Teaching Tripod?
➢ How do I determine how much time to allocate to each element of the ID process?

WHY DO INSTRUCTION LIBRARIANS NEED SOMETHING DIFFERENT?
While various versions of the ID process already exist, many of them were developed as a means to quickly train large groups of people on specific tasks such as operating machinery or using complex forms of technology. While the overall principles of ID can certainly be applied to educational situations, they often need some modification to make them suitable to the more cognitive endeavors associated with education in general (Dick 1987, Morrison et al. 2011, Reiser 2012) and ILI in particular. Furthermore, while instruction librarians could certainly use the types of ID developed for use in schools and universities, these approaches tend to address the design of instruction for full-length courses. So traditional ID approaches may seem too elaborate for the one-shot type of instruction that still is very much a major part of ILI. What instruction librarians need is a more streamlined approach, something that is flexible and adaptable so it can be used both for full-length courses as well as one-shot classes, and one that

can be completed in a relatively short period of time if necessary (Bell and Shank 2007; Farmer 2011; Goodman 2009). We could even refer to this as "ID lite." In other words, instruction librarians need an approach that can be expanded when they are working in the full-course mode, and streamlined when they have limited development time, as is often the case for one-shots.

THE TEACHING TRIPOD APPROACH IN A NUTSHELL

The need for "ID lite" for ILI brings us to what I have come to call the "Teaching Tripod" approach. This type of ID concentrates on the link between expected learning outcomes (ELOs), learning activities, and assessment. By identifying gaps in the learners' knowledge and abilities, and developing outcomes based on those gaps, you can ensure that your instruction is relevant and useful to your learners (Bell and Shank 2007; Branch and Merrill 2012; Dick, Carey, and Carey 2011). You then use those outcomes to create opportunities for learners to interact with the material, and to demonstrate the attainment of those outcomes—thus filling in the gaps in their understanding, skills, and knowledge (Cottam and Dowell 1981; Kaplowitz 2012; Miller and Bratton 1988).

These three elements (outcomes, activities, and assessment) are crucial to the design and development of any instructional offering. And they offer an easy to follow methodology that can be adapted for any type of ILI—face-to-face (F2F) or online—and for any length instruction—full course or one-shot (Booth 2011, Kaplowitz 2012). See figure 3.1 for a brief overview of the Teaching Tripod.

BEYOND THE TEACHING TRIPOD: NEEDS ASSESSMENT, IMPLEMENTATION/DELIVERY

Clearly the three pieces of the Tripod are not meant to operate in isolation. In order to create appropriate ELOs, you need to have some background information about your learners and their information literacy needs. Sometimes you may have the luxury of being able to do in-depth research on your learners ahead of time. Other times you rely on information provided by your instructional partners—especially in the K–20 environments. And more often than perhaps you would like, you have to base your ELOs on your informal interactions with your learners during reference-desk exchanges and consultation appointments, casual conversations, and your general knowledge of the overall learner population. In any case, you must base your ELOs on what, in your best professional knowledge and experience, learners need to know in order to satisfy their information literacy needs.

Once you know what you want learners to attain from the instruction, you can then create learning opportunities (activities) as well as comprehension checks (assessments) to ensure that learning has indeed happened. When the three parts of the Teaching Tripod are in place, you can move on to organizing the activities and assessments into a logical sequence (sequencing) and sharing the instruction with your learners (implementation/delivery) (Grassian and Kaplowitz 2009; Booth 2011; Kaplowitz 2012; Morrison et al. 2011).

FITTING IT ALL TOGETHER

By taking a step back and not jumping into instruction without some systematic thought you will improve the likelihood that your instruction will address your learners' information literacy needs and that they will profit by the experience of working with you in an instructional setting (Farmer 2011; Grassian and Kaplowitz 2009; Kaplowitz 2012).While the amount of time you spend on needs assessment and implementation/delivery will vary from situation to situation, the three Teaching Tripod pieces are crucial to the design of any type of instruction and must always be a part of your ID process.

ELOs provide the framework for instruction. They describe your expectations—what skills, behaviors, and strategies you want learners to be able to perform following instruction. Once you determine what you want learners to take away from the instructional experience, you can decide how to provide them with opportunities to attain those outcomes. In other words, you can come up with ways in which your learners can interact with the material in order for learning to occur. To do so you turn to your instructional bag of tricks to select the types of

FIGURE 3.1

The Teaching Tripod in Brief

➢   What do your learners need to know? (Expected Learning Outcomes)

   ○   Identify what learners need to be able to do in order to accomplish a specified goal.

➢   How will they learn it? (Activities)

   ○   Create learning activities that allow the learners to interact with the material to be learned so that they can attain the identified outcomes.

➢   How will we know they learned it? (Assessment)

   ○   Develop ways in which learners can demonstrate the attainment of the identified outcomes.

learning activities that seem to be most appropriate to help your learners attain the outcomes you have set for the instruction. Activities in this sense are being defined in the broadest sense and can include anything from the more teacher-centered lecture/demo approach, to structured question and answer, collaborative group work, problem- or case-based exercises and other more learner-centered approaches.

Finally, you will make sure to include some way to have learners demonstrate that they have in fact attained the outcomes you want learners to attain as a result of the instructional experience. In other words, you include some type of assessment for each of the learning outcomes you have set. If you do not assess the attainment of each outcome, you have no way of knowing if your instructional endeavors have been effective. Furthermore, assessments help learners reflect upon and gauge their own progress as well as provide feedback to instructors on how well (or not) the instruction is progressing (Branch and Merrill 2012; Grassian and Kaplowitz 2009; Miller and Bratton 1988).

In some cases activities can serve double duty and can provide some assessment information. When you give learners the opportunity to practice what they are learning during the instruction itself you can uncover misconceptions and other problems as you go along. This also gives you the chance to make midstream corrections (reviewing the material, offering additional examples, repeating and rephrasing points, etc.) that gets the learners back on the right track.

CONTEXT, LEAD TIME, AND SCOPE

The three parts of the Teaching Tripod are all interrelated and are crucial to your ID process if you wish to provide effective instruction. Each of these pieces (as well as the additional aspects of ID referred to above) will be examined in more detail in later chapters in this book. This chapter will discuss how the Tripod relates to the other aspects of ID and will offer suggestions about how to determine the amount of time you might wish to allocate to each part of the ID process.

Deciding when you need to go beyond the Tripod itself, and the degree to which you should do so is a complex issue. Your decisions often depend on external circumstances such as how the instruction was initiated, where it will take place, contact time for F2F offerings, software and accessibility issues for online offerings, and so forth. Of course the biggest deciding factor in many cases is how much time you have for your planning and preparation. If time is short, you may have to concentrate on the ELOs, activities, and assessment pieces and spend very little time on the other aspects of the ID process.

You will also need to consider the scope of the instruction you are developing. Full-length courses require a bit more planning than a one-shot. Planning for a full-length course actually has two layers of complexity—one for the overall course and one for each of the individual classes or segments of the course. Hopefully if you are involved in designing and developing a full-length course, you have the time necessary to do a thorough job. Keep in mind that when working on a full-length course, you need to have the overall structure (course goals and outcomes, sequence of topics being addressed, course assessments) in place before you begin. But you may not have the time to completely develop each of the individual classes or segments. However, since the course will run for several weeks or months, you can address each of the individual segments as they come up over time.

GOING BEYOND THE TRIPOD

Clearly you should never embark on any kind of instruction (F2F or online) without a systematic and thoughtful consideration of ELOs, activities, and assessment. But how do you decide on how much time we need to spend on ID elements such as needs assessments and implementation/delivery? In order to answer this question requires some honest self-reflection on your part. What do you already know about the instructional situation? Try using the worksheet in figure 3.2 to do this preliminary analysis.

FIGURE 3.2

How Much Do I Already Know?

You are considering designing an ILI offering for a specific group of learners. But how much do you already know about the instructional situation? On a scale of 1 to 5 with 5 being "extremely" and 1 being "not at all," rate your familiarity with the following:

➢ Learners' characteristics   1   2   3   4   5
   (demographics, backgrounds, cultures, ethnicities, languages spoken, etc.)

➢ Learners' information needs   1   2   3   4   5

➢ Learners' previous ILI experience   1   2   3   4   5

➢ The teaching space (for F2F)   1   2   3   4   5
   (layout, equipment, seat arrangements)

➢ The software available to design and present the instruction (for online)   1   2   3   4   5

➢ The content to be taught   1   2   3   4   5

➢ Learners' technological capabilities   1   2   3   4   5

➢ Learners' hardware and accessibility issues   1   2   3   4   5

Once you have determined what you already know, you can make more informed decisions about how much or how little time needs to be expended in the needs assessment (information gathering stage) and implementation/delivery (marketing, logistics, presentation, and materials preparations) pieces of the ID process. The more you already know, the less time you will need for any additional needs assessment. This is especially true if you have worked with the population (or a similar one) before. However, if this is a "new to you" group of learners or "new to you" content, it is a good idea to allocate some extra time for gathering background information about the learners, their information needs, their previous ILI experience if any, and/or the content to be addressed in the instruction.

If you are working in an instructional setting that is familiar to you, whether it is a physical space or working with software you have used before, your implementation/delivery phase can also be streamlined. But if you are going to be working in unfamiliar territory, you will need to expend a bit more time and energy to learn what can and cannot be accomplished given the limitations and constraints of the space and/or software. You may also have to spend additional time in the implementation/delivery segment to make sure that the ways in which you plan to present the material (in your F2F meetings or online) are appropriate to the instructional environment in which you will be teaching.

Your own past experience with the content you will be teaching will also impact the amount of time you will need to spend on the implementation/delivery phase. If you have taught this content before, you probably have a pretty good idea about the amount of information that is appropriate for a given F2F time frame or what works best in the online environment available to you. And you may even have instructional materials you can repurpose for this new instruction. But if you are tackling something new, you should allocate extra time for testing the instructional package in advance. You may wish to do test runs with colleagues or a sample of the population. These preliminary tryouts will help you identify possible sequencing and/or implementation/delivery issues. Furthermore, if this is a F2F endeavor, rehearsing the material should help you gain confidence and improve your overall presentation skills. For online instruction, preliminary testing can identify problems with the organization of the information and potential navigation issues. Accessibility issues can also be tested during this tryout period.

FURTHER CONSIDERATIONS

Having determined your level of familiarity with the various aspects of the instructional situation, you can make a best-guess estimate about how much time you will need to devote to the Tripod elements and to the needs assessment and implementation/delivery components of your ID process. To fine-tune that estimate will require a little more analysis of the instructional situation. Here are some things you need to consider.

How Was the Instruction Initiated?

➤ *Reactive Mode*—The decision to offer instruction is based on your own experiences answering questions or working directly with learners. So little, if any, additional needs assessment will be required, and you can move right into the Tripod phases. The amount of time you need to spend on implementation/delivery will depend on where instruction is taking place (in your own library space or elsewhere). Extra time may be needed for outreach and marketing in the implementation/delivery stage in order to "sell the instruction" to institutional partners and learners.

➤ *Interactive Mode*—The instruction was requested by a partner/collaborator outside of the library. So the requester will probably be able to provide most of the needs assessment data needed. He or she may even be willing to work collaboratively with you on the Tripod phases, especially in terms of determining appropriate ELOs. The time spent on implementation/delivery will depend on where instruction is taking place (in library space or elsewhere). However, the requester can help with this as well, especially if instruction is taking place in his or her space. Little or no time will be needed for the outreach, marketing, or scheduling parts of implementation/delivery, especially if the requester is requiring attendance.

➤ *Proactive mode*—In this mode the impetus to design instruction comes from you. You decided the time had come to do an in-depth review of your learners' information needs in order to identify any areas where new ILI efforts might be needed. This mode, therefore, requires expending a lot of effort in the needs assessment stage. Once that data is in hand, you can use what you learned as you work out the Tripod details. This mode will also require the most implementation/delivery effort. In short, you will need to allocate a considerable amount of time for the entire ID process (Grassian and Kaplowitz 2009).

How Much Do I Already Know about the Target Population and My Learners' Information Literacy Needs?

➤ If you are very familiar with your population already, or have recently done thorough needs assessments, you can concentrate on the Tripod elements. The time you will need to spend on implementation/delivery will depend on who initiated instruction, where instruction will take place, etc.

➤ If this population is new to you, or if you have decided to examine the relevance, appropriateness, and effectiveness of your current offerings, you will have to devote extra time to needs assessment activities, which in turn will inform your Tripod elements. The amount of time you need to spend in the implementation/delivery stage will depend upon the type of instruction you decide to offer based on the results of your needs assessment.

How Much Preparation Time Do I Have?

➤ If you only have a limited amount of time (less than two weeks) you will by necessity have to focus most of your efforts on the three Tripod phases. This is often the case in instruction initiated in the interactive mode. Generally in this mode you receive a request for instruction that is expected to take place fairly close to the time of the request. A limited time frame may also occur if your library has added or updated some resource (online catalog, database, etc.) and you feel that some instructional support will help learners make better use of the new and/or updated resource.

➤ If you have a moderate amount of time (more than two weeks but less than two months) you may be able to do additional needs assessments to learn more about your learners and their needs. The amount of time you allocate for implementation/delivery will depend in part on other external factors (where you are teaching, previous experience with this instruction, etc.). Outreach and marketing may have to be limited, and pretesting the instruction/materials may also have to be streamlined. The slightly longer time frame tends to occur for instruction that you decide to develop based on your own experiences with your learners (reactive mode).

➤ If you have the luxury of more than two months you can expand your ID process to include thorough needs assessments and spend additional time on implementation/delivery. You can field-test your materials on a representative sample of the target population, review the results of the test, and revise the material as needed. You will also be able to devote a bit more time to outreach and marketing to bring the new instructional effort to the attention of your learners and institutional partners. Instruction that has arisen out of the proactive mode of initiation requires the longest lead time, as more attention should be paid to all aspects of the ID process. This is especially true if there is any kind of substantial cost associated with developing the new instruction, such as in creating online tutorials or instructional videos.

How Much Contact Time Will I Have?

➤ Obviously, planning for a full-term course will require a greater time commitment than would be needed for a one-shot. While the Tripod elements are crucial for either type of instruction, ID for full-length courses would ideally be based on an in-depth understanding of the target audience. So the instructor should conduct thorough needs assessments to ensure he or she has a solid understanding of the audience and its instructional needs. Furthermore, the complexity of a full-length course with its multiple segments often requires extra effort in the implementation/delivery stage.

➢ Planning for the individual segments of a full-time course can concentrate on the three Tripod elements since most of the other information is already in place from the overall course planning work. However, you may still have to spend a little bit of time on the implementation/delivery element for each individual segment to make sure everything is in place for the types of activities and assessments scheduled for them.

➢ The amount of effort you need to put into planning for one-shots will depend a great deal on the answers to the other questions discussed here. For example, how the instruction was initiated, how much you know about the target audience, how much preparation time you have, how much contact time you have, and whether this is new or a revised instruction.

Is This a New Instructional Offering or a Revision of an Older One?

➢ You can really streamline the process if you are revising/revamping already developed instruction. Use what you learned from the previous offering to tweak the Tripod elements. Did the original sequence seem to work or do you think the material should be reorganized? Were there problems related to implementation/delivery in terms of space, time frame, facility, etc., that need to be addressed?

➢ On the other hand, if you are starting from scratch, you will need to allocate more time to each of the ID elements. So if you are designing something completely new, you should make sure you have the necessary time to devote to needs assessment and implementation/delivery.

Can I Repurpose Materials Already on Hand?

➢ This is obviously related to the previous point. If you are revising a previously offered instructional endeavor, you probably have a great deal of material you can use for this offering as well. That will help streamline the Tripod components themselves since you already have ELOs, activities, and assessments that can be used. It will also cut down on the time you need to spend on implementation/delivery.

➢ However, even if this is a new instructional effort, you may find that you have materials on hand that with a little revision would be suitable for this instructional effort. The amount of material you can repurpose will obviously impact how much time you need to spend on the Tripod elements themselves as well as on the implementation/delivery phase.

Will I Be Teaching in a Face-to-Face (F2F), Online, or Blended Format?

➢ While much is the same for all three of these formats, each one requires special considerations as well.

➢ Obviously, the Teaching Tripod phases are necessary regardless of the format being used for the actual instruction. And you still need to base your Tripod phases on what you know about the learners (needs assessments). However, implementation/delivery issues vary a bit for each of these delivery modes.

➢ For example, any computer-based instruction (fully online or blended) will require examining your target audience's experience with and access to technology. And assessing learning may also require some extra attention, especially for online tutorials, which learners can access remotely at any time. Implementation/delivery may require technical expertise and/or working with someone else who has that expertise, thereby adding to the time needed to get this instruction ready for use.

➤ F2F offerings require consideration of contact time in order to determine how much you can reasonably expect to address in the given time frame, a thorough understanding of the space and equipment available to you for the instruction, an examination of the physical layout of the space to ensure the activities you plan can be executed in the F2F environment, and so forth. How little or how much time you need to expend in the implementation/delivery stage will depend on how familiar you are with the content to be addressed as well as with the physical parameters of the teaching space you will be using.

➤ For more on planning for the three different delivery modes (F2F, online, and blended) see *Information Literacy Instruction: Theory and Practice* (Grassian and Kaplowitz 2009) and *Transforming Information Literacy Instruction Using Learner-Centered Teaching* (Kaplowitz 2012).

Is There Anything Else That I Should Consider?

➤ Any instructional offering can have its unique characteristics. While the above points probably cover most situations, you may discover you need to adjust the entire planning process based on some other circumstances.

➤ It is often helpful to run your ideas past a colleague to ensure you have not missed any potential pitfalls.

➤ And remember that the best-laid plans can still go wrong. If this happens, try to be flexible and adaptable and make note of the problems so you can try to adjust for them in future offerings.

Figure 3.3 contains a worksheet that can guide you through as you fine-tune your ID process for the task at hand. Once you have determined the answers to the worksheet questions, you can decide how much effort you need to expend in the Tripod, needs assessment, and implementation/delivery components of your ID process.

WRAP-UP

The three Teaching Tripod elements are central to most ideas regarding ID. Other component pieces such as needs assessments are also important, since they supply background data for the Tripod elements. Needs assessments tell us what learners need to learn (identifies gaps in knowledge/skills) and to some degree inform us about the type of activities and assessment that will work, that is, what will appeal to the target population. For example, teaching methodologies that are appropriate for adults may not work with children and teens. Seniors may also need some special consideration when selecting what to include in instruction, how much technology to use and/or teach, and the methods selected to address the content. Learners for whom English is not their primary language may be more comfortable with demonstrations and hands-on practice rather than any activities that require listening skills such as lectures, or reading large amounts of text either on-screen or in handouts. They may also feel uncomfortable about speaking up in class in any kind of interactive discussion activity. Finally, your learners' levels of computer abilities will determine the types of instructional technology you can use for teaching purposes, the complexity of the technology you choose as the content of your instruction, as well as the pace of hands-on computer exercises.

The implementation/delivery piece builds on what you have decided for your Tripod elements. The relationship between needs assessment and the Tripod is addressed in chapter 4 as well as the types of information you should try to gather to inform you about what should go into the Tripod. This chapter also discusses levels of needs assessments—that is, how to adjust based on time constraints and type of instruction you are designing.

Chapter 9 looks at how to build on your Tripod planning during your implementation/delivery stages. Topics covered in chapter 9 include how to market your instructional product effectively, suggestions on how to reach out to and communicate with your community (both your learners and your institutional partners), logistical details (scheduling, staff, space, furniture, equipment, technology, etc.), as well as delivery concerns (preparing yourself and your materials).

FIGURE 3.3

An Analysis of the Instructional Situation

Complete this worksheet to help you reflect on what you already know about the ILI you are designing so you can decide how much energy and time you need to devote to your needs assessments, your Tripod elements, and your implementation and delivery components.

➢   How was the instruction initiated (reactive, interactive, or proactive)?

➢   What do I already know about the target population and my learners' information literacy needs?

➢   How much time do I have to prepare the instruction?

➢   How much contact time will I have (both in terms of full-length course versus one-shot and amount of time for each segment or class)?

➢   Is this a brand-new instructional offering or am I revising/revamping an already developed instructional offering?

Instruction librarians often express trepidation regarding the amount of time they feel is necessary for systematic and thorough ID. However, if you are dedicated to offering effective instruction, you must devote time and energy to the ID process. Furthermore, as you start using the Tripod approach, you will begin to build a library of outcomes, activities, and assessments that can be modified and reused with many different classes/online offerings—especially in the case of one-shots. You might think of the time you spend in planning as an investment for the future—providing you with a repository of ID ideas from which to draw. So ID gets faster as you get used to using the Tripod. Plus you get better at writing outcomes and matching outcomes with activities and assessments for particular audiences with each instruction you develop using this approach. And you gain experience deciding how much or how little time you can reasonably spend in the entire ID process. The more you engage in the Teaching Tripod approach to ID, the more efficient you will become as you design the most effective, engaging, and relevant instruction for your learners (Grassian and Kaplowitz 2009; Kaplowitz 2012; Morrison et al. 2011).

In a way this process is ongoing and never really ends. As you offer your instruction you not only are constantly checking to make sure your learners are attaining the ELOs you have set for the experience, you also engage in critical observation of the instruction itself to pinpoint areas that may need improving. You may even discover that your outcomes need tweaking or enhancing. Every time you teach, you are testing the effectiveness of the instruction itself, which often leads you back to the beginning of the Tripod once again or suggests that you need to do a little more information gathering, that is, needs assessment. Each teaching experience helps you learn even more about your learners and their information needs—confirming or refuting your original ideas—and leading you to review and possibly revise the outcomes you have developed for future instructional offerings. See chapter 10 for more on how the end of each ID process is often the beginning of the next. Continually reviewing, reflecting on, and revising your instructional offerings not only helps you improve the effectiveness of your ILI, it also encourages you to keep your instruction fresh and relevant, and supports your growth and development as teachers.

WHAT STUCK?

As ILI coordinator, you are concerned about how your librarians are planning their instructional efforts. You are not convinced they are developing the most relevant, engaging, and effective courses, classes, and online tutorials. You are especially concerned that your instruction librarians are not including ways to determine if learners are gaining any new appreciation for information literacy or obtaining any new information literacy–related skills or strategies that will help them address their future information needs. However, you are sympathetic to the constraints under which your librarians are working—especially in terms of workload and lead time available for planning specific instruction. But you also feel very strongly that every instructional offering should have specific, clear, observable, and measurable ELOs, should consist of engaging ways for learners to interact with the material to be learned, and should offer learners opportunities to exhibit the attainment of the expected outcomes. It is up to you to convince your fellow librarians to try something that may be a new approach to ILI planning for them. Complete the worksheet in figure 3.4 to help you develop a workshop that will introduce the Teaching Tripod approach to your colleagues.

FIGURE 3.4

An Introductory Workshop on the Teaching Tripod Approach to ID

Complete this worksheet to help you develop a workshop on the merits of the Teaching Tripod approach to ID for ILI.

➢ Make a list of three to five points about the advantages of using the Teaching Tripod approach. Use these points during a short (five to ten minutes) marketing-type persuasive presentation for your librarians.

➢ Now create a thirty- to forty-five-minute workshop that gives your instruction librarians a chance to try out the Tripod approach on classes currently being taught and/or on some new instruction endeavor being considered. Model the Tripod approach by developing the following elements:

   ○ Write at least three expected learning outcomes for this session. What do you hope your colleagues will be able to do following the instruction?

   ○ Develop the activities you will include in your session that will help your colleagues attain the outcomes set.

   ○ Design appropriate assessments that will provide opportunities for your colleagues to demonstrate the attainment of the outcomes.

➢ At the end of the session, share how you used the Tripod to design the instruction just completed.

REFERENCES

Bell, Stephen, and John D. Shank. 2007. *Academic Librarianship by Design*. Chicago: American Library Association.

Booth, Char. 2011. *Reflective Teaching, Effective Learning*. Chicago: American Library Association.

Branch, Robert M., and M. David Merrill. 2012. "Characteristics of Instructional Design Models." In *Trends and Issues in Instructional Design and Technology*, edited by Robert A. Reiser and John V. Dempsey, 8–16. Boston: Pearson.

Cottam, Keith M., and Connie V. Dowell. 1981. "A Conceptual Planning Method for Developing Bibliographic Instruction Programs." *Journal of Academic Librarianship* 7 (4): 22–28.

Dick, Walter. 1987. "A History of Instructional Design and Its Impact on Educational Psychology." In *Historical Foundations of Educational Psychology*, edited by John Glover and Royce Roning, 183–200. New York: Pleum.

Dick, Walter, Lou Carey, and James Carey. 2011. *Systematic Design of Instruction*. 7th ed. Boston: Allyn & Bacon.

Farmer, Lesley S. J. 2011. *Instructional Design for Librarians and Information Professionals*. New York: Neal-Schuman.

Goodman, Valeda Dent. 2009. *Keeping the User in Mind: Instructional Design and the Modern Library*. Oxford: Chandos.

Grassian, Esther, and Joan Kaplowitz. 2009. *Information Literacy Instruction: Theory and Practice*. 2nd ed. New York: Neal-Schuman.

Kaplowitz, Joan R. 2012. *Transforming Information Literacy Instruction Using Learner-Centered Teaching*. New York: Neal-Schuman.

Miller, Marian I., and Barry D. Bratton. 1988. "Instructional Design: Increasing the Effectiveness of Bibliographic Instruction." *College and Research Libraries* 49 (6): 545–49.

Morrison, Gary R., Steven M. Ross, Howard K. Kalman, and Jerrold E. Kemp. 2011. *Designing Effective Instruction*. 6th ed. Hoboken, NJ: Wiley.

Reiser, Robert A. 2012. "What Field Did You Say You Were in? Defining and Naming Our Field." In *Trends and Issues in Instructional Design and Technology*, edited by Robert A. Reiser and John V. Dempsey, 1–7. Boston: Pearson.

4

What Do I Need to Know?

You have convinced me that using the Teaching Tripod instructional design (ID) approach would be useful for my Information Literacy Instruction (ILI) planning and now I am ready to try my hand. But I want to make sure that my instruction will be relevant and appropriate for my learners. How do needs assessments contribute to the Tripod process?

You probably think you know a lot about your learners and their needs already. And you most likely do know a great deal about them from your day-to-day interactions at the reference desk, during consultation appointments, from your experiences in ILI sessions, and from casual conversation with your learners. But are you sure your anecdotal information is up to date? Perhaps new needs have surfaced that have not as yet come to your attention. Maybe the demographics in your target population have shifted a bit. And how well do you understand the climate, culture, and politics of the institution in which your library is located? Who are the key players in your environment? What do these key players value? How do new programs gain the support necessary to get them approved and implemented? Being familiar with your institutional environment will help you decide what type of ILI would have the most chance of success and with whom you could partner to help make your ILI ideas a reality.

Engaging in some form of background research about your population, their needs, and your institutional culture can help you ensure that the information you are using as the basis for your Teaching Tripod elements is accurate, will allow you to create the most appropriate ILI for your audience, and will help you select an approach that has the greatest chance of being accepted by your library, your audience, and your institution. Furthermore, it is always a good idea to do a reality check before you proceed to make sure that you have the resources (staff, equipment, space, technology, etc.) to implement your ideas, the time to complete the ID process, and the expertise to create the materials (print or online) you wish to use.

QUESTIONS TO CONSIDER
- ➢ What types of information/data should I be collecting before I start working on the Teaching Tripod elements?
- ➢ How do I gather this information?
- ➢ Where would I find this information?
- ➢ How do I use the information I gathered to inform my ideas during the Teaching Tripod process?

IDENTIFYING THE PROBLEM—WHAT IS THE KNOWLEDGE GAP?

Why did you decide that offering some kind of instructional support should be considered? What motivated you to take on this often complicated, complex, labor-intensive, and time-consuming task of developing some new form of ILI? Did something in your environment change causing you to think that a new ILI endeavor is needed? As mentioned in chapter 3, the impetus for developing a new instructional offering can take many different forms—reactive (as a reaction to your experiences with learners), interactive (in coordination with your institutional partners), or proactive (from your own expertise, and from your desire to enhance your ILI program and add new elements to it) (Grassian and Kaplowitz 2009). You have probably experienced all three modes of instructional initiation in your own practice. So think about your own ILI offerings and take a moment to complete the worksheet in figure 4.1 regarding how instruction is initiated in your environment.

Regardless of the starting point, the first thing you need to do is identify the problem. Is there something your learners need to do, some information they need to gather, some skill they need to acquire, and/or some resource they need to learn about that would enhance their information literacy abilities? Do your learners seem frustrated and discouraged by their inability to find the most appropriate, authentic, and relevant information to address their information needs? If so, would some form of instructional support ease their way? In order to answer this question, you need to know more about the learners themselves and their particular information needs.

NEEDS ASSESSMENTS—AN OVERVIEW

If you wish to make informed decisions about when and how to develop new instructional offerings you need to have a solid understanding of your learners, the environment, and the realities of your own situation. In order to do so, you need to have up-to-date and accurate information. In other words, you need to perform some kind of needs assessment. During this pre-Tripod part of the ID process you will need to gather information on the following:

➤ Your learners—In order to gather data about learners and their information needs, needs assessments look at such things as demographics, past ILI experiences, educational goals, and so forth.

➤ Your environment—You also need to examine your institution or community's culture, climate, and politics. This is a good opportunity to find out who in your institution/community might share your interest in ILI and could be potential partners for you.

➤ Your situation—Looking at your library's resources to determine what types of instruction can be supported given the current situation (staffing, facilities and equipment, funding, time allocations, training needed, etc.) can serve as a definite reality check. Are your ideas even feasible given what you have available to you? This is also the time to look at the rest of your ILI program to see how the new offering will impact it. Does the new offering supplement current offerings or can it replace ones already being done? Are some of the current offerings poorly attended or outdated, and so could be dropped to make room for the new offering (Booth 2011; Grassian and Kaplowitz 2005, 2009; Morrison et al. 2011)?

Let's examine each of these three aspects of a needs assessment in a bit more detail.

Needs Assessment—Part 1: Finding Out about Your Learners

Gathering information about your learners can take a variety of forms from casual to systematic. Instruction librarians often formulate some impressions about possible knowledge gaps from the types of questions that are asked at reference-desk exchanges or other interactions with their learners. In some cases these informal needs assessments may be enough to cause you to decide that instruction would be helpful, and you can move directly

FIGURE 4.1

How ILI Is Initiated in My Library

Think about the various types of ILI offered in your library. Give one example of ILI that was initiated via each of the three approaches (reactive, interactive, and proactive).

Reactive mode example (initiated as response to existing situation)

➢   What prompted the decision to develop a new ILI offering?

➢   Did you collaborate with anyone on this ILI and if so, who?

➢   Who was the intended audience for this ILI?

➢   What type of ILI did you decide to offer?

Interactive mode example (initiated at the request of someone outside the library)

➢   What prompted the decision to develop a new ILI offering?

➢   Did you collaborate with anyone on this ILI and if so, who?

➢   Who was the intended audience for this ILI?

➢   What type of ILI did you decide to offer?

Proactive mode example (initiated based on librarian's expertise and knowledge of ILI and a desire to enhance the current ILI program)

➢   What prompted the decision to develop a new ILI offering?

➢   Did you collaborate with anyone on this ILI and if so, who?

➢   Who was the intended audience for this ILI?

➢   What type of ILI did you decide to offer?

into the Teaching Tripod portion of your ID process. This is especially true if you feel that the situation is urgent and needs to be addressed quickly.

On the other hand, these informal experiences may cause you to think that further exploration into your learner population would be helpful. So you decide to undertake more formal and systematic ways to gather this information about your learners and the characteristics they exhibit. Various offices and agencies in your community or institution can provide a great deal of data regarding the demographics of your target audience. You will want to find out the ages, ethnicities, and cultures represented by your learners, their previous educational experience, as well as any ILI they may have already encountered. Is English a second language for some of your learners and if so, what are their first languages (Freiberg and Driscoll 2005; Morrison et al. 2011)? Census reports, city-planning offices, zoning commissions, and other government agencies can be useful starting points for the public library environment. The city and state education agencies and boards of education can provide this type of information for school librarians. If you work in the college or university setting, try working with the registrar's office as well as any office that provides support to special portions of the campus population (student services, students with disabilities, international students, transfer students, reentry students, or groups that work with students for whom English is a second language). Human resources offices might be a good source of information in the corporate or special library setting. Other sources of information might be administrators, community leaders, and members of local organizations and special interest groups (Grassian and Kaplowitz 2009).

If time permits, you might also wish to engage in some data gathering of your own through the use of interviews, focus groups, and surveys/questionnaires. In addition to providing the demographic data you need, these will also allow you to find out more about perceived information needs directly from the learners themselves, and/or those who work most directly with them (employers, classroom teachers/faculty, supervisors). By talking to your learners, you can discover what information they are most frequently looking for and where they are encountering difficulties or are becoming frustrated. Asking employers, supervisors, or teachers/faculty their information literacy expectations for their staff or students can also be enlightening. Keep in mind that any of these more formal and systematic approaches can be time consuming, labor intensive, and require a certain level of expertise. But they also can provide the most accurate and in-depth information about your learners (Grassian and Kaplowitz 2005, 2009; Veldof 2006).

Another way to discover what types of ILI skills your learners need is to examine your institution's mission statement and look for references to information literacy or related concepts. If information literacy is mentioned directly, how is it defined? It is always a good idea to know what your parent institution means by information literacy to make sure you are all in agreement. Knowing how others in your setting define information literacy can not only help you develop appropriate ILI, it can also open up lines of communication with potential partners in your environment.

Professional organizations may also offer some insight into the types of skills that are expected of people preparing for certain fields (academic, corporate, technical, etc.). Knowing what is expected of your learners by those will be looking at them for entry into higher levels of education or the workplace can give you much food for thought about the types of information literacy skills you wish to include in your ILI. Don't forget to talk to technology experts in your environment. They can help identify access issues as well as facilitate your understanding of the levels of technology expertise that may exist among your learners (Grassian and Kaplowitz 2009).

Needs Assessment—Part 2: Finding Out about Your Environment

An in-depth understanding of your learners is only one part of your information gathering. You also need to examine the overall context in which you are operating. That is, you need to do some research about the climate, culture, and politics of your parent organization, institution, or community. You may have discovered a great deal about your learners and have a firm idea of what types of ILI they need to be successful both in your environment and beyond. But in order to make your ideas a reality, you must be able to implement them. And to do so you need to know how your environment works. That is, you should have a firm understanding about how your library fits into the bigger picture in which it is operating. Identifying who needs to be convinced that your ideas have merit, as well as who might be potential supporters and collaborators increases the likelihood that your ILI ideas will become a reality (Grassian and Kaplowitz 2005). Who are the stakeholders in the situation you are examining? In other words, who will be affected by any information literacy deficits exhibited by your learners? Obviously, your learners represent one important stakeholder group. But don't forget the groups from whom you solicited information about your learners as described above.

The levels of information literacy learners exhibit directly impact teachers and faculty in the K–20 world. Without a solid grounding in information literacy, learners may not be able to complete tasks assigned to them efficiently and effectively. Administrators in these environments may also be counted as stakeholders since they must uphold institution standards as well as those set by accreditation agencies. The levels of information literacy exhibited by those who are seeking employment also affect the quality of the workforce. So you can count employers among your stakeholders. Community leaders, library board members, and those in political office may also have some interest in having an educated and information literate population. If you are working in the public library setting, don't forget to explore these groups as potential stakeholders and possible partners. Look for goals that you and your stakeholders have in common. Identify how what your stakeholders value overlaps with the goals of your ILI. Once they see what is in it for them, your stakeholders will be more likely to both support your ideas and work collaboratively with you to achieve those common goals (Grassian and Kaplowitz 2005; Raspa and Ward 2000; Rubin 1998).

Another thing to consider is how change and innovation is viewed in your environment (both within your library and in the larger institution or community). Do you work within a risk-taking, nimble, fast-moving environment that is willing to try new things even if they have the possibility of failure? Or is your environment a more conservative one that approaches innovation a bit more cautiously? Who are the decision makers? What is the nature of power within your organization/community? Is it top down or more distributed? In other words, whom do you have to convince in order to get a new ILI endeavor (or any new idea) approved—both among your direct coworkers and supervisors and in the larger environment)? Identifying and cultivating the change makers and getting their support will go a long way to ensure your ideas are heard and can move forward (Grassian and Kaplowitz 2005; Schneider 1994; Todaro 2001).

Don't forget to look at the context within your library as well. For example, when considering adding instruction, it is a good idea to look at your current ILI offerings to see where the new endeavor would fit in. Could current offerings be modified to meet the identified instructional need? You should also consider if any of your current offerings could be canceled to make way for the new class or course. Further, you should take a look at any instructional material (print or online) that could be repurposed for the proposed instruction. Last, but certainly not least, you need to have a firm understanding of where ILI fits into the priorities in your library. Is ILI clearly defined as part of the library's mission, and if not, why isn't it? Does your library administration value and support ILI? How do your colleagues (both teaching librarians and those who are not directly engaged in teaching) feel about ILI? Knowing how both your administration and your colleagues view ILI will help you frame the way in which you propose your ILI ideas within your library.

Needs Assessment—Part 3: Finding Out about Your Situation

Finally, you need to do some introspection and reflection on what is possible given the situation in which you are operating. Although you may have identified a real need and have some great ideas about how to address that need, you have to be sure that the cure is not worse than the disease. In other words, you must engage in some thoughtful reality checking. What types of ILI solutions are achievable given your staffing, facilities, workload demands, time constraints, and so forth? If you were to add a new form of ILI how would that impact not only those directly engaged in ILI, but the rest of your library staff as well? This is a good time to get as many people as you can from within the library involved in the planning process. Having others assist in the ID process will help to garner their support as well as their goodwill. Plus, you will be tapping into a broader pool of experience and expertise, which could result in a stronger, more effective ILI endeavor (Grassian and Kaplowitz 2005, 2009; Veldof 2006).

This is also a good time to review the strengths of your instruction librarians and what, if any, additional training might be needed to support changes in your ILI. Look at everything that might be involved in new offerings. How comfortable are your librarians in both F2F and online instruction? Would your instruction librarians benefit from some updating and revitalizing of their F2F teaching methods? Are there types of presentation or other instructional software that your librarians should know about? Has your library added new resources that your librarians need to review before teaching about them? Identifying training needs will not only ensure a smoother implementation process, it will also help you determine how much implementation time you will need to allocate as you get both the materials and those who will be teaching the content ready for the new ILI offering.

DETERMINING THE CONTENT OF YOUR NEEDS ASSESSMENT

As you can see, there are lots of aspects to a thorough needs assessment. However, as has already been discussed in chapter 3, how much of a needs assessment is necessary will depend on many factors such as how instruction was initiated (reactive, interactive, and proactive), how much lead time you have for your ID, the scope of the instruction (one-shot versus full-length course), whether or not you have worked with this audience before, and so on.

To review some of the points made in chapter 3, we can see for example that the proactive approach where you are trying to identify gaps in your ILI program and come up with new ILI initiatives requires the most intensive and complete needs assessment. In the reactive approach, on the other hand, you have already identified a need based on your interactions with your learners. So although there may be some additional information that might prove useful, reactive instruction generally does not require as much in-depth needs assessment as do those initiated proactively. In the interactive approach, the person who requested the ILI will probably be able to supply most of the information you need. However, while he or she may have a general idea that it would be useful for learners to gain more information literacy skills, the exact nature of those skills may not be as clear. That is where you come in, and it is also where some form of needs assessment might be useful to help you explore the exact nature of the information needs and any gaps in knowledge exhibited by the particular target audience in question. It might also provide some addition insight for the requester as well.

Obviously the more time you have available for your ID process, the longer you have for the type of information gathering that is necessary for your needs assessment. If you only have a few days or even a few weeks, it might be necessary to go with what you already know, and use the instruction itself as a way to gather a bit more information about the learners and their needs. You can always do a brief needs assessment at the beginning of a F2F session, or have learners complete some kind of online survey prior to coming to class or beginning an online tutorial. You can use that data to do some slight modifications to your instruction in a F2F session. In the online environment, this needs assessment data can be used to offer learners suggestions about the most appropriate path through the material to address their information needs. This will help learners focus on what they need to learn and build on what they already know.

You should also consider the scope of your instruction—that is, are you getting ready for a one-shot or a full-length course—when deciding the extent of any needs assessment you might wish to do. You may need to do a bit more research on your audience if you are developing a full-length course than you would for a one-shot.

Furthermore, you usually have (or ought to have allocated) more time to get ready for a full-length course than you might have for the one-shot situation.

Your familiarity with the target audience also factors into your needs assessment decisions. If you are working with a group that you have already worked with before, you may know a great deal about these learners and their information literacy needs and can do just a quick update type of needs assessment. However, if this is a new audience for you, it would be helpful if you could factor in a bit more time for your needs assessment efforts in order for you to learn more about them. Please see chapter 3 for more on this topic as well as worksheets to help you determine how much of a needs assessment would be appropriate for your specific, current situation.

Regardless of the type of needs assessment you undertake, the first thing you need to do is identify where there are gaps in your own understanding of the situation. Once you pinpoint the types of information that would be most helpful you can then move on to brainstorming where to find that information. This really boils down to coming up with the answers to the following three questions:

➤ What do I know?
➤ What do I need to find out?
➤ How will I find out?

So before you begin your ID process, take a few moments to complete the worksheet in figure 4.2.

NEEDS ASSESSMENTS AND THE TEACHING TRIPOD

Clearly the information attained by doing needs assessments feeds directly into what you will include in the three Teaching Tripod elements. First and foremost, the more you know about your learners and their information needs, the more appropriate and relevant will be the expected learning outcomes (ELOs) you write for your ILI. Having done your homework, you can now feel more secure that you have selected the type of ELOs that will empower your learners to find the information that is useful and important to them.

Furthermore, the more you know about your learners the better equipped you will be to select the type of learning activities that will be most engaging and effective for them. And finally you will be able to select appropriate types of assessment techniques to help you determine that your learners have in fact attained the outcomes you set for the instruction.

You will also find that this needs assessment information is valuable in the implementation/delivery stages of your ID process. Knowing how your environment works (culture, climate, and politics) will go a long way in helping you gain the support you need to bring your ILI ideas into being. And considering the realities of your situation (staffing, timing, facilities, etc.) will ensure that you will not be developing ILI that will be a burden on your library, but will in fact fit in well with other ILI offerings already in place, and that will have the support of those with whom you work. For more on how needs assessments supports implementation/delivery issues, see chapter 9.

NEEDS ASSESSMENTS AND ILI

Performing some kind of needs assessment is a crucial part of all ID for any type of instruction, and ILI is no exception. In some ways instruction librarians operate at a disadvantage in regard to knowing their audience. Their interactions with their learners may be few and far between in both the public and special library setting. In the K–20 environment instruction librarians most often are working with the direct curriculum teachers rather than being the teacher of record. Even when they teach full-length courses, they may not be as involved with the larger

FIGURE 4.2

Getting Ready for a Needs Assessment

Complete this worksheet to help you plan for your needs assessment.

What Do I Know?

➤ Who are my learners (demographics, educational and ILI background, etc.)?

➤ What information gaps seem to exist in my learners' ILI skills, knowledge, and abilities?

➤ Who are my potential partners and/or stakeholders?

➤ What attitudes toward ILI are held by the members of the organization and by those within the library?

➤ What do I know about organizational climate and culture?

➤ Can I identify any potential constraints/limitations resulting from current levels of staffing, funding, facilities, time frame, and so forth.? If so, what are they?

What Do I Need to Find Out?

➤   Is there anything I need to add to what I already know?

➤   Is there anything else I might need to know? If so, what might that be?

How Will I Find Out?

➤   What offices or agencies within my organization or community might have the data I need?

➤   Who in my organization or community might supply additional information about my potential learners and their needs?

➤   Who in my organization or community might supply additional information about the environment (culture, climate, politics) within which I will be working?

➤   What outside agencies, professional organizations, potential employers, governmental departments might be able to supply insight into the information literacy needs of my target audience?

student population as their discipline teacher colleagues. So instruction librarians often must rely on what others know about their learners in order to develop the type of ILI that will be useful.

Taking a moment to at least consider what, if any, type of needs assessment is necessary and appropriate every time you are thinking about developing a new class or course is a worthwhile endeavor as it will allow you to make intelligent and informed decisions about the amount of effort you need to expend in your ID process. And if you decide that you know enough about your learners and their needs to move directly into the Teaching Tripod aspect of planning, you can feel comfortable that you are making that decision based on sound thinking and not just because you are anxious to get the process started.

Full-blown and extensive needs assessments are not undertaken lightly as they require a great deal of effort, time, and expertise. And for the most part, you do know a lot about your learners, your organizational or community environment, and the constraints under which you are operating in your own library setting. So you may decide that you only need to do some brief data gathering in order to update your ideas. However, you should also take care not to become complacent about what you know (or think you know) regarding your learners, your environment, and your situation. You might wish to consider including doing an extensive needs assessment every two to five years in your long-term ILI planning to ensure that the information you are basing your ID ideas on is accurate, and that you are still developing relevant and useful ILI. Keep in mind that whatever data you collect from any kind of needs assessment—be they large or small in scope—can feed into these more extensive needs assessments providing useful contacts, data, and other information for these two- to five-year efforts (Grassian and Kaplowitz 2009).

WRAP-UP

Instruction librarians all know quite a bit about their learners from their various interactions with them—in the library, in the classroom, or in informal exchanges with learners in their shared environment. But if instruction librarians are to engage in systematic ID, they also need to go beyond these informal and often anecdotal ways of gathering information. Understanding what comprises a needs assessment, what questions you need to ask, what types of data you need to gather, and where to find the data you need about your learners, your environment, and your own library situation helps you make thoughtful decisions before you embark on the Teaching Tripod aspects of ID. And if you decide that you don't need to do additional information gathering for a specific situation, that decision will be based on a firm grasp of how needs assessments contribute to the overall ID process.

WHAT STUCK?

You feel your librarians have now bought into the idea of instructional design for their ILI offerings and are excited about the possibilities of using the Teaching Tripod approach as a way to structure their planning. But they have expressed the opinion that their hands-on experience with your learner population has supplied them with all the background information they need. With all that experiential familiarity under their belts they feel ready to jump into the actual Teaching Tripod stage of the ID process.

You are concerned that they may be basing their decisions on outdated information or are less informed about your learner population than they may think. So you decide to develop a brief introduction to the concept of needs assessment to help them gain some insight into this important pre-Tripod aspect of ID. Please complete the worksheet in figure 4.3 to help you create "talking points" as you prepare to discuss needs assessments with your colleagues.

How you present this information is up to you. You could develop an interactive workshop, do a brief presentation during a staff meeting, create and distribute some print material, or develop a web page that covers this material. You are the best judge of the most appropriate way to reach your colleagues and persuade them of the necessity of considering what if any type of needs assessment is appropriate as they do their ID for ILI.

FIGURE 4.3

Talking Points about Needs Assessments

What would be the best way to introduce the topic of needs assessments to your colleagues? Your responses to the following questions should help you organize your thoughts as you prepare to discuss needs assessments with your fellow instruction librarians.

➢   How would you describe the concept of needs assessments to your colleagues?

➢   What would you like to share about the advantages of doing needs assessment prior to engaging in the Teaching Tripod process?

➢   How would the different ways in which instruction is initiated help your learners to gain more insight into the concept of needs assessments?

➢   How would you help your colleagues determine how much or how little a needs assessment should be done under a variety of different circumstances?

REFERENCES

Booth, Char. 2011. *Reflective Teaching, Effective Learning*. Chicago: American Library Association.

Freiberg, H. Jerome, and Amy Driscoll. 2005. *Universal Teaching Strategies*. Boston: Allyn & Bacon.

Grassian, Esther, and Joan Kaplowitz. 2005. *Learning to Lead and Manage Information Literacy Instruction*. New York: Neal-Schuman.

———. 2009. *Information Literacy Instruction: Theory and Practice*. 2nd ed. New York: Neal-Schuman.

Morrison, Gary R., Steven M. Ross, Howard K. Kalman, and Jerrold E. Kemp. 2011. *Designing Effective Instruction*. 6th ed. Hoboken, NJ: Wiley.

Raspa, Dick, and Dane Ward. 2000. "Listening for Collaboration: Faculty and Librarians Working Together." In *The Collaborative Imperative: Librarians and Faculty Working Together in the Information Universe*, edited by Dick Raspa and Dane Ward, 1–18. Chicago: Association of College and Research Libraries—American Library Association.

Rubin, Hank. 1998. *Collaboration Skills for Educators and Nonprofit Leaders*. Chicago: Lyceum.

Schneider, William E. 1994. *The Reengineering Alternative*. Burt Ridge, IL: Irwin.

Todaro, Julie Beth. 2001. "The Effective Organization in the 21st Century." *Library Administration and Management* 15 (3): 176–78.

Veldof, Jerilyn. 2006. *Creating the One-Shot Library Workshop: A Step by Step Guide*. Chicago: American Library Association.

What Will My Learners Be Able to Do?

Expected Learning Outcomes

Now that I have gathered my background information, I feel confident that I have identified my learners and can describe their information literacy needs. I have also familiarized myself with the institutional climate within which I must operate, and have decided what type of information literacy instruction (ILI) would have the best chances of succeeding in my environment given that climate as well as any limitations and/or constraints that exist in my own library. So why can't I just start outlining my proposed ILI?

As an instruction librarian your area of expertise is information literacy. You know how to define it, what skills are needed to be information literate, and how to teach those skills. So it stands to reason that once you know who your learners are and what they need to learn about information literacy in order to satisfy their information needs, you can draw upon your own knowledge base to design an effective ILI class, website, or online tutorial. RIGHT???? Actually, that is not entirely true. While it is possible to come up with ILI based on your own experience and expertise, designing effective and well-organized ILI takes a bit more thought.

Think of it as creating a recipe or developing a road map for your ILI. The aim of this element of the Teaching Tripod is to make sure that your ILI will help learners accomplish what is necessary in order to address their information needs. Writing expected learning outcomes (ELOs) ensures that your ILI includes the ingredients/signposts (skills and information) learners need and will provide them with the recipe/directions (strategies) that will enable them to find the information they seek (Grassian and Kaplowitz 2009).

QUESTIONS TO CONSIDER
➢ Why should I write ELOs for my ILI?
➢ What are the characteristics of ELOs?
➢ How do ELOs relate to the other two elements of the Teaching Tripod?
➢ How do I decide which ELOs to include in my ILI?
➢ How do I write effective ELOs?

ARTICULATING YOUR INSTRUCTIONAL INTENT

Completing some type of needs assessment helps you discover the skills, knowledge, and abilities that are necessary for your learners to attain in order to satisfy their information needs. Now comes the interesting part—translating those ideas into instruction. The information you gathered in your needs assessments allowed you to gain a better understanding of your learners and the specific situation in which you are working. Hopefully it also helped you identify any information literacy–related knowledge gaps your learners may have. Your next task is to decide the types of instructional interventions that will best address these knowledge gaps.

The first step in developing instructional interventions is to articulate the overall intent of your proposed instruction—in other words, your instructional goal(s) for the ILI. Goals describe what you want your learners to accomplish—that is to say, what you would like learners to take away from the instruction. Since goals are meant to give an overview of the instruction, they can be written in broad, general strokes using words such as "understand," "learn," and "know." Taking the time to organize your thoughts into coherent statements enables you to design targeted instruction that will be effective, engaging, and useful to your learners (Grassian and Kaplowitz 2009).

While goals are often written in these general terms, ELOs describe the actual behaviors and skills learners will need to attain to achieve these specified goals. In other words, they indicate what learners need to be able to do in order to reach the goals set for the instruction (Farmer 2011; Grassian and Kaplowitz 2009; Morrison et al. 2011). For example, the goal of your instruction might be that learners know how to find relevant articles on their topic. ELOs indicate what they need to be able to do to complete that goal. In this case they would need to select appropriate databases, design effective search strategies using those databases, evaluate search results for relevancy, and refine searches to improve results.

Even the briefest of investigations into the literature related to ELOs will yield what might appear to be an overwhelming amount of information. One particular point of potential confusion is the use of the terms "objectives" and "outcomes." Many writers in the fields of pedagogy and instructional design (ID) differentiate between these two concepts. When that is the case, objectives are intended to describe the behavior learners are expected to be able to exhibit following instruction, and outcomes describe how they will actually exhibit that behavior. So returning to the database-searching example from above, one of the objectives would be selecting an appropriate database and the ELO would be that learners demonstrate that they can pick the most appropriate databases for a given topic from a list of possible options.

The difference between objectives and outcomes, therefore, is real but fairly subtle. To further complicate matters, many writers either use the terms interchangeably or describe both in very similar terms. So for the purpose of working with the Teaching Tripod approach, I have combined both ideas under the one heading of ELOs. As we continue to explore this idea, keep in mind that the intent of an ELO is to indicate both what is to be learned and how the learner will exhibit having learned it.

WHAT DO EXPECTED LEARNING OUTCOMES LOOK LIKE?

ELOs describe how the instruction will impact your learners. In other words, they specify how your learners will be changed as a result of participating in instruction. ELOs are intended to answer two questions:

➢ What will learners be able to do following instruction?
➢ How will you know they can do it?

As such, they need to be written in a specific way. So ELOs must adhere to the following rules.
    ELOs:

➢ Are written from the learners' perspective.
➢ Describe observable actions.
➢ Are measurable.
➢ Are written in the active voice (i.e., using active verbs)

Following these four simple rules allows you to avoid the most prevalent mistake people make when writing ELOs—that is, using words that are more appropriate for describing instructional goals such as "know" or "understand." The reason that these types of words are not suitable for ELOs is that they are neither observable nor measurable. In order to answer your two questions "What will learners be able to do following instruction?" and "How will you know they can do it?" your outcomes need to describe ways in which learners can demonstrate that they have in fact attained the ELOs you have set for them (Grassian and Kaplowitz 2009).

Another way to look at this is to think about why you are writing ELOs in the first place. The purpose of ELOs is to help you determine the content of your instruction, assist you in developing ways in which learners can interact with the material to be learned in order to attain the proposed ELOs, and point out how learners can demonstrate that they have learned the material addressed in the instruction. So while we cannot directly observe how someone understands a concept, we can write outcomes that indicate the action a learner will take in order to demonstrate that understanding.

Let's return to that database-searching example described above. The goal of that instruction was to have learners know how to find relevant articles on their topic. While we cannot observe "knowing," we can observe learners selecting appropriate databases to search, developing effective search strategies, executing and refining searches as needed, and so forth. So we are putting our goal into operational terms by creating observable and measurable ELOs that support the attainment of the broad instruction goal.

HOW EXPECTED LEARNING OUTCOMES RELATE TO THE OTHER ELEMENTS IN THE TEACHING TRIPOD

In a very real way ELOs create the framework upon which you hang the rest of your planning process. Outcomes help you organize and structure your instruction, suggest learning activities that will enable learners to interact with the material in a productive and useful way, and indicate what needs to be assessed in order to determine if the instructional goals were reached (Battersby and Learning Outcomes Network 1999, Mager 1997b). ELOs are the starting point from which the rest of the Teaching Tripod will grow. So both the learning activities and assessment elements of the Tripod build upon the ELOs you set for the instruction. See figure 5.1 for a graphical representation of how the three Tripod elements are interrelated.

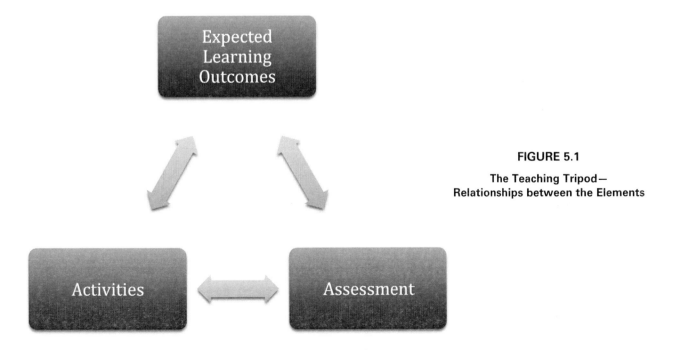

FIGURE 5.1

**The Teaching Tripod—
Relationships between the Elements**

The idea underlying this approach to ID is often referred to as "backward design" (Wiggins and McTighe 2006). Rather than starting with what you think you should teach, you begin your ID process by looking at the end product—that is, what you want your learners to be able to do as a result of instruction. You begin at the end and use that end point to decide how you can get your learners there—thus the term "backward design."

Once you have identified this end point, you can engage in what is known as task analysis (Mager 1997a; Morrison et al. 2011). Basically, task analysis asks you to look at the end product (the instructional goal) and break it down into its component parts (what learners need to be able to do to reach that goal). Each of those component parts becomes a specific ELO. Once you have your ELOs, you can think about the types of learning activities that will allow your learners to attain each of these outcomes. In other words, you can decide upon the ways in which you want learners to interact with the material in order to achieve all the ELOs set for the instruction.

Each ELO must be addressed during instruction through some type of instructional activity. Here the term "activity" is being used in the broadest sense. Having learners listen to you lecture on the topic or view a demonstration of the material or strategy you want them to learn can be viewed as one type of activity. However, keep in mind the observable and measurable rules for outcomes. So while material can be addressed in these relatively passive ways, you should also include something that will help you observe learners' grasp of the material and that allows them to demonstrate the attainment of the ELO. We will return to the idea of how learners can interact with material in observable and measurable ways in chapter 6, which deals with the learning activities element of the Tripod.

While every ELO must have an associated activity, not every activity you include in your instruction needs to relate to the designated ELOs. However, if an activity does not address one of your ELOs, you should ask yourself why you are including that activity in your instruction. Does it have a purpose? Or is it just something you thought would be fun to include? Remember that learners can grasp only so much in a given instructional interaction. So try to avoid overloading them with material that is not critical to the instructional goal. A review of activities versus ELOs can help you home in on the most important elements of your instruction and will help you to "trim the fat" by eliminating those less relevant activities from the overall instruction. These extra activities can be held in reserve and included in the instruction if time permits. On the other hand, if you feel that the activity is critical to the instruction, you might wish to review your outcomes to see if you left something out in your ELO list.

Doing a task analysis not only helps you determine the activities you need to include, it often suggests the order in which the elements should be addressed. So another way that writing ELOs and doing task analysis pays off is that they help you sequence your instruction. We will return to this concept of sequencing in chapter 8.

Finally, having written ELOs informs the assessment component of your ID process. In the same way that each ELO needs to be addressed by a specific learning activity, you also must include some way for learners to demonstrate the attainment of all the ELOs. In other words, the attainment of all the ELOs must be assessed. Assessments can be formal or informal. They can be part of the instruction itself or can occur at a later time. But without an assessment of each ELO, you have no way of knowing if your instruction was effective or if the instructional experience was a complete waste of time for all concerned.

Many of the active learning exercises that instruction librarians often include in their ILI can be used as informal assessment measures. As you watch learners try out newly acquired skills in some kind of hands-on practice or collaborative learning activity, you can also gauge the attainment of the associated ELO. Much of the assessments typically done in ILI one-shots rely heavily on this more informal approach to assessment. The assessment element of the Teaching Tripod will be addressed in more detail in chapter 7.

You probably have ELOs in mind every time you design any kind of ILI. But you may not be articulating them in any formal way, nor have actually written them down. However, you probably understand the ELOs that underlie your instructional ideas better than you may think you do. Reflect on some ILI you have already designed and then complete the worksheet in figure 5.2. You may be surprised to discover that when you reflect on your ID process you were already thinking in terms of ELOs.

FIGURE 5.2

ELOs in My ILI

Whether or not you think in terms of ELOs when you design your ILIs, you should have a pretty good idea about what you are trying to accomplish with your interactions with your learners. Think about an ILI you already teach and then answer the following questions:

➤ Look at a class or online learning activity you have already designed. What do you think were the ELOs you had in mind for this instruction?

➤ Did you clearly articulate these outcomes for yourself and/or for your learners? Why or why not?

➤ Now look at the ELOs you described in answer to the first question. What did you include in your ILI to help learners attain each of the ELOs? Describe any lecture segments, demos, exercises, or other activities that were part of your ILI.

➤ Finally, how did you determine if the ELOs described above were attained? In other words, how did you assess if your learners learned what you intended them to learn?

DECIDING WHAT TO INCLUDE

As we have already discussed, deciding upon ELOs for any given instruction is directly related to your needs assessment and what you already know about your learners and their needs. Needs assessments help you determine the content of your ILI by identifying the skills, knowledge, and strategies your learners need to acquire in order to address their specific information needs. ELOs also help you avoid overloading your learners with unnecessary material by allowing you to "trim the fat" in your instruction. Articulating your instructional ELOs lets you concentrate on what is absolutely necessary for your learners to learn and points out "nice but not crucial" elements you may have included in your ILI.

Be rational about the number of ELOs that can be addressed in a given time frame for synchronous (in real time) instruction whether it is for F2F or live online. While this may be a fairly intuitive notion for synchronous instruction given the time constraints involved, you should also think about limiting the number of ELOs in your asynchronous online material. Although learners can usually interact with asynchronous sites at their own pace and on their own schedule, learners can easily be overwhelmed and turned off by overly ambitious and complicated online instruction (Morrison and Anglin 2005). Whether you are designing synchronous or asynchronous instruction, try to think like a novice. What was it like for you when you first tried to learn this material? Select only the most critical items for your ELOs. Remember that you can always refer learners to additional material (print or online), or recommend additional ILI for more complex material if appropriate.

One way to look at this is to think in terms of "need to know," "nice to know," and "extra bells and whistles." Use whatever background information you have on your learners and their levels of experience—educational, technological, and ILI—to help you figure out what your learners already know. Determining their experience levels will help you decide what you should include in your ILI. Extremely inexperienced learners will have to start at the most basic "need to know" level, while you may be able to start more experienced ones at a more advanced point in the process.

Once you selected the "need to know" items, you can go on to decide what also might be the "nice to know." These would be skills, strategies, or behaviors that are not absolutely necessary to fulfill the instructional goal, but might result in a bit more sophisticated results. Your learners can function without them, but some learners might appreciate these extra tips. The same holds true for the "extra bells and whistles." These are the items that are not necessary at this point, but might be of interest to learners as they gain some experience with the basic material.

Whether to go beyond the "need to know" ELOs depends both upon the level of your learners and any time constraints you might have for your instruction. The shorter the contact time for synchronous (in real time) instruction whether it is face-to-face (F2F) or online, the more selective you need to be when choosing ELOs. You might wish to restrict yourself to three to five ELOs if you are only going to be interacting with learners for an hour or so. However, having a few "nice to know" and "extra bells and whistles" ELOs can come in handy in a variety of situations. For example, if your learners attain the basic ELOs quicker than you anticipated, perhaps because they were more experienced than you originally thought, they might appreciate learning some more sophisticated and complex material.

Being prepared with this additional material can also come in handy when faced with questions that may go beyond the scope you intended for the instruction. Since you already considered these possible ELOs, you also will have thought about ways to address them. So you probably will have some activities, demos, or speaking points at your fingertips to answer these additional questions. Of course, the amount of time you can devote to these extra points will depend on how much time you have in total, and how quickly (or not) your learners are attaining the basic ELOs you set. If time is running short, and/or if only one or two of your learners seem to be at this more advanced level, you can always set up some individual consultations with them. And these consultations will be easy to do since you already have the requisite material ready to go.

As already mentioned above, although it might appear that asynchronous online instruction such as online tutorials should allow you the opportunity to address more ELOs than synchronous instruction with its contact time constraints, even asynchronous instruction has an overload potential. Learners can still be overwhelmed by the instructional content if the ILI is attempting to address a large number of ELOs. Asynchronous instruction does offer some ways to address this issue by the careful use of organization and navigation principles. For example, you can organize the asynchronous material into the three levels discussed above and then offer learners the opportunity to move through the "need to know" material first and select any of the other "nice to know" or "extra bells and whistles" material if and when they feel they need it. Furthermore, since these asynchronous online instructions are usually available for a length of time, learners can choose to do the basic material first. They can try their hands at applying what they learned, and then return to the tutorial to either review parts of the basic information and/or move on to the more complex material (Kaplowitz 2012).

WRITING EXPECTED LEARNING OUTCOMES

Many people choose to skip writing formal outcomes because the idea of putting their thoughts into words feels awkward, intimidating, and maybe even a little bit daunting. But taking the time to articulate what you want your learners to take away from your instruction often can help you clarify your ideas. As a result, your instruction may be more appropriate, coherent, and better organized, and will provide your learners more of a chance of attaining the instructional goal(s). Finally, once you have articulated your ELOs you will be ready to move on to creating engaging learning activities that will enable your learners to attain the ELOs you have set (the learning activities element of the Tripod). Plus you will have identified what learners will have to do in order to demonstrate they have attained those ELOs (the assessment element of the Tripod).

There are various ideas in the ID and education literature about how to write ELOs. However, all these notions agree upon the fact that an ELO must adhere to the four rules or guidelines we have already touched upon above. To reiterate, ELOs are written from the learners' perspective, describe observable behaviors, are measurable (can be assessed), and are written in the active voice (use active verbs). The simplest format for an ELO is as follows:

➤ After instruction, learners will be able to [insert behavior/skill].

However, when you first are trying your hand at all this, you might want to use a more expanded approach. One way to do this is to use what has been referred to as the ABCD formula (Cruickshank, Jenkins, and Metcalf 2009; Elliott et al. 2000). In this methodology for writing ELOs, each of the elements (ABCD) is explicitly described. The letters in the ABCD formula stand for

A = Audience

B = Behavior

C = Condition

D = Degree

Audience

Details about the learners are included in the "audience" element. The audience can be described in a number of ways depending upon your environment. For K–20, the grade level as well as the curriculum being learned is usually part of the audience component. For example, the audience in this environment might be described as high school juniors in an American history class. In a public library the audience might be senior citizens or adults for whom English is a second language. In the corporate or special library setting the audience might include job title as well. So in this setting the audience might be researchers in the research and development division of a biotechnology company.

Behavior

The behavior element is, of course, the heart of the ELO and describes what you expect learners to able to do following instruction. This is where those active verbs go as well. Here are some examples of ELOs for the "audience" examples from the previous paragraph:

➤ High school juniors in an American history class will be able to select relevant articles for their research paper.
➤ Senior citizens for whom English is a second language will be able to evaluate the quality of websites found.
➤ Researchers in the research division of a biotechnology company will be able to identify technical reports/patents that are related to their current research project.

Active Verbs

Let's take a moment to talk about active verbs before moving on to the C and D elements of the formula. The above three examples used the active verbs "select," "evaluate," and "identify." The value of using these types of words is that they describe observable and measurable actions. Fortunately for those of us who write ELOs, help in selecting appropriate verbs is available in the form of Benjamin Bloom's *Taxonomy of Educational Objectives* (1984) and the updated version published almost twenty years later (Anderson and Krathwohl 2001). The value of these taxonomies lies not only in that they suggest verbs for you to use, but also that they associate the verbs with a hierarchy of comprehension levels from basic to complex. In Bloom's original work these levels (starting with the most basic) are knowledge, comprehension, application, analysis, synthesis, and evaluation. The updated version changes the nomenclature to remember, understand, apply, analyze, evaluate, and create. See figures 5.3 and 5.4, respectively, for a sample of verbs that are associated with the levels for each of the two taxonomies.

The verbs listed in these two figures are just a sample of the verbs associated with the comprehension levels in the two taxonomies. Refer to the taxonomies themselves for the complete lists.

Affective Outcomes

Before moving on to the next two ELO elements (C and D) let's take a moment to address how to deal with affective outcomes. While it is fairly easy to see how ELOs can be written for the type of cognitive outcomes described above, you might also be interested in having your instruction impact your learners' attitudes, opinions, and feelings as well. These affective outcomes are a bit more difficult to develop, as it is often a challenge to figure out how changes in learners' affect will be observed and measured. In order to comply with the rules for writing outcomes, you will have to come up with a way for learners to demonstrate the expected change in affect. In other words, you have to come up with observable behaviors from which you can infer that the affect has been changed as a result of your instruction (Cruickshank, Jenkins, and Metcalf 2009; Grassian and Kaplowitz 2009). One way to do this is to administer some kind of questionnaire or survey that measures the learners' attitudes, opinions, or feelings both prior to and following the instruction and compare the learners' responses. Another way to measure affective outcomes is to observe changes in behavior related to that attitude, opinion, and/or feeling. Let's say you are interested in alleviating technophobia through your instruction. You could write the following affective ELO:

➤ After instruction learners (in the target audience) will choose to use computer-based resources as least as often as print resources.

FIGURE 5.3

Bloom's Taxonomy—Comprehension Levels and Suggested Verbs

Knowledge

- ➢ Define
- ➢ Describe
- ➢ Identify
- ➢ List
- ➢ Recall
- ➢ Recognize

Comprehension

- ➢ Classify
- ➢ Distinguish
- ➢ Explain
- ➢ Give examples
- ➢ Locate
- ➢ Select

Application

- ➢ Apply
- ➢ Choose
- ➢ Demonstrate
- ➢ Illustrate
- ➢ Predict
- ➢ Relate

Analysis

- ➢ Analyze
- ➢ Categorize
- ➢ Compare
- ➢ Contrast
- ➢ Differentiate
- ➢ Infer

Synthesis

➢ Arrange
➢ Combine
➢ Construct
➢ Develop
➢ Summarize
➢ Synthesize

Evaluation

➢ Assess
➢ Conclude
➢ Evaluate
➢ Judge
➢ Justify
➢ Rate

FIGURE 5.4

Anderson and Krathwohl's Revised Taxonomy—Comprehension Levels and Suggested Verbs

Remember

- ➢ Define
- ➢ Identify
- ➢ List
- ➢ Recall
- ➢ Recognize
- ➢ Relate

Understand

- ➢ Choose
- ➢ Cite examples of
- ➢ Discriminate
- ➢ Explain
- ➢ Put into own words
- ➢ Select

Apply

- ➢ Apply
- ➢ Demonstrate
- ➢ Generalize
- ➢ Illustrate
- ➢ Interpret
- ➢ Utilize

Analyze

- ➢ Analyze
- ➢ Conclude
- ➢ Determine
- ➢ Differentiate
- ➢ Infer
- ➢ Predict

Evaluate

➢ Appraise
➢ Assess
➢ Critique
➢ Evaluate
➢ Judge
➢ Rate

Create

➢ Arrange
➢ Construct
➢ Create
➢ Design
➢ Develop
➢ Produce

This sets up an activity in which you ask learners to find some specific kind of information and allow them to choose the type of resources they wish to use (print versus computer based) to address this information need. Have your learners try to find some type of information at the beginning of the instruction, and then set another similar information-seeking task for them after the instructional experience. If learners use more computer-based resources following instruction than they did prior to instruction, you can infer that they are less technophobic than they were before you worked with them. So you have not only given your learners a chance to practice their newly acquired attitude, you have given yourself a way to assess that affective change.

While writing affective ELOs can be a bit more challenging than those for cognitive ones, wishing to have your instruction positively impact your learners' affect is a legitimate goal. If learners are too intimidated or anxious to use library-recommended resources they will limit the resources they select when searching for the information they need. Furthermore, library anxiety is still a major impediment to learners being willing to come into your facilities or access your libraries remotely. Including affective outcomes that aim to increase learners' comfort level and enhance their confidence in their abilities to find the information they need will go a long way to reduce library anxiety in your learners (Grassian and Kaplowitz 2009).

Condition

So we have now addressed the audience and behavior components of ELOs. That brings us to C, or condition. The condition describes the situation in which the learner will be interacting with the material in order to demonstrate attainment of the ELO. Let's expand on the sample ELOs already described.

➢ The condition for the high school juniors looking for relevant articles for their research papers would be that after searching appropriate databases, learners are able to select relevant articles for their research papers.

➢ In the case of the senior citizens learning how to evaluate websites, the condition would be that after executing a well-structured web search, senior citizens are able to apply a set of evaluative criteria to determine the most authoritative and trustworthy ones.

➢ And the biotechnology researchers would be able to identify relevant technical reports from the search results attained after utilizing appropriate/recommended online or print resources.

In general, the condition is under your control. The condition describes the parameters you establish for the instruction—that is, the resources you are introducing and making available for the learners' use in addressing their information needs.

Degree

The last component of the ABCD formula is D, which stands for degree. This element describes the level at which learners must demonstrate the ELO in order to be said to have attained the outcome. Most often used in ELOs for credit-bearing instruction as a way to determine grades, you can also include this element in your workshops and one-shot instructions as well. See below for examples of degree for both credit-bearing courses and for nongraded ILI.

➢ Degree for credit-bearing courses—Example: high school students. In credit-bearing courses, the degree generally is related to a grade or score on a product, project, or test. So the references that those high school students included in their papers might be evaluated for quality and relevance and given a score on the appropriateness, relevance, and authoritativeness of the material. And in order to be said to have attained this outcome, learners must earn a grade of 75 percent or more.

➤ Degree for nongraded ILI—Example: senior citizens in a public library or researchers in a biotechnology company. Since many ILIs are not directly graded, the inclusion of degree in your ELOs may not be necessary. Of course, you may choose to include them if you like, but they would be a bit more informal. So you might take a look at the results learners obtained after they performed their database, website, or technical report resource searches and check to see how many of the results meet your standard of quality. You might use the results of this informal review to determine if learners have attained the ELO in question or if you need to do a bit more work with them either during the instruction itself and/or as a follow-up. In other words, you might decide that if learners don't seem to find appropriate and relevant material at least 75 percent of the time, then they have not attained the ELO, and you need to go back and go over that material again. Since the degree of attainment is generally determined in a fairly informal way in many ILI endeavors, librarians often opt to skip the degree element when writing their ELOs.

EXPECTED LEARNING OUTCOMES FOR INFORMATION LITERACY INSTRUCTION

While Bloom's taxonomy and its 2001 update can be very useful in structuring ELOs for ILI, it is helpful to use professional standards developed for librarians in order to determine what types of behavior you wish your learners to exhibit. In other words, you need to know how the library profession characterizes the attributes of an information literate person. Fortunately, professional library associations especially in the K–20 environment (American Association of School Librarians 2013; Association of College and Research Libraries 2013a) have developed standards for information literacy as have many professional organizations in the various academic disciplines (Association of College and Research Libraries 2013b). These can be used as a starting point when you are developing ELOs for your ILI endeavors, and can be further customized to fit your specific situation (Grassian and Kaplowitz 2009).

PUTTING IT ALL TOGETHER

Before we complete this discussion of ELOs and how to write them, let's go back to those sample outcomes from above and see what they would look like if we included all four of the elements from the ABCD formula.

➤ In the case of the high school students, the ABCD outcome might look like this:
"After having searched appropriate databases for their topics, high school juniors in an American history class will be able locate relevant articles at least 75 percent of the time."

➤ The expanded outcome for the senior citizens could be:
"After performing a well-designed web search, senior citizens will be able to evaluate the quality of the websites found at least 75 percent of the time."

➤ And finally, the expanded ELO for the biotechnology researchers might read:
"After using recommended resources for technical reports/patents, researchers in the biotechnology company will be able to identify reports/patents that are relevant to their research at least 75 percent of the time."

While these expanded ELOs might seem a bit cumbersome and overly complex at first, they do help to clarify exactly what you have in mind. As such, they perform a useful service as you begin your ID process. You can use the basic format ("After instruction, learners will be able to [insert behavior here]") as you proceed as a kind of shorthand, all the while keeping in mind that the pared-down outcome is really standing in for the more detailed one. The basic ELOs are also useful if you wish to share your outcomes with your learners either verbally or in the form of handouts in your F2F classes, or at the beginning of any online tutorials or other online instruction. Many instructors in the F2F setting will have the ELOs listed on the board at the beginning of the class or just describe them as part of the introduction to the session. Learners often appreciate this advance notice of what they should expect from the instruction. However you wish to share your ELOs with your learners, make sure they are in a format that is clear and easy to understand and not so overly complex that they intimidate or confuse your learners.

Now let's see if you can apply the above material to your own ILI. Try your hand at developing some ELOs for an ILI that you typically teach by completing the worksheet in figure 5.5.

WRAP-UP

Writing ELOs can seem like a scary, daunting, and formidable task if you have never done them before. However, the more you practice the easier it becomes. Furthermore you will find that over time you will create a library of ELOs that can be reused with little or no modification in a number of different ILIs. Whenever the idea of sitting down to write formal ELOs seems like more effort than it is worth, remind yourself that the payoff for doing so is more effective instruction—instruction you can feel confident is including what your learners need to learn in order to feel empowered about their abilities to find trustworthy, authoritative, quality material that addresses their information needs. And writing ELOs will assist you as you work with the other two elements of the ID process—selecting appropriate learning activities, and determining how you will be assessing the effectiveness of your ILI.

WHAT STUCK?

Now that you and your colleagues have done the necessary data gathering for your needs assessments, you all feel ready to start designing your ILI endeavors. Many of you have heard about ELOs and have even done some reading on the subject. But none of you have much experience writing them. You decide that multiple heads may be better than one and invite your colleagues to a brown-bag lunch during which you could all collaborate on writing ELOs for various instructional situations. You decide to kick off the lunch by sharing an example of your own. Figure 5.6 offers you a possible outline for your presentation.

FIGURE 5.5

Formalizing ELOs

If you are new to writing ELOs, you may feel a bit overwhelmed or unsure about how to begin. Use this worksheet to help you get started.

➤ Go back to the worksheet you completed in figure 5.2. Use the brief formula "After instruction, learners will be able to [insert behavior here]" to write a basic version of each of the ELOs you listed there.

➤ Now expand on those ELOs by identifying the ABCD elements for each ELO.

   ○ Audience: Who is your audience (age, academic level, demographics, languages spoken, any other relevant characteristics)?

   ○ Behavior: What do you expect your learners to be able to do following instruction? This may be very similar to your basic version, but you may wish to elaborate a bit more at this point.

   ○ Conditions: Under what constraints or conditions will the learners be working?

   ○ Degree (Optional): What is the degree to which learners must demonstrate the ELO in order to be said to have attained the outcome?

➤ Finally, write expanded versions of each of your ELOs using the ABC (and, if appropriate, D) elements of the ABCD formula for writing ELOs.

FIGURE 5.6

What Are ELOs and Why Use Them?—A Brown-Bag Presentation

Use this worksheet to help you prepare an outline for your workshop on writing ELOs.

➤ Start off by reviewing the concept of ELOs. Complete the following statements to help you frame your thoughts for this review.

○ Writing ELOs is important because:

○ The correctly written ELOs have four specific characteristics. Those characteristics are:

○ The formula for a brief version of an ELO would be as follows:

○ A more complete version of an ELO would follow the ABCD formula. What do each of these letters stand for?

➤ Next, share the results of a needs assessment you conducted by describing what you learned about your audience, their information needs, the institutional environment (as appropriate), and the current library situation that might impact potential ILI.

○ After my needs assessment, I identified the following knowledge gaps:

➤ Now describe a few ELOs you developed based on your needs assessment.

○ Based on my needs assessment, I decided that my ELOs should be:

➤ Finally, share how your ELOs helped you choose learning activities and assessments for your ILI.

    ○ Using my ELOs as a guideline, I choose the following learning activities and assessments for my ILI:

➤ Now it's their turn

    ○ Ask your colleagues to come up with possible ELOs for some of their ILIs.

    ○ This can be done as a brainstorming exercise, or if you think your colleagues would be more comfortable with an anonymous approach, have them write their ideas on large sticky notes that you collect and display around the room.

    ○ What are some ELOs you think they might suggest?

➤ Collaborative exercise—fine-tuning ELOs

    ○ After deciding on possible ELOs, have your colleagues do some kind of collaborative exercise (small group, think/pair/share, etc.) in which pairs or groups work together to review and revise their proposed ELOs to make sure they adhere to the writing guidelines introduced in your discussion.

    ○ Don't forget to leave some time for pairs/groups to share their final results.

    ○ The directions you would give for this activity are as follows:

➤ What are the take-aways?

    ○ End the session by asking your colleagues what their "take-aways" might be from this meeting.

    ○ Use this activity as a way for your colleagues to review and sum up the session.

    ○ List five to ten things you hope your colleagues will take away from this session below:

REFERENCES

American Association of School Librarians. 2013. "AASL Standards for the 21st Century Learner." American Library Association, http://www.ala.org/aasl/standards-guidelines/learning-standards

Association of College and Research Libraries. Instruction Section. 2013a. "Information Literacy Competency Standards for Higher Education." http://www.ala.org/acrl/standards/informationliteracycompetency

Association of College and Resource Libraries. Instruction Section. 2013b. "Information Literacy in the Disciplines." American Library Association. Accessed June 17, 2013. http://wikis.ala.org/acrl/index.php/Information_literacy_in_the_disciplines

Anderson, Lorin W., and David R. Krathwohl. 2001. *A Taxonomy of Learning, Teaching and Assessing: A Revision of Bloom's Educational Objectives.* Boston: Allyn & Bacon.

Battersby, Mark, and Learning Outcomes Network. 1999. *So What's a Learning Outcome Anyway?* ERIC Centre for Curriculum, Transfer and Technology. http://files.eric.ed.gov/fulltext/ED430611.pdf

Bloom, Benjamin Samuel. 1984. *Taxonomy of Educational Objectives.* Boston: Allyn & Bacon.

Cruickshank, Donald R., Deborah Bainer Jenkins, and Kim K. Metcalf. 2009. *The Act of Teaching.* 5th ed. Boston: McGraw-Hill.

Elliott, Stephen N., Thomas R. Kratochwill, Joan Littlefield Cook, and John F. Travers. 2000. *Educational Psychology : Effective Teaching, Effective Learning.* 3rd ed. Boston: McGraw-Hill.

Farmer, Lesley S. J. 2011. *Instructional Design for Librarians and Information Professionals.* New York: Neal-Schuman.

Grassian, Esther, and Joan Kaplowitz. 2009. *Information Literacy Instruction: Theory and Practice.* 2nd ed. New York: Neal-Schuman.

Kaplowitz, Joan R. 2012. *Transforming Your Information Literacy Instruction Using Learner-Centered Teaching.* New York: Neal-Schuman.

Mager, Robert Frank. 1997a. *Goal Analysis: How to Clarify Your Goals So You Can Actually Achieve Them.* 3rd, completely rev. ed. Atlanta: Center for Effective Performance.

———. 1997b. *Preparing Instructional Objectives: A Critical Tool in the Development of Effective Instruction.* 3rd ed. Atlanta: Center for Effective Performance.

Morrison, Gary R., and Gary J. Anglin. 2005. "Research on Cognitive Load Theory." *Educational Technology Research & Development* 53 (3): 94–104.

Morrison, Gary R., Steven M. Ross, Howard K. Kalman, and Jerrold E. Kemp. 2011. *Designing Effective Instruction.* 6th ed. Hoboken, NJ: Wiley.

Wiggins, Grant, and Jay McTighe. 2006. *Understanding by Design.* Upper Saddle River, NJ: Prentice Hall.

What Will My Learners Be Doing During Instruction?

Selecting Instructional Methods

So based on what I learned from my needs assessment I have determined the appropriate expected learning outcomes (ELOs) for my information literacy instruction (ILI). Why can't I just tell my learners what they should know and show them a few resources that will help them attain those ELOs? Once I have shared this information with them won't they then be able to satisfy their information needs?

Your aim for any ILI should be that the interaction has a positive impact on your learners, one that empowers them to fulfill their information needs. ELOs describe what you want learners to be taking away from your instruction. After participating in your ILI, learners should have acquired new skills, attitudes, and knowledge, and as a result will have improved their information gathering abilities and be more information literate individuals. The activities you include in your ILI allow learners to interactive with appropriate material so they can attain the ELOs set for the instruction and thus become better equipped to locate the information they need and critically evaluate that information for credibility and relevance (Bell 2008; Bell and Shank 2007; Dempsey and Van Eck 2012). Remember that ELOs describe what learners will be able to do following instruction. Instructional activities give learners a chance to develop the new behaviors and skills that will help them attain the ELOs you have selected for them. Activities allow learners to explore the material in productive ways, to practice using newly acquired skills, and to apply these skills (i.e., transfer learning) to a variety of situations.

Furthermore, research from a variety of fields (education, psychology, neuroscience, etc.) all support the idea that merely telling learners what you think they need to know may not be the most effective way of teaching. Although you may wish to start with a descriptive overview of the material to set the stage (the conceptual framework) and provide some relevant background information, people do not really learn something until they are actively involved with it (Kaplowitz 2012). You can't just describe what needs to be learned and expect that your learners will now know what to do. You need to offer learners ways to acquire that information in some active way so that it becomes personally meaningful to them and becomes part of their own knowledge base. So selecting instructional activities to support learning is a key part of designing any kind of effective instruction—ILI included.

A great deal has already been written on various types of instructional methods and the advantages and disadvantages associated with each type. While the following may refer to some of that material, an in-depth discussion of various methodologies is beyond the scope of this book. Keep in mind that this chapter is intended to help you move from your ELOs to the selection of instructional activities. So this chapter will address the various methodologies from that viewpoint and discuss how you can use what you know about different types of activities to help your learners attain your ELOs.

QUESTIONS TO CONSIDER
➤ What is learner-centered teaching and how does it relate to selecting learning activities for my ILI?
➤ What does research on how people learn tell me about the activities I should use in my ILI?
➤ How do my ELOs relate to my learning activities?
➤ What are the pros and cons of the major types of instructional methods?
➤ Why should I consider a mix of methods?
➤ How do activities relate to assessment?
➤ How do delivery format, technology, and accessibility concerns impact my selection of instructional activities?

LEARNER-CENTERED TEACHING: GETTING YOUR LEARNERS INVOLVED

Hopefully you now are beginning to see how ELOs relate to the activities you will be including in your ILI. But perhaps you are still asking yourself why lecturing and demonstrating resources is not sufficient for learning to occur. As already indicated above, there is a vast body of research directed toward answering that question. And the overwhelming findings from that work are that having learners actively involved is the way to go. In general this approach is called learner-centered teaching (Kaplowitz 2012; McCombs and Miller 2007) and is based on principles derived from research into how people learn (Bransford et al. 1999; Bransford et al. 2000). One of the foundational documents on learner-centered teaching comes from the American Psychological Association. This document describes the characteristics of learner-centered teaching based on an amalgamation of research results from psychology, education, and other related fields (American Psychological Association Work Group of the Board of Educational Affairs 1997). Current advances in the neuroscience of learning also indicate that learner-centered teaching causes changes in areas of the brain related to learning and memory (Kaplowitz 2012).

So what does all this research tell us about how people learn? First of all, it says that learning does not happen in a vacuum. While we may each interact with material on our own and use that interaction to formulate ideas about how the world works, we must test our ideas out in a community setting. In other words, we must collaborate with other learners in order to verify our ideas. A second factor in how people learn is that we do not learn anything until we actively explore it. In other words, learners need to be involved in the learning process itself—not by just listening, but by taking an active role in the experience. That is, they need to participate in the instruction in an active way (Bransford et al. 1999; Doyle 2011; McCombs and Miller 2007). Finally, the research indicates that learners need to connect to the material at hand. They must see the relevance of what is being learned to their own lives and find a way to make it their own. If learners do not take an active part in the experience, they will not gain very much from it. So in a way, learners are being asked to take on some measure of ownership for the learning process. And instructors are asked to share the responsibility for learning with their learners. Furthermore, learners are asked to be conscientious group members, taking responsibility not only for their own learning, but also for that of others in the group. This can happen in a number of ways—by giving learners some say in how they will interact with the material to be learned, how their learning will be assessed, the resources they will explore, and/or the topics they will research (Kaplowitz 2012).

Allowing learners to take some responsibility for the learning process not only improves learning, it also results in enhanced self-confidence and self-esteem. Learners feel a sense of ownership of the material and are more directly connected to it. The more learners feel ownership of and a connection to the material, the more likely the newly learned material will become incorporated in their own worldview. As a result, learners will become more comfortable and confident about their abilities to use their new abilities in the future. Incorporating learner-centered teaching practices therefore helps to reduce library anxiety and in some cases technostress as well (Grassian and Kaplowitz 2009; Kaplowitz 2012).

To further understand why learner-centered teaching practices help learners succeed in instructional encounters, we need to take a short side trip into the field of memory. In order for learning to really occur, information must move from the learners' transient and somewhat ephemeral short-term memory into their more permanent long-term memory. Including a variety of learner-centered-teaching-based activities in your ILI allows this to happen in several ways. First, it offers the learners a break. Since short-term memory has a limited capacity, if you are continually addressing new topics, you run the risk of overloading the learners' short-term memory. So some of the newer material will push out some of the older stuff. To avoid that situation, you need to incorporate periods in which learners work on what is currently in their short-term memory, process it, and as a result allow it to move into long-term memory. Stopping for reviews, structured question-and-answer or discussion activities, hands-on practice, collaborative group exercises, reflection, and so on, give the learners those necessary breaks. And if structured correctly these learner-centered-teaching-inspired breaks can also give learners a chance to apply the newly learned material. Furthermore, allowing learners to actively engage with the material enables them to construct their own meaning about what they are learning, and organize it in such a way that is relevant to them—thus increasing the chances that they will be able to access these newly acquired ideas when they need them in the future (Kaplowitz 2012; Marlow and Page 2005).

In short, learner-centered teaching emphasizes getting the learner involved in a variety of ways. It calls for active participation on the part of the learners—moving the learner from the passive listener role to an actively involved and responsible one. This is turn asks the instructor to rethink his or her teaching role. Often referred to as moving from the sage on the stage to the guide on the side persona (King 1993), instructors are encouraged to do less talking and showing, and more facilitating of the learners' experiences. The instructor, in this view, is not the only or even the dominant voice in the learning process. He or she sets the stage, provides the learners with the tools needed, and then allows learners to interact with the material in a productive and relevant way so that they can form a personal connection to and understanding of the material to be learned. The learner-centered perspective asks instructors to share the instructional power base by allowing learners to take on some of the responsibility for their own and as well as that of their fellow learners' instructional experience. I like to summarize the various learner-centered teaching principles into three overall themes—collaboration, participation, and responsibility, or CPR for short (Kaplowitz 2012).

LEARNER-CENTERED TEACHING AND YOU

So how do you as the instructor put CPR into action? To create a learner-centered experience for your learners, you must do three things:

➢ Listen
➢ Engage
➢ Inspire

Listen

First of all, you listen to your learners by exploring their needs through the needs assessment techniques described in chapter 4. You make sure that you are basing your instruction on what your learners have shared with you about their information needs, not on what you think they need to know. Second, you listen to them during the learning experience itself. That is, you keep your eye on them as they learn the material so that you are alert to any misconceptions or difficulties they may be having as they interact with the material. You also take their questions seriously and try to answer those expressed concerns in a respectful and supportive fashion. Finally, you listen to your learners through your assessments, which help to inform you about how well your learners have attained the ELOs you originally set for the instruction (Vella 2000).

Engage

Second, you engage your learners by selecting topics that are of relevance to them and by allowing them to collaborate with you in some way on the format, content, and structure of the instruction. One way to engage your learners is to provide lots of opportunities for learners to interact with the material themselves. Another way is to set aside time for learners to discuss the topics being addressed both with you and with each other. Including some structured question-and-answer segments can help you guide your learners through the material while keeping their attention and interest alive. Engagement also comes from allowing learners to apply newly learned material in meaningful ways. Offering some form of hands-on practice, either individually or in groups, on practical examples to which the learners can relate not only gives learners the opportunity to demonstrate what they have learned, it also promotes transfer of learning. And as mentioned above, stopping for activities also gives learners the change to process information in their short-term memory and to transfer it to the more permanent long-term storage (Bransford et al. 1999; Grassian and Kaplowitz 2009; Weimer 2003).

Inspire

Finally, we want to make sure that learners gain confidence in their newly learned abilities and feel empowered to apply these new ideas to future information needs. In other words, our learners should complete our ILI feeling comfortable about searching for information, confident that they can find the most useful and relevant information to fulfill their needs, and inspired to apply their new knowledge, skills, and abilities to any problems they encounter in the future (Grassian and Kaplowitz 2009).

For more on the concepts of listen, engage, and inspire, see *Transforming Information Literacy Instruction Using Learner-Centered Teaching (*Kaplowitz 2012) as well as the second edition of Grassian and Kaplowitz's *Information Literacy Instruction: Theory and Practice* (2009).

LETTING GO—LEARNER-CENTERED TEACHING AND CONTROL

Many instruction librarians express concern about moving to a more learner-centered practice because they don't want to put so much of the instruction in the hands of the learners. Furthermore, they worry that because participatory activities and exercises are generally more time consuming than the more teacher-centered activities such as lecture and demonstration, they will be limited in how much can be addressed in a given ILI experience. While it is true that you probably will have to allocate more time to an activity than you might to a lecture segment dealing with the same material, if your aim is to have your learners attain your ELOs, then the trade-off is well worth it. Yes, you may have to include less material than you might like when using learner-centered teaching practices, but your learners have a better chance of gaining something valuable from the session than if you just told them everything you think they need to know.

Remember the "less is more" idea that asserts it is better to address a few topics effectively than many topics superficially (Grassian and Kaplowitz 2009; Kaplowitz 2012). The more you try to fit into a given instruction, the more likely the learners will be overwhelmed, stressed, and unable to process the material. They may remember nothing from the session except that there is so much to learn, there is no way they can succeed at the tasks addressed. Learners may feel even more anxious at the end of instruction than they did when they started it. Obviously that is something you want to avoid. Giving learners time to work with and process what they are learning increases the likelihood that they will attain the ELOs you set for them, and will feel more confident and comfortable about their abilities to address their information needs in the future.

Although on the surface it may look like the instructor who practices the learner-centered approach to teaching is no longer in charge of the learning, that is far from the reality. In truth learner-centered teaching practices require the instructor to be even more conscientious about what transpires during instruction. It is up to the instructor to select the types of activities that will assist learners to attain specific ELOs. He or she must also provide the learners with clear, well-organized directions, allocate an appropriate amount of time to each activity, and monitor progress to make sure learners are moving through the material in the given time frame. This is of course most important in the synchronous situation with its time constraints, but even asynchronous learner-centered teaching approaches need to be well organized, clear, and selective in the amount of material learners are expected to absorb at any one time (Kaplowitz 2012). The learner-centered instructor does not just hand over complete control to the learners. Instead he or she shares control with the learners and empowers them to accomplish the tasks set for them. Working in a learner-centered teaching environment requires that the instructor be extremely well prepared and organized, so that all the material can be worked with as intended. The learner-centered instructor is always in charge, even if it looks like the learners are running the show. The logistics of instruction (organization, timing, and sequencing) will be covered in more detail in chapter 8.

Before moving on to an examination of the different types of activities available to you, take a moment to review the concept of learner-centered teaching by completing the worksheet in figure 6.1.

USING EXPECTED LEARNING OUTCOMES TO STRUCTURE INSTRUCTION

Now that you have a better understanding about why to include instructional activities in your ILI, it is time to consider how ELOs help you structure your instruction. Writing ELOs is not just to organize your thoughts and help you decide upon the correct content for your instruction. They are intended to guide you as you develop the actual instructional experience as well as to point out what learners need to do to demonstrate the attainment of the instructional goal(s). So ELOs serve a very practical purpose in the instructional design process as you move on to select how you will share the material with your learners.

One way to do this is to reexamine all the ELOs you set for this instruction and think about one or more activities that would help learners attain each ELO. You can rely on your own expertise or you can explore the many books and websites that offer suggestions about effective instructional activities.

When making your selections keep in mind that it is important to pick activities that match up with the level of comprehension indicated by each specific ELO (Morrison et al. 2011). For example, if your ELO says learners will be able to locate or recall something, your exercise should not ask them to evaluate or apply. And the opposite also holds true. If your aim is to have learners be able to apply, synthesize, or evaluate, don't ask them to just recall or recognize (as in listing names of resources or selecting ones from a given list). It often helps at this point to refer back to Bloom's taxonomy or its more current update (Anderson and Krathwohl 2001; Bloom 1984), whichever you used to structure your ELOs. Check which level of comprehension—knowledge, comprehension, application, analysis, synthesis, and evaluation (Bloom) or remember, understand, apply, analyze, evaluate, and create (Anderson and Krathwohl)— your ELO is aimed at and select your activities accordingly (Morrison et al. 2011). Before describing this process any further, let's take a break in the discourse. Use the worksheet in figure 6.2 to help you try your hand at matching outcomes to activities.

FIGURE 6.1

What Do You Know about Learner-Centered Teaching?

The concept of learner-centered teaching might be a new one for you. Or you may already be quite familiar with it. Answer the following questions to review both what you already know about the subject and to help you pinpoint what you still need to know about it.

➤   How does learner-centered teaching differ from more traditional teacher-centered (i.e., lecture/demo) approaches?

➤   What are some of the reasons that learner-centered teaching is thought to be a more effective way to teach?

➤   List some of the underlying principles of learner-centered teaching.

➤   Describe some examples of learner-centered teaching practices.

➤   How would you incorporate learner-centered teaching practices into your own ILL?

FIGURE 6.2

ELOs and Levels of Comprehension

Come up with three to five ELOs for one of your own ILIs. You might wish to refer back to the ones you wrote in chapter 5 or come up with some new ones. Indicate the level of comprehension you want your learners to attain via each ELO. Space is provided for five ELOs.

INSTRUCTIONAL GOAL(S)

➢ Expected Learning Outcome:

  ○ Level of comprehension from Bloom or Anderson and Krathwohl:

➢ Expected Learning Outcome:

  ○ Level of comprehension from Bloom or Anderson and Krathwohl:

➢ Expected Learning Outcome:

  ○ Level of comprehension from Bloom or Anderson and Krathwohl:

➢ Expected Learning Outcome:

  ○ Level of comprehension from Bloom or Anderson and Krathwohl:

➢ Expected Learning Outcome:

  ○ Level of comprehension from Bloom or Anderson and Krathwohl:

SELECTING YOUR ACTIVITIES

Hopefully you are now eager to try your hand at selecting activities that allow your learners to attain the ELOs set for the instruction. Many different types of activities are available for your instructional use. In general you can view activities on a continuum from teacher centered to learner centered (Cruickshank, Jenkins, and Metcalf 2009; Freiberg and Driscoll 2005; Slavin 2011). However, regardless of whether the activities you chose are more teacher centered, learner centered, or somewhere in between, you must make sure that what you ask learners to do in the activity you select for a given ELO will allow learners to attain the outcome described. So always keep in mind the level of comprehension described in each ELO as you select the activities you plan to include in your instruction.

Descriptions of instructional activities are readily available in the many books, articles, websites, and other publications that are dedicated to effective teaching practices. For more on this, see the appendix at the end of this book. However, for the purposes of our current discussion, it might be useful to examine activities from the broad perspective of the teacher-centered to learner-centered teaching continuum.

Keep in mind that although some activities appear to be more appropriate to higher levels of comprehension than others, any activity can be used for any ELO provided you ask the learners to perform appropriately during that activity. So if the ELO specifies knowledge or comprehension, learners should be asked to identify or describe the material in some way. If the ELO is concerned with synthesis or analysis, learners should be asked to go beyond description to these higher-order modes of thinking. And if the ELO is concerned with application and/or evaluation, you should probably give learners the chance to take what they have learned and try to use it hopefully in an authentic, real-life-type situation. Now let's turn our attention to the various broad categories of activities generally associated with instruction starting with the most teacher-centered methodologies of lecture and demonstration (also known as modeling).

Lecture/Demo

In these techniques the teacher is completely in charge and engages in a one-way communication with the learners. That is, the instructor is talking at the learners, not with them. Learners are placed in a passive, receptive, listener role. Teacher-centered approaches such as these have the advantage of allowing the instructor to share his or her expertise and to address large amounts of information in a relatively short period of time. Lectures, and to some degree demos in which effective strategies and techniques are modeled, allow the instructor to summarize, synthesize, and organize a lot of information in a logical, systematic fashion. They also give the learners a glimpse at how an expert views the field (Cruickshank, Jenkins, and Metcalf 2009; Kaplowitz 2012). However, it is important to limit the amount of time you place your learners in this passive role as people find it difficult to concentrate on large amounts of material for extended periods of time. So if you talk at your learners for too long, you may lose their attention as well as possibly overloading their ability to store information. Lecture/demos of more than ten or fifteen minutes have been shown to lose their effectiveness (Bligh 2000; Brookfield 1990). Furthermore, placing learners in this passive, receptive role does not allow them to interact with the material in a way that will help them attain the ELOs set for the instruction. So it is probably a good idea to intersperse more participatory activities into any teacher-centered scenario. However, lectures and demos can be very useful as they give the learners an overview of the material to be learned and a conceptual framework for the instruction to come, and provide them with the basic knowledge needed to move on to the more active type of instructional experiences.

The lecture/demo does not have to be a totally passive experience for the learner. Research has shown that interspersing pauses or a break during the lecture at appropriate intervals also helps improve retention. This is especially true if learners are required to perform some note-taking-related task during the break, such as writing summaries, comparing notes with another student, and/or formulating questions based on the material and then endeavoring to come up with answers to their own or their neighbors' questions (Aiken, Thomas, and Shennum 1978; Davis and Hult 1997; King 1992). In short, anything that asks the learner to think about the lecture material and do something with what they have just heard improves retention of the material over just listening to the lecture even when the learner has been taking notes. These more active listening approaches help learners construct their own mental model of the material, connect the new information to what they already know, and improve their chances of being able to use that information in the future (Mayer 2010, Wittrock 2001, 1974).

Another way to help provide a little more learner engagement when using the lecture/demo method is through the use of partial or skeletal notes. In this technique instructors provide some form of incomplete notes—either in standard outline form or as a graphic organizer. This approach is often referred to as an "empty outline" (Angelo and Cross 1993; Kaplowitz 2012). This outline provides a conceptual framework for the material and can serve as a way to help learners focus on the key elements of the material (Ausubel 1977; Katayama and Robinson 2000; Kiewra et al. 1991). To create even more learner engagement, you can intersperse structured question-and-answer segments into your lecture/demo at the end of each lecture section before you move on to the next topic. So let's move on and take a look at that technique.

Structured Question and Answer

In these types of activities the instructor leads the learners through the material by posing questions and providing feedback regarding the responses; this represents a move toward learner-centered teaching. While the instructor is still "running the show," the learners are placed in a more active role. Here the instructors and learners begin to engage in a two-way conversation or dialogue about the material. Many instructors find this an easy and somewhat more comfortable way to move into more learner-centered territory and use structured question-and-answer segments as a way to break up lecture/demos into reasonable and manageable chunks for their learners. Another advantage to this approach is that it provides learners with the opportunity to put the material into their own words and gives them a bit more ownership of and responsibility for the learning process (Cruickshank, Jenkins, and Metcalf 2009; Eggen and Kauchak 2010). While structured question-and-answer techniques tend to be most useful for getting learners to demonstrate their basic understanding of the material, and are most often associated with knowledge and comprehension types of ELOs, you can also structure the questions so that they challenge learners to think on the higher comprehension levels. For example, you can ask learners why specific resources might be more suitable for specific types of information needs than others and thereby get them to think in terms of application and/or evaluation.

Discussion

Moving even closer to the learner-centered end of the spectrum is the discussion method. Discussions give the learners even more of a role in the learning process. Here the instructor sets a problem or describes a situation for the learners to address either as a whole group or in smaller subgroups. Discussion introduces the concept of multiway communication since learners are talking to each other as well as to the instructor. In fact, the most effective discussions are the ones in which the instructor's voice is the one least heard (Kaplowitz 2012). Once the discussion is set in motion, the instructor becomes a watchful guide and only inserts his or her own comments in response to direct questions from the group or to correct any misconceptions being raised. The instructor keeps an eye and an ear on the discussion and calls it to a halt when it seems appropriate. He or she often closes the discussion segment by summarizing and synthesizing what was addressed during the discussion period or asks the learners to do so. As in the case of structured question-and-answer activities, discussions allow learners to articulate their ideas in their own words. They also provide learners with a chance to exchange ideas with their peers, gain insight into other people's points of view, and practice respectful listening (Davis 2009; McKeachie and Svinicki 2006). Here again the way you structure the discussion relates to the ELO you are trying to address with the activity. So learners can be asked to discuss anything from selecting appropriate resources (knowledge or comprehension) to comparing and contrasting (synthesis and analysis), and/or critiquing different resources or strategies (evaluation).

Of course, discussions are only successful if everyone is willing to participate. The instructor must also make sure that everybody is given a chance to voice his or her views and that everyone's opinions and comments are treated with equal respect. It is not really a true discussion if only one or two voices dominate the conversation. So it is up to the instructor to make sure this does not happen and to ensure that the discussion does not veer off into areas not directly related to the topic at hand. One way to address this issue is to start the discussion with an activity called think/pair/share. In this type of exercise, learners are given the discussion topic and told to think about their responses to it for a couple of minutes. Then they are put into pairs to talk about what each person came up with. Finally, pairs are asked to share the results of their paired conversations, which then can serve as the kickoff to a larger discussion within the entire group. The advantage to think/pair/share is that it allows everyone to have a voice and express his or her ideas even if it is to only one other person. Furthermore, although many people are reluctant to speak up in a large group, they are often more willing to exchange ideas in this more protected pair situation. In addition, giving everyone time to mull over his or her ideas privately first increases the likelihood that each learner will have something to say. Finally, learners are given the chance to vet their ideas with their partners, and even the shyest of learners might then feel comfortable enough to voice their ideas to the larger group after having already checked out their thoughts in the smaller paired setting (Grassian and Kaplowitz 2009; Kaplowitz 2012).

Hands-On Practice

While discussions do turn the conversation over to the learners, hands-on practice activities really move the instruction into learner-centered territory. Generally used after learners have had some experience with the material through some of the already mentioned techniques, hands-on practice allows learners to work directly with and process the material to be learned (Cruickshank, Jenkins, and Metcalf 2009). While hands-on practice can be used to help learners initially explore the material to be learned (knowledge and comprehension), it is generally more useful as a way for learners to attain some of the higher-order outcomes such as application and evaluation. Practice also provides even more opportunities for learner control especially if learners are allowed to solve whatever problem the instructor has set for them using resources of their own choice, and/or if the learners are allowed to use the resources to find information on topics of their own choice.

The ability to incorporate hands-on practice is often dependent upon the number of learners involved and of course, the resources and equipment available to the learners. It can be difficult for instructors to monitor large numbers of learners at one time and to make sure that none of them are going astray or becoming frustrated by their inability to find the material they need on their self-selected topics. Furthermore, since people learn at different speeds, some learners may finish earlier than others. Those who finish early may become bored, while those who take a bit longer may feel pressured or inadequate to finish the task. Here again the instructor must be ready for all possible situations—perhaps by having additional tasks available for the early finishers, and offering extra support to those who are struggling to complete the activity. Those who use hands-on practice in their ILI often ask colleagues, more advanced students, or staff to help out as rovers during these segments so that the instructor does not have to juggle all the learners alone (Grassian and Kaplowitz 2009; Kaplowitz 2012).

Collaborative Group Work

While hands-on practice offers the learners a measure of independence in and control over their learning, the instructor still maintains a good deal of oversight. He or she generally sets the parameters for the practice by designating the materials and resources to be used—usually based on what was just addressed in the previous in-structional segment. So for example, if the most recent material introduced a number of different resources, the hands-on activity would center on having learners use those particular resources. While hands-on practice can be done individually, in pairs, or in small groups, the more learner-centered types of collaborative group work gener-ally involves giving the learners some sort of problem to solve (often referred to as problem-based learning or PBL) and then allowing the group some freedom in selecting the resources and strategies used to solve that problem.

Collaborative group work allows learners to practice what they have learned, and gives them the opportunity to apply that learning to some relevant and hopefully real-world-type situation. Collaborative group work takes the learner-centered approach to the next level, by allowing learners a greater degree of latitude in the way they inter-act with the material as well as providing them with the opportunity to learn from each other in a social learning situation (Barkley, Cross, and Major 2004; Cooper et al. 2000; Johnson, Johnson, and Smith 2007). Learners often find it easier to comprehend new information when their peers explain it in terms to which they can relate than when that same information is presented by the instructor. Furthermore, those who engage in this peer teaching seem to also gain from the experience. Putting material into teachable and relatable terms is often an excellent way to review and solidify one's own understanding of the material (Grassian and Kaplowitz 2009; Kaplowitz 2012).

Collaborative group work can be done in the online setting as well as either in the synchronous or asynchronous setting. Groups are formed and are presented with a task or problem to solve. But learners are interacting with each other online rather than in person. The synchronous setting works much the same as a face-to-face one with groups interacting online and in real time. Discussion boards or forums are often used to accomplish this type of activity when learners are working together in an asynchronous mode (Ko and Rossen 2010, Palloff and Pratt 2007).

While collaborative group work offers a great deal of advantages, it does have some drawbacks of its own. In general, this type of activity takes more time than other types of activities. Furthermore, group dynamics can also be an issue. So it is helpful to set some guidelines for collaborative group work ahead of time and perhaps precede it with a brief discussion on how to work productively in groups. Finally, since the groups are working independently of you and each other, it is important to make sure you are monitoring the activities in each group. Monitoring group activity, especially in the asynchronous online setting, often requires a rather large time commitment on the part of the instructor, as he or she must keep tabs on the various groups and their progress through the material. Here again, recruiting colleagues to assist you as rovers in the face-to-face setting or to help you monitor the online activities comes in handy. Since collaborative group work generally takes more instructional time than other types of activities, you should make sure you are getting enough bang for your instructional buck. In other words, ask yourself if the time being allocated to the group work will have a large enough instructional payoff to justify the time spent. Collaborative group work is generally aimed at helping learners attain higher levels of comprehension. So if your outcomes involve synthesis, application, and/or evaluation, collaborative group work is an extremely appropriate activity to incorporate in your ILI (Kaplowitz 2012).

In some ways, collaborative group work is more an approach to organizing the learners than an entirely unique method. Many of the activities already touched upon can certainly be done in small groups instead of individu-ally or in pairs. For example, the think/pair/share approach can be expanded into think/pair/square/share. In this version, the third step (preceding sharing with the group at large), would be for two pairs to combine after their pair discussion to form a larger (four-person) square to allow for pairs to compare their ideas with each other. Structured question-and-answer approaches can also be modified into collaborative work by placing the learners into small groups and having each group work on the questions you pose and then report back findings to the larger group.

Two additional methods that make use of collaborative group learning are the "jigsaw" and the "pass the prob-lem" techniques. In "jigsaw," material to be learned is divided up among the groups. Each group learns about a particular resource, strategy, concept, and so forth. After a set amount of time, the groups are re-formed by having members of each of the original groups assigned a number—1, 2, 3, 4, and so forth. Then new groups are formed for each of those numbers. The resulting groups now include representatives from each of the prior groups. Therefore, each newly formed group can profit by what was learned about the material in the first grouping. Members of the new groups are then instructed to teach each other what they learned during the first part of this activity, or work collaboratively to apply the material to solve a problem set for them by the instructor. This is a great technique if you have a lot of resources you wish to share with the learners and not enough time to do so. In the first round each group learns about one of the resources. In the second round each member of the new groups teaches what he or she learned in the first round. So the net result is that all the learners are exposed to everything you wanted them to explore (Aronson 1978; Brown and Campione 1996; Kaplowitz 2012).

In "pass the problem," each of the small groups is presented with one part of the overall problem and works on its piece for a given period of time. Each group then passes its work to the group next to it. Each subsequent group provides additional ideas and then passes it on to the next group. This goes on for several rounds until the pieces of the problem return to the original group that worked on them. In the end everyone has worked on all parts of the problem. Again, this can be a fairly time-consuming activity, but it does offer the advantage of getting everyone involved in all parts of the problem at hand (Cruickshank, Jenkins, and Metcalf 2009; Kaplowitz 2012).

One last word on collaborative group work in general. It is always wise to allot some time following the small-group activities for full-group sharing in order to give your learners the most effective experience. You may not have time for each group to present its findings, but the more groups you can allow to do so, the better. The small groups can then see the commonalities and differences in their thinking and may gain even more understanding of the material. If you are working in a synchronous situation, time is going to be a deciding factor. However, you can supplement the synchronous contact time by using some kind of online resource—a blog, wiki, discussion forum, or the like—for groups to share their thoughts after the synchronous experience. Obviously the asynchronous setting is already set up to do this online sharing. Once learners have been given a chance to share their ideas, you may also wish to do some kind of summary or wrap-up that further brings all the ideas together (Kaplowitz 2012).

Reflection

Probably the most learner centered of all the approaches, reflection allows each learner to review, synthesize, and generally think about what he or she just learned. It can be used to assist learners with any level of comprehension, but reflections tend to ask learners to bring together everything they learned and comment on how they might use that new information. Reflection lets each learner put the material into perspective in a way that is personally meaningful. In general, the questions learners are asked to reflect on are aimed at the synthesis, analysis, application, and/or evaluation levels of comprehension. Many instruction librarians incorporate some variation on the "minute paper" or other classroom assessment techniques (Angelo and Cross 1993) either at the end of the entire instruction or at specific points during it to give learners the chance to engage in this type of reflection. The "What Stuck?" sections that appear at the end of each chapter in this book are meant to serve as reflection activities for you, the reader.

While most reflections are done in written format—on paper in the face-to-face format or as part of some kind of electronic format in the online setting—they can also be done in a more collaborative way that allows everyone to benefit from each person's ideas. Online reflections can be posted anonymously in an open forum so that everyone can read all the reflections and learn from them. Reflections can be done in a dynamic and engaging way in the face-to-face setting as well. One approach is to have learners call out what they learned from the session and for you or an appointed recorder to write the ideas on the board or flip chart sheets. You can also do the "What Stuck?" reflections as a game. Divide the class into groups (or have them return to groups they have worked in throughout the session) and tell them they each have a set amount of time to come up with a list of "What Stuck?" (for example, ideas, concepts, resources, techniques) from the preceding instruction. Provide flip chart sheets for each group to create its list. At the end of the set time, review the lists, count up the entries, and proclaim a winner. You can award small gifts to the members of the winning team. And because you want your learners to leave on a positive note, everyone else in the class also receives some kind of token (Kaplowitz 2012).

Moving to this game idea as a way to end in-person classes has several advantages. First of all, it shares with all types of the reflection, the advantage of having learners summarize the material themselves and put it into their own words. Furthermore, the game aspect provides an activity that appeals to the more competitive learners in the group as a change of pace from all the collaborative group work learner-centered teachers usually include. Finally, it is a fun and upbeat way to end a class that maybe changes learners' ideas about ILI and shows that instruction librarians can not only provide valuable information, they can do so in an engaging and invigorating and maybe even inspiring fashion (Kaplowitz 2012). Plus these types of refection activities can serve as an informal assessment of the instruction. By reviewing the "What Stuck?" lists after instruction is over, you can get a pretty good idea of what learners found meaningful and important from the material you shared with them. We will return to the idea of activities as assessment later in this chapter as well in chapter 7.

Hopefully the above brief introduction to the range of methods from teacher centered to learner centered has provided you with some ideas about how to select an appropriate instructional activity for each of your ELOs. Test out your ability to do so by completing the worksheet in figure 6.3. Note that this is an expansion of the worksheet that appeared in figure 6.2 above.

GETTING AND KEEPING LEARNERS' ATTENTION—THE CASE FOR MIXING METHODS

We all started out as learners and as such we all probably have particular instructional methods that we like more than others. As a result, we might incorporate those methods into our teaching more often than those we don't care for as much. While that is understandable, concentrating on one or two types of activities can be detrimental to effective learning. The major reason for this has to do with attention and motivation. You must capture and sustain your learners' attention throughout the instruction in order to have them interact with the material in a productive way. And you must provide them with reasons why it will benefit them to learn the material you are addressing. In other words, you need to make sure your learners have sufficient motivation to participate in the instructional experience.

Attention and motivation are interrelated. People pay more attention to information that has personal relevance to them. And it is often up to you to point out how they will benefit from the instructional experience. In order words, you must provide them with the answer to the "What's in it for me?" question. Once you have captured their attention by showing learners what they will get from participating, learners' motivation should increase.

However, getting their attention is only the first step. You must also make sure that their attention is sustained throughout the instructional experience. And the best way to do that is to include a variety of ways for the learners to interact with the material. People may become restless or bored if they are engaged in one type of activity for too long—most notably the lecture/demo format. However, breaking up lectures into smaller chunks and incorporating other types of activities not only helps sustain interest, it also enables learners to process the information more efficiently.

Instructional Myths—Learning Styles and the Learning Pyramid

Before we leave this topic, let's address a couple of what might be called "instructional myths" that are often cited as the justification for mixing methods—the learning styles issue and the learning pyramid. First let's look at

FIGURE 6.3

Selecting Appropriate Activities

Refer back to the ELOs and levels of comprehension you described in figure 6.2. Now add an instructional activity for each of these ELOs. Make sure the activity you select is consistent with the level of comprehension described in the ELO for which it is intended. Space is provided for five ELOs.

INSTRUCTIONAL GOAL(S)
➤ Expected Learning Outcome:

○ Level of comprehension:

○ Instructional activity:

○ Reason for selecting this activity:

➤ Expected Learning Outcome:

○ Level of comprehension:

○ Instructional activity:

○ Reason for selecting this activity:

➢ Expected Learning Outcome:

○ Level of comprehension:

○ Instructional activity:

○ Reason for selecting this activity:

➢ Expected Learning Outcome:

○ Level of comprehension:

○ Instructional activity:

○ Reason for selecting this activity:

➤ Expected Learning Outcome:

○ Level of comprehension:

○ Instructional activity:

○ Reason for selecting this activity:

the concept of learning styles. While it may certainly be true that learners often express a preference for interacting with material to be learned in a particular way (reading, watching, listening, hands-on practice, discussion, etc.), there is no definitive research evidence to support the fact that learners actually learn more when material is provided in their stated preferred fashion (Kratzig and Arbuthnott 2006). Furthermore, research has also shown that learners may not be the best judges of their own "learning style." They may say they like to work in one way, but when observed that is not how they are actually working with the material.

In addition, despite what we may think is our optimal learning situation, we have all had to learn how to cope with the various ways material is presented to us—in our so-called preferred way or not. The bottom line is that while styles may in fact exist, they don't seem to provide any valuable insight into how to organize our instruction. And even if they did provide some insight, working with that information would not be cost effective (Coffield et al. 2004; Pashler et al. 2008; Sanderson 2011). Most of us do not have the time, money, or expertise to "test" our learners' styles. And what would we do with the information if we were able to do that testing? Would we provide several ways to interact with the same information? Could we? So the morale of this learning styles research is that we mix methods not because we are trying to "reach" different types of learners, but because it is the best way to capture and sustain attention and motivation. All types of learners profit by this "mixing it up" because it helps learners to remain engaged in the instructional experience.

That brings us to the second instructional myth—most often referred to as the learning pyramid. You have probably all encountered this pyramid somewhere in your experience as a teacher. It is the notion that people remember 10 percent of what they *READ*, 20 percent of what they *HEAR*, 30 percent of what they *SEE*, 50 percent of what they *HEAR and SEE*, 70 percent of what they *SAY or WRITE*, and 90 percent of what they *SAY AS THEY DO AN ACTIVITY*. As appealing as that notion might be, once again an exploration of the literature shows there is no solid, research-based data to support it (Booth 2011; Lalley and Miller 2007; Molenda 2004). Even the numbers themselves should make us raise an eyebrow and question the so-called data. The percentages are just too perfectly distributed with each number being a multiple of 10 and the spacing of categories somewhat even to have arisen from any real-world experimentation (Holbert and Karady 2008).

While considerable doubts remain as to the origins of the learning pyramid and the "data" used to develop it, instructors in all fields should be grateful to the thinking it inspired in educators in general and instruction librarians in particular. Interest in the learning pyramid sparked the conversations that ultimately led to activities-based instruction and contributed to the rise of a more learner-centered approach to teaching. The data may be flawed, but the idea that grew out of the pyramid concept is that it is more effective to have learners work directly with material and to gain experience with it in a number of different ways (Carlson 2009).

Although the pyramid itself may not have any data to back it up, the research done in the area of memory capacity and storage referred to above does support the concept if not the data itself. As already discussed, short-term memory storage has a limited capacity. According to Miller's classic article, short-term memory is limited to seven plus or minus two chunks of information (1956). Often referred to as cognitive load (Lohr and Gall 2007; Paas, Renkl, and Sweller 2003; Sweller, van Merrienboer, and Paas 1998), this constraint severely limits how much a person can store in his or her short-term memory at any one time. Once short-term memory reaches its capacity, no new information can be processed unless something is removed. So if we try to teach too much in a given time frame, the earliest material may not be retained as new information is presented.

It is like trying to pour more water into an already full glass. The excess spills out and is lost—something we want to avoid in our teaching (Kaplowitz 2012). So once again we see the value of mixing up the ways in which learners are asked to interact with the material to be learned. Interspersing activities that allow the learners to work directly with material that has just been learned gives them the break they need to process the material and move it to more permanent and seemingly limitless storage associated with long-term memory.

So mixing methods leads to more effective instruction for a number of reasons. It helps capture and sustain attention. It increases motivation by providing learners with different ways to see "what is in it for them," and it addresses the issue of cognitive load increasing the capacity of learners to absorb information. Plus, mixing methods creates a more dynamic, engaging, and fun learning environment in which learners and instructors work together productively. In the end using a variety of methods gives learners the best chance to reach the instructional goal(s) set for the instructional experience.

The worksheet in figure 6.4 lists all the participatory activities described in this chapter. Lecture/demo is excluded, as it is a more passive, teacher-centered way to address material. Create examples for the five activity types that would allow learners to attain an ELO for each of the various levels of comprehension listed. For example, if you plan to use structured question and answer to address a knowledge ELO, you might ask learners to define and or give examples of terms or concepts from material already shared with learners—perhaps via the lecture or demo method. Note that you may choose between knowledge or comprehension for one example, application or analysis for a second, and synthesis or evaluation for a third, for a total of three examples for each of the different activity types.

ACTIVITIES TO ASSESSMENT

Including a variety of instructional activities in your ILI can pay off in a number of ways. As already discussed, mixing methods helps to capture and sustain learners' attention. Obviously this is a crucial element to effective instruction. If learners are not paying attention to you, they cannot benefit from your instruction. Furthermore, more participatory learner-centered approaches seem to increase learner engagement and thus increases the chances that your learners will attain the ELOs you set for the instruction (Kaplowitz 2012).

Participatory learner-centered activities also provide the instructor with some informal assessment data. As you observe learners interacting with the material to be learned—through question-and-answer exchanges, discussion, hands-on practice, group work, and/or reflection—you can get some idea about how much (or little) your learners have gotten out of your instruction. Interspersing activities allows you to ensure that your learners have gained what you intended from the material, as well as to see that they have not developed any misconceptions and/or incorrect habits. Instructors often use these informal assessment opportunities as comprehension checks. These information assessments help instructors determine if learners are ready to move on to the next instructional segment or if the instructor needs to make some "on-the-spot" modifications in the session—going back over already addressed material in some way before allowing learners to interact with any new material (Kaplowitz 2012; Grassian and Kaplowitz 2009).

Assessment will be discussed in more detail in chapter 7. However, keep this "double-duty" potential of instructional activities in mind when including them in your sessions. While every ELO must be assessed in some way to ensure the effectiveness of the instruction, not all of them need to be assessed by formal methods. In fact, many instructional librarians rely heavily on these more informal assessment approaches especially in their one-shot or stand-alone ILI endeavors. Since they generally do not confer grades on their learners and often do not have any kind of formal interactions with them following their ILI, these informal, activities-based assessments may be all instruction librarians have to assess their learners' success, as well as the effectiveness of their instruction.

INSTRUCTIONAL CONTEXT—DELIVERY MODE, TECHNOLOGY, AND ACCESSIBILITY

Selecting relevant and appropriate activities for your ILI is obviously a very important part of the ID process. However, your instruction does not exist in a vacuum. When deciding on what you will include in your instruction you

FIGURE 6.4

Using Activities with Different Levels of Comprehension

Complete this worksheet by describing how you would use each activity type to help your learners attain an ELO for the various levels of comprehension listed. Remember that each activity can be used for any level as long as it is structured appropriately.

Structured Question and Answer

➢ Knowledge or comprehension example:

➢ Application or analysis example:

➢ Synthesis or evaluation example:

Discussion

➢ Knowledge or comprehension example:

➢ Application or analysis example:

➢ Synthesis or evaluation example:

Hands-On Practice

➢ Knowledge or comprehension example:

➢ Application or analysis example:

➢ Synthesis or evaluation example:

Collaborative Group Work

➢ Knowledge or comprehension example:

➢ Application or analysis example:

➢ Synthesis or evaluation example:

Reflection

➢ Knowledge or comprehension example:

➢ Application or analysis example:

➢ Synthesis or evaluation example:

must also consider the context in which you are working, the technology available to you, the appropriateness of that technology both to your situation and your instructional goals, as well as accessibility issues. Let's take a look at each of these issues in more detail.

Delivery Mode (Format)

While most of the activity types were developed in and for the F2F format, with a little thought, planning, and imagination they can all be adapted for an online environment as well. Some suggestions for doing so have already been mentioned in the various activity descriptions above. The field of online instruction and distance education is a vital and rapidly evolving one. A little bit of research will yield a vast array of information on how to design effective, engaging, activities-based online instruction.

Both the F2F and the online format have their advantages and limitations. Using a blended or hybrid format is an excellent way to maximize the advantages of both formats while minimizing some of the issues associated with each of them. For example, one of the problems with the more learner-centered teaching approaches in the F2F situation is that not everyone is comfortable with or willing to participate at the level required by many of these activities. This is especially true of reflective types who need a bit more time to formulate their thoughts before responding in class and/or are a bit reluctant to voice their views in such a public setting. This is where discussion boards and other online tools that allow for exchange of ideas can come into play. Discussions can begin in the F2F (or synchronous online setting) and then continue in some asynchronous online fashion allowing those reflective or more reticent learners an opportunity to also have their voices heard.

While blended environments are most often used in full-length courses, you can also take advantage of the blended idea when teaching your one-shot or stand-alone ILI sessions. One big drawback of any synchronous instruction, whether it is F2F or online, is time constraints. Synchronous instruction has a set time limit. Your contact time has a beginning and an end point, and it is up to you to decide how much and what will be addressed during that period. Making these decisions can often be painful as we always seem to want to give our learners more than is reasonable for them to absorb in the time frame we have. Since we don't want to stress their memory and learning capacities, we often leave things out or only briefly address them even if we think they are relevant and important to our instructional goal(s).

But what if you start thinking a little outside of the synchronous time frame box to see if you can expand your contact time by involving learners with the material either before or after you are working with them directly? One easy way to do this is to provide paper handouts that review the material, add material that there was not enough time to include in the synchronous contact time, or give exercises that allow learners to practice their newly acquired skills after instruction has occurred. Or you can contact learners ahead of time and provide them with some foundational material and/or ask them to perform some preliminary work with the material to be addressed as a way of piquing their interest. Asking your learners to perform some task and bring their results to class not only allows you to see what they already know, but often helps illustrate to them that they have something to learn—that is, points out "what's in it for them" regarding your instruction.

While paper handouts are fairly easy to generate and use, they do have the drawback of being somewhat ephemeral. People lose them or don't remember they have them when faced with a situation in which they might be helpful. And of course there is also some cost involved in producing the paper handout. However, you can compensate for some of these issues by mounting your supplementary material on your library website. The information is then available wherever and whenever the learner needs it—before or after the actual synchronous experience.

You can also make use of various web tools to engage your learners in online exchanges of ideas much like the discussion boards so common in online courses. Provide a place on your website for learners to ask questions or make comments about the material planned for an upcoming instruction. This can also be a sort of informal needs assessment for you as you monitor the types of questions being posed. And don't forget to provide a place for learners to keep the conversation going after the instruction is over. While we often share our e-mail addresses with our learners and urge them to contact us if they have further questions, providing a discussion-type space for them allows learners to continue to interact with each other as well as with us.

These approaches to expanding contact time work for stand-alone, drop-in type classes often seen in the public and special library world, as well as those one-shots so often taught for specific classes in the K–20 world. In the case of the latter, while you can always use your own library website as the platform for your materials, it might be better to see if the curriculum instructor has an online site. If so, it may be even more effective to see if you can obtain space there. You can not only monitor what is going on in the class and perhaps be proactive about offering help if you are noticing any issues related the learners' information needs, you will also be a presence in the course allowing learners to contact you directly if they have questions or are encountering difficulties finding the information they need.

While it is clear how adding online components to synchronous instruction (whether the format is F2F or online) can offer all kinds of benefits, adding some F2F time to online instruction also has its benefits. The biggest complaint that learners make about online instruction is that they feel isolated and alone in the environment. Getting online learners to view themselves as part of a learning community and to work collaboratively in a participatory manner is often a challenge. But adding even one F2F component to your online instruction during which learners are given the opportunity to get to know and interact with their fellow learners (and with you) can go a long way to counter these feelings of isolation.

Courses that are taught primarily in the asynchronous online format often have a F2F kickoff session where learners and the instructor get together in the same physical space to help create a feeling of community for the learners who may not have any other opportunity to interact with the instructor and/or fellow learners except via the asynchronous online environment. Having one F2F meeting before the asynchronous instruction begins adds a personal touch to what is often viewed by learners as a fairly isolating and cold form of educational interaction.

In the synchronous online format one of the first "meetings" is often dedicated to some icebreaker type of activity in which learners are encouraged to share their personal goals for taking the course and/or something about themselves as learners and as people. As in with the initial F2F session for asynchronous instruction, the goal of this session is to make people feel connected to each other in a more personal way.

While it is more challenging to incorporate F2F encounters into the more stand-alone online material exemplified by online tutorials, for example, providing learners a place to exchange ideas, questions, and concerns with each other and with you can often help to alleviate some of the negative feelings associated with online instruction. You could do this in a number of ways. One way would be to hold informal brown-bag lunches or other "open house" types of meetings every so often in the library and invite members of your population to come and exchange their thoughts with you and each other. You can also provide some kind of online version of this through the use of some form of chat room approach, discussion board, or other type of web technology that allows you to interact with learners and hopefully also gives them some opportunity to interact with each other as well. It is often comforting for learners to see that they are not alone in their concerns and that others are facing the same issues and challenges as they are when engaging in their quests for information. New types of online tools are being developed all the time. Do some exploring to see what you can come up with to help you be more inclusive and to get your learners more involved with the online material you are providing for them.

Technology

Advances in instructional technology have opened up a whole new world of opportunities in the way you can reach out to and teach your learners. However, just because a particular technology is available to you, does not mean you have to use it. Remember that your motivation for using something in your instruction should be driven by what you hope your learners will gain from the encounter, not by the activity or technology itself. In other words, choose technology (as with all instructional activities) based on how well they suit your learners, the instructional situation, the environment in which you are working, and above all how well the activity or technology helps your learners accomplish the expected learning outcomes (ELOs) set for the instruction (Grassian and Kaplowitz 2009; Kaplowitz 2012; Palloff and Pratt 2007). It is very easy to be seduced by some new instructional technology that is being touted as the next big thing. After all, you want your instruction to appeal to your learners. You know that many of your learners spend a good deal of their time interacting with some kind of technology in their everyday lives. And you think that if you stick to the more traditional types of instruction, you will look as if you are behind the times. But base your technology-related decisions on how well (or not) the use of that technology will benefit your learners.

Accessibility

One more thing to consider when making instructional technology decisions is the issue of accessibility. Here again, the more you know about your learners the better when it comes to deciding if a particular technology will work with your target population. Technology comes with a myriad of issues—both software and hardware. So you must ask yourself a number of questions before including a particular type of technology in your instructional arsenal. First of all, keep in mind that just because you know how to use some type of technology does not ensure that your learners do as well. Think about whether learners will need special hardware and/or software to take advantage of the technology and if they have access to those types of hardware and/or software. For example, while flash animations are eye catching and engaging, they do not work on certain types of handheld devices. So some of your learners may become frustrated when trying to access your material if it is in that format.

Online videos are also an interesting way to present information. However, the more complex they are, the more difficult they are to download—especially if learners have older, less powerful computers. Again, you want to avoid frustrating learners by requiring them to wait long periods of time for your instruction material to appear. And in this day of instant gratification anything longer than a few seconds is considered long.

Furthermore, you want to make sure that your materials are accessible to the entire range of your learners, including those with visual or auditory disabilities. If you do decide to use some kind of technology that may be difficult for some of your learners to access, make sure the same information is also available in an alternative format for your learners with these specific needs. Take a look at the principles referred to as the Universal Design for Learning (UDL) to assist you in your instructional technology–related decisions (CAST 2011). These principles are intended to help instructors deal with a variety of accessibility issues. While the UDL principles and guidelines were developed to accommodate working with instructional technology, they are also good rules to live and teach by for F2F instruction as well (Kaplowitz 2012).

WRAP-UP

As you can see, using a variety of instructional activities pays off in many, many ways. Research has shown that participatory learner-centered teaching is more effective and engaging than the more passive teacher-centered ways of teaching. Although both lecture and demo have their place, they should be used carefully and sparingly. Teacher-centered approaches are most effective if they are used to lay the groundwork for the more active learning experiences you have included. Asking learners to participate in learner-centered activities not only gives them the opportunity to really get involved in (and take some responsibility for) their learning experience, it allows learners to work collaboratively with each other in the type of social setting that is often very reminiscent of the way they gather and absorb information in their everyday lives.

Furthermore, these types of activities give you as the instructor a way to monitor ongoing instruction and to make midstream corrections as needed. Finally, since learners take a measure of control of and responsibility for their own learning, each session you teach takes on a slightly different aspect. You may be pleasantly surprised by some of the directions your learners take. Those who practice the learner-centered teaching approach often comment that they are less likely to suffer symptoms of instructional burnout—even when teaching the same material over and over again. The content may be the same and the activities may be identical, but what your learners do with those activities will be unique to the particular group with whom you are working. So rather than having your instruction feeling like the "same old same old" every time you teach, each instructional encounter can be a new and exciting opportunity to interact with your learners. You won't become bored with your instruction, and as a consequence neither will your learners.

WHAT STUCK?

While you are quite taken with the idea of trying your hand at a more learner-centered teaching approach, several of your colleagues have expressed reservations about leaving the more comfortable lecture/demo–type teaching they have been using for years. You decide to bring everyone together for a discussion of the advantages and drawbacks of using learner-centered, activities-based instruction. To make sure that all pertinent points are covered by this session, complete the worksheet in figure 6.5.

Once you have completed the worksheet, you can them determine how you will address these issues with your colleagues. You might include some brainstorming exercises on how they feel about assessment. You could put your colleagues into groups and ask them to discuss the advantages and disadvantages of the different forms of assessment. You could facilitate a group discussion on the advantages of mixing methods, and so on. Don't forget to include some kind of closure exercise that asks your colleagues to reflect on what they learned from the workshop—not only to help them review the material for themselves, but also as a way for you to gather some assessment data about their experience.

FIGURE 6.5

What Will Learners Do? Selecting Learning Activities

Complete this worksheet to prepare yourself for your discussion of the various learning activities options discussed in this chapter. Then use the worksheet sections as a way to frame your session for your colleagues.

Learner-Centered Teaching

➢ What does research tell us about how people learn?

➢ What are the major principles associated with learner-centered teaching?

➢ What are the advantages of learner-centered teaching?

➢ What, if any, are the drawbacks or concerns associated with learner-centered teaching?

ELOs and Instructional Activities

➢ How do ELOs help you select instructional activities?

➢ How do you determine if you have selected an appropriate activity for a specific ELO? Refer to levels of comprehension (Bloom or Anderson and Krathwohl) as a way to answer this question.

Most and Least Used Methods

➤   What are two methods do you use the most? Why do you think you use these more than other methods?

➤   Which two methods do you use the least? Why do you think you avoid these two methods?

➤   Which methods do you think your colleagues use the most? Why do you think these methods are so popular?

➤   Which methods do your colleagues seem to avoid using? Why do you think these methods are avoided?

Advantages and Drawbacks of Various Activity Types

➤   Lecture/demo

○   Advantages:

○   Drawbacks:

➤ Structured Q&A

  ○ Advantages:

  ○ Drawbacks:

➤ Discussion

  ○ Advantages:

  ○ Drawbacks:

➤ Hands-On Practice

  ○ Advantages:

  ○ Drawbacks:

➤ Collaborative Group Work

  ○ Advantages:

  ○ Drawbacks:

➤ Reflection

  ○ Advantages:

  ○ Drawbacks:

Mixing Methods

➤   All methods have their advantages and drawbacks. Mixing methods has been shown to be an effective approach to teaching. Instruction is improved when you teach using a variety of methods because:

Final Reflection

➤   After reflecting on the material you read in this chapter, in what way do you think you might change your own ILI practices?

REFERENCES

Aiken, Edwin G., Gary S. Thomas, and William A. Shennum. 1978. "Memory for a Lecture: Effects of Notes, Lecture Rate, and Information Density." *Journal of Educational Psychology* 67 (3): 439–44.

American Psychological Association Work Group of the Board of Educational Affairs. 1997. *Learner-Centered Psychological Principles: A Framework for School Reform and Redesign*. Washington, DC.: American Psychological Association.

Anderson, Lorin W., and David R. Krathwohl. 2001. *A Taxonomy of Learning, Teaching and Assessing: A Revision of Bloom's Educational Objectives*. Boston: Allyn & Bacon.

Angelo, Thomas, and Patricia Cross. 1993. *Classroom Assessment Techniques: A Handbook for College Teachers*. San Francisco: Jossey-Bass.

Aronson, Elliot. 1978. *The Jigsaw Classroom*. Beverly Hills, CA: Sage.

Ausubel, David. 1977. "The Facilitation of Meaningful Verbal Learning for the Classroom." *Educational Psychologist* 12 (2): 162–78.

Barkley, Elizabeth F., K. Patricia Cross, and Claire Howell Major. 2004. *Collaborative Learning Techniques: A Handbook for College Faculty*. San Francisco: Jossey-Bass.

Bell, Stephen. 2008. "Design Thinking." *American Libraries* 39 (1/2): 44–49.

Bell, Stephen, and John D. Shank. 2007. *Academic Librarianship by Design*. Chicago: American Library Association.

Bligh, Donald A. 2000. *What's the Use of Lectures?* San Francisco: Jossey-Bass.

Bloom, Benjamin Samuel. 1984. *Taxonomy of Educational Objectives*. Boston: Allyn & Bacon.

Booth, Char. 2011. *Reflective Teaching, Effective Learning*. Chicago: American Library Association.

Bransford, John D., Ann L. Brown, Rodney R. Cocking, and National Research Council. 1999. *How People Learn: Bridging Research and Practice*. Washington, DC: National Academy Press.

———. 2000. *How People Learn: Brain, Mind, Experience and School*. Washington, DC: National Academy Press.

Brookfield, Stephen. 1990. *The Skillful Teacher: On Technique, Trust and Responsiveness in the Classroom*. San Francisco: Jossey-Bass.

Brown, Ann L., and Joseph C. Campione. 1996. "Psychological Learning Theory and the Design of Innovative Environments: Procedures, Principles and Systems." In *Contributions of Instructional Innovations to Understanding Learning*, edited by Leona Schauble and Robert Glaser, 289–325. Mahwah, NJ: Erlbaum.

Carlson, Jon D. 2009. "Who Are You Wearing? Using the Red Carpet Question Pedagogically." *International Studies Perspectives* 10 (1): 198–215.

CAST. 2011. "Universal Design for Learning Guidelines—Version 2.0." National Center on Universal Design for Learning. Accessed May 29. http://www.udlcenter.org/aboutudl/udlguidelines.

Coffield, Frank, David Moseley, Elaine Hall, and Kathryn Ecclestone. 2004. *Learning Styles and Pedagogy in Post-16 Learning: A Systematic and Critical Review*. London: Learning and Skills Research Center.

Cooper, James L., Jean MacGregor, Karl A. Smith, and Pamela Robinson. 2000. "Implementing Small-Group Instruction: Insights from Successful Practitioners." *New Directions for Teaching and Learning* 81: 63–76.

Cruickshank, Donald R., Deborah Bainer Jenkins, and Kim K. Metcalf. 2009. *The Act of Teaching*. 5th ed. Boston: McGraw-Hill.

Davis, Barbara Gross. 2009. *Tools for Teaching.* 2nd ed. San Francisco: Jossey-Bass.

Davis, Martha, and Richard Hult. 1997. "Effects of Writing Summaries as a Generative Learning Activity During Note Taking." *Teaching of Psychology* 24 (1): 47–49.

Dempsey, John V., and Richard N. Van Eck. 2012. "E-Learning and Instuructional Design." In *Trends and Issues in Instructional Design and Technology*, edited by Robert A. Reiser and John V. Dempsey, 281–89. Boston: Pearson.

Doyle, Terry. 2011. *Learner-Centered Teaching: Putting the Research into Practice.* Sterling, VA: Stylus.

Eggen, Paul, and Don Kauchak. 2010. *Educational Psychology: Windows on Classrooms.* Upper Saddle River, NJ: Merrill.

Freiberg, H. Jerome, and Amy Driscoll. 2005. *Universal Teaching Strategies.* Boston: Allyn & Bacon.

Grassian, Esther, and Joan Kaplowitz. 2009. *Information Literacy Instruction: Theory and Practice.* 2nd ed. New York: Neal-Schuman.

Holbert, Keith E., and George G. Karady. 2008. "Removing an Unsupported Statement in Engineering Education Literature." In Proceedings of the 2008 American Society for Engineering Education Pacific Southwest Annual Conference, Flagstaff, AZ, March 27–28.

Johnson, David W., Roger T. Johnson, and Karl A. Smith. 2007. "The State of Cooperative Learning in Postsecondary and Professional Settings." *Educational Psychology Review* 19 (1): 15–29.

Kaplowitz, Joan R. 2012. *Transforming Information Literacy Instruction Using Learner-Centered Teaching.* New York: Neal-Schuman.

Katayama, Andrew D., and Daniel H. Robinson. 2000. "Getting Students 'Partially' Involved in Note-Taking Using Graphic Organizers." *Journal of Experimental Education* 68 (2): 119–33.

Kiewra, Kenneth A., Nelson F. Dubois, David Christian, Anne McShane, Michelle Meyerhoffer, and David Roskelly. 1991. "Note-Taking Functions and Techniques." *Journal of Educational Psychology* 83 (2): 240–45.

King, Alison. 1992. "Comparison of Self-Questioning, Summarizing, and Notetaking-Review as Strategies for Learning from Lectures." *American Educational Research Journal* 29 (2): 303–23.

———. 1993. "From Sage on the Stage to Guide on the Side." *College Teaching* 41 (1): 30–35.

Ko, Susan, and Steve Rossen. 2010. *Teaching Online: A Practical Guide.* 3rd ed. New York: Routledge.

Kratzig, Gregory P., and Katherine D. Arbuthnott. 2006. "Perceptual Learning Style and Learning Proficiency: A Test of the Hypothesis." *Journal of Educational Psychology* 98 (1): 238–46.

Lalley, James P., and Robert H. Miller. 2007. "The Learning Pyramid: Does It Point Teachers in the Right Direction?" *Education* 128 (1): 64–79.

Lohr, Linda. L., and James E. Gall. 2007. "Representation Strategies." In *Handbook of Research on Educational Communications and Technology*, edited by J. Michael Spector, M. David Merrill, Jeroen van Merrienboer, and Marcy P. Driscoll, 85–96. New York: Erlbaum.

Marlow, Bruce A., and Marilyn L. Page. 2005. *Creating the Constructivist Classroom.* Thousand Oaks, CA: Corwin.

Mayer, Richard. 2010. "Merlin C. Wittrock's Enduring Contributions to the Science of Learning." *Educational Psychologist* 45 (1): 46–50.

McCombs, Barbara.L., and Lynda Miller. 2007. *Learner-Centered Classroom Practices and Assessments: Maximizing Student Motivation, Learning, and Achievement.* Thousand Oaks, CA: Corwin.

McKeachie, Wilbert J., and Marilla Svinicki. 2006. *McKeachie's Teaching Tips.* 12th ed. Boston: Houghton Mifflin.

Miller, George A. 1956. "The Magic Number Seven, Plus or Minus Two: Some Limits on Our Capacity for Processing Information." *Psychological Review* 63 (2): 81–97.

Molenda, Michael. 2004. "On the Origins of the 'Retention Chart.'" *Educational Technology* 44 (1): 64.

Morrison, Gary R., Steven M. Ross, Howard K. Kalman, and Jerrold E. Kemp. 2011. *Designing Effective Instruction.* 6th ed. Hoboken, NJ: Wiley.

Paas, Fred, Alexander Renkl, and John Sweller. 2003. "Cognitive Load Theory and Instructional Design: Recent Developments." *Educational Psychologist* 38 (1): 1–4.

Palloff, Rena M., and Keith Pratt. 2007. *Building Online Learning Communities: Effective Strategies for the Virtual Classroom.* San Francisco: Jossey-Bass.

Pashler, Harold, Mark McDaniel, Doug Rohrer, and Robert Bjork. 2008. "Learning Styles: Concepts and Evidence." *Psychological Science in the Public Interest* 9 (3): 105–19.

Sanderson, Heather. 2011. "Using Learning Styles in Information Literacy: Critical Considerations." *Journal of Academic Librarianship* 37 (5): 376–85.

Slavin, Robert E. 2011 *Educational Psychology.* 10th ed. Upper Saddle River, NJ: Prentice Hall.

Sweller, John, Jeroen van Merrienboer, and Fred Paas. 1998. "Cognitive Architecture and Instructional Design." *Educational Psychology Review* 10 (3): 251–96.

Vella, Jane. 2000. *Learning to Listen, Learning to Teach.* 2nd ed. San Francisco: Jossey-Bass.

Weimer, Mary Ellen. 2003. "Focus on Learning, Transform Teaching." *Change* 35 (5): 49–54.

Wittrock, Merlin C. 1974. "Learning as a Generative Process." *Educational Psychologist* 19 (2): 87–96.

———. 2001. "Teaching Learners Generative Strategies for Enhancing Reading Comprehension." *Theory into Practice* 24 (2): 123–26.

How Will You Know?

Assessing Information Literacy Instruction

Now that I have written my outcomes and am ready to select activities based on those outcomes, I feel as if my instructional planning is complete. Although I understand the value of assessment, unless I am teaching a full-length graded course or need to provide accountability data for my stakeholders, I don't see the need to assess my learners. Furthermore, with the limited contact time I have for many of my information literacy instruction (ILI) one-shots and stand-alone workshops, I really don't want to set aside time for assessment activities that will limit my abilities to provide my learners with the information I wish to share with them. In addition, I don't feel as if I have the experience or expertise to design quality assessment activities.

Why should you assess your ILI? It is really very simple. You assess because you want to know if your instruction had a positive effect on your learners. If you have bought into the Teaching Tripod approach, you have begun your instructional planning by writing expected learning outcomes (ELOs). You also have begun to consider the types of learning activities you want to incorporate into your instruction so that learners get the chance to interact with the material in order to attain those outcomes. Having gone to all that trouble, don't you want to include a way to find out what your learners actually got out of the instructional experience? Assessment provides valuable information that can be used to improve learning, increase instructional effectiveness, and garner crucial support from your stakeholders. The bottom line is that without this third piece of the Tripod, you have no way of knowing if your learners learned anything from the instructional experience, or if the instruction was just a waste of everyone's time (Grassian and Kaplowitz 2009; Kaplowitz 2012).

QUESTIONS TO CONSIDER
- ➤ How does assessment relate to the other elements in the Teaching Tripod, namely, outcomes and activities?
- ➤ What does assessment tell me about my ILI?
- ➤ What are some issues related to assessment?
- ➤ What types of assessments are available to me?
- ➤ How do I pick the right assessment for my purposes?

ASSESSMENT AS PART OF THE TEACHING TRIPOD

Assessment is the last element in the Teaching Tripod. Without assessment the Teaching Tripod is incomplete. Moreover, each of the three Tripod elements (ELOs, activities, assessment) is interrelated and mutually supportive. If the intent of writing ELOs is to articulate what you want learners to be able to do following instruction, then you need a way to find out if they can in fact "do it." Therefore, you need to offer learners an opportunity to demonstrate that they have attained instructional goals and outcomes so that you can assess your learners' progress (Farmer 2011; Johnson and Dick 2012). That is why you should start thinking about assessment as soon as you finish writing your ELOs (Grassian and Kaplowitz 2009; Kaplowitz 2012; Morrison et al. 2011). Look over your completed ELOs and decide how you plan to assess each one. And use these decisions to help you structure your instruction. View the learning activities you are considering as both opportunities for your learners to attain ELOs, and as potential ways for you to assess their progress. Will watching your learners interact with the material be enough of an assessment for your purposes, or do you think you need to add more formal assessment approaches? As you review your ELOs keep in mind that each and every one of your outcomes needs to be assessed in some way—either through observational means or via some specialized type of assessment technique.

Remember that the three Tripod elements work as an interrelated unit. Outcomes lead to both activities and assessment. Assessment is intended to measure the attainment of outcomes. And activities can serve both as a way for learners to attain outcomes and as a method for assessing learner success. So all three elements are vital to effective instructional design (ID). Take a moment to consider your own ILI practice as it relates to assessment. Complete the worksheet in figure 7.1 to help you reflect on how much assessment you are already doing, the types you generally use, and what might be holding you back from incorporating more assessment into your ILI.

THE CONCEPT OF ASSESSMENT

Assessment is kind of like spinach. We all know it is good for us, but we don't always want to have much to do with it. The thought of assessing our ILI is often viewed with trepidation. Perhaps you don't feel you have the expertise nor do you really see the need for it—especially in your one-shots. But that is because you are viewing assessment from a very limited perspective—the more formal and methodical types of assessment either associated with student grading, or with accountability.

However, there is more to assessment than accountability and grading. Assessment also provides constructive feedback that can help improve the instructional experience for your learners, and can help you improve the instruction for the future. This type of assessment is frequently more informal than accountability or grading assessment, and often takes place during the instructional experience. Assessment for accountability and grading assessment, on the other hand, generally occurs after instruction has been completed (Grassian and Kaplowitz 2009; Kaplowitz 2012).

When you think about assessment from this perspective, you might discover that there is more assessing going on in your instruction than you realized. Do you watch your learners explore material that you have shared with them? Do you monitor their behavior during hands-on practice and/or exercises? Do you ask questions about the material or encourage interactive discussion on topics being examined? Do you collect the learners' exercises or worksheets after hands-on practice or group activities? If so, you are engaging in this more informal type of assessment. Keep in mind that if you don't include any kind of measure of effectiveness in your ILI, you have no way of knowing if the activities you selected are helping (or hindering) your learners in their quest to attain the instructional goals and outcomes you have set for the experience.

Most of us do this type of informal assessment all the time, perhaps without even thinking about calling it assessment. In face-to-face synchronous instruction, we tend to watch for that "glazed over" look that implies that we have "lost" our learners. They are no longer paying attention to us or to the material we are sharing with them. When our learners seem to be confused, overwhelmed by the material, or just plain bored, that signals us that we need to do something to get their attention back—slow down the pace, review the material, rephrase it or present it in a different format, offer additional examples, introduce a different type of activity, and so on.

FIGURE 7.1

Reflecting on Your ILI

How much assessment do you include in your ILIs? What do you do and why? What if anything holds you back from doing more assessment? Complete this worksheet to help you reflect on your assessment practices.

➤ On a scale from 1 to 5 with 5 being "always" and 1 being "never," how often do you include something that could be thought of as assessment in your ILI offerings?

                    1   2   3   4   5

➤ If you do include assessment, give some examples of the types of assessments you generally use.

➤ If you never include assessment or only do it occasionally, what holds you back from assessing your instructional endeavors?

➤ What, if any, changes would you be willing to make in your ILI in order to include more assessment in your instructional offerings?

This monitoring of attention during instruction is sometimes referred to as checking for "with-it-ness" (Kounin 1970), as in the learners are still with us or we have lost them somehow and need to make some changes in the way we are working with them.

As you monitor for "with-it-ness," you are also looking for evidence that your learners are attaining the ELOs set for the instruction. You can use the information you gain from these informal assessments to help learners gauge their own progress toward the ELOs. By providing them with constructive feedback on the various learning activities in which they are engaging, learners can self-assess how well they are doing as well as identify areas that need some improvement. Furthermore, informal assessments can be used to help you make midstream corrections and improve your instruction on the spot (Grassian and Kaplowitz 2009; Kaplowitz 2012).

Accountability assessments, on the other hand, require a great deal of careful planning and generally involve formal data collection as well as some type of reporting mechanism. Obviously if you are teaching a full-term course, you will need to provide your learners with a grade that hopefully reflects the degree to which they have mastered the material you shared with them. Most courses include built-in assessment methods such as examinations, written papers, and/or projects with scoring guidelines (sometimes called rubrics) for evaluating the quality of the learners' work.

Assessments done in order to provide information to stakeholders with the intent of garnering continued or increased support for your ILI programs are another form of accountability assessments. These assessments generally require a written report that summarizes the findings and includes recommendations for the future. Accountability assessments can take a variety of forms, such as longitudinal studies to assess the long-term effect of instructional programs, or research comparing the relative merits of different methods of instruction. Regardless of the form, accountability assessment tends to involve systematic data collection, statistical analysis, and some kind of summary and synthesis of findings. As a result they are time consuming, labor intensive, and often costly. Assessments of this type are therefore undertaken only when absolutely necessary, and generally have their originals in some outside force such as accreditation cycles in the academic and/or school settings or funding reviews in most, if not, all library settings.

The decision to undertake either accountability or constructive feedback assessments depends on why you are doing the assessment as well as its intended audience. Regardless of the type of assessment you are involved in, what you are looking at is how well your learners have attained the ELOs set for the instruction. When you use informal means to observe your learners interacting with the material you are sharing with them, you are doing so as a way to gauge the progress toward the goals and outcomes of the instruction and to provide further assistance as needed. Learners in full-length credit courses receive grades that are intended to indicate how well they attained each course ELO. Accountability assessments look at the overall impact of your ILI and are also measured in terms of how well learners have attained ELOs—either in regard to a particular type of ILI or the ILI program overall. Does your ILI seem to help learners become information literate as described by some outside standard set by a professional association either within librarianship or in a specific discipline? Does completing a particular ILI class or course result in learners attaining skills that help them in their other studies? What impact do your ILI classes or courses have on your learners' abilities to gain employment, or in other ways satisfy their ongoing, lifelong information needs? All these assessments must have something to measure, and what they measure is the attainment of whatever ELOs are associated with the class, course, or program (Booth 2011; Kaplowitz 2012; Miller and Bratton 1988). No matter what type of assessment you are doing, the information you learn should be recorded in some way and used when you review and revise your instruction for the next time you plan to teach this material (Grassian and Kaplowitz 2009; Kaplowitz 2012; Morrison et al. 2011).

TIMING—BEFORE, DURING, AND AFTER

Although we generally think of assessments as being placed at the end of instruction, assessments can occur before and during instruction as well. Where you place your assessment activity depends upon what you are trying to learn about your learners (Farmer 2011; Kaplowitz 2012). Here are some things to consider when you are deciding where to place your assessment.

"Before" Assessments

Are you trying to determine what learners already know and need to know so that you can select your ELOs for the instruction? Obviously these are assessments that are done before instruction—as you are doing initial planning. Chapter 4 examines these "before" needs assessments in detail, but keep in mind that you can do quick assessments at the beginning of a face-to-face or a synchronous online session by asking some relevant questions, doing a brief survey using online tools such as SurveyMonkey or online polling software, or by administering some kind of pretest. You can find out about your learners' previous experience in searching for information, how they feel about doing this type of research, and how confident (or not) they are that they are finding what they need. You can also do a reality check at this point to make sure that whatever you thought brought the learners to you is actually what they need to know. We sometimes make assumptions about our learners' skill levels, past experiences, and specific needs based on what we already think we know about this group, or because of some background information we have gotten from whoever requested the instruction. It is always a good idea to verify that these assumptions are correct by checking with the learners themselves.

If you are working in an asynchronous online environment, you can also include some of these more or less on-the-spot "before" type assessments. For example, online tutorials can include a self-test that helps learners decide if the instruction is relevant, and/or helps learners select the parts of the tutorial that would be most appropriate for them. These self-tests can also be used for ILI courses taught entirely online. Learners can self-assess if the course seems like a good way to address their needs. You can also include some self-assessment to help learners decide if online learning is for them. Not everyone works well in the more self-directed environment associated with online or distance learning. So it is a good idea to give learners a chance to decide ahead of time if they should choose an online learning option. Many "see if online learning is right for you" self-assessments exist for use with your learners (Cerro Coso Community College 2011; MiraCosta College 2011; Sierra College 2011).

Contacting learners ahead of time or gathering some preliminary information before the actual instruction begins can ensure that you are on the right track with the ELOs you have selected, and that learners will gain what they need from your instruction. It also lets them know that you really care about them and want to do the best job you can in supporting their library research (Grassian and Kaplowitz 2009; Kaplowitz 2012).

"During" Assessments

As already mentioned, the learning activities you include in your instruction can also provide informal assessment data during the actual instructional experience. You just need to develop a mind-set that views what is happening during these activities as "mini-assessments." Of course, your main role during activities is to act as a facilitator or guide to help your learners work through the material, but you should also be taking note of how well they seem to be able to work with the material you have shared with them. Pay particular attention to places where learners seem to be having difficulties or have gotten some incorrect ideas. These points call for midstream corrections—stopping to go over the material again in some fashion to ensure that learners are able to correctly apply the newly learned material.

Don't forget that assessment never ends. Every time you teach you should be looking for ways to improve your instructional effectiveness. "During" assessments can be used to gather this very crucial information. Keep a record of points where learning may have gone awry for use when you review and revise the instruction before offering it again. As you reflect on what happened (good or not so good) during the instruction, you will be able to identify any aspects of the instruction that might benefit from adjustment for future offerings. Perhaps your ELOs were incorrect or overly ambitious for this group and you need to rethink them? Or maybe some of your activities need to be reorganized, replaced by other types of activities, or in some other way modified. This type of "during" assessment is generally referred to as formative because the information you collect can be used to improve the learning experience during instruction as well as provide you with feedback on the overall effectiveness of the instruction and maybe even spark ideas for future improvements (Booth 2011; Johnson and Dick 2012; Kaplowitz 2012; Morrison et al. 2011).

"After" Assessment

When most people hear the word "assessment," they think about activities that occur when instruction has been completed. As already discussed, assessment can take place at various points in the instructional process. We have already discussed the "before" and "during" types of assessments. So now let's take a closer look at what falls under the heading of end-point assessment. "After" assessments can happen at the very end of an individual class or instructional segment, or it could be scheduled for some time in the future. The point is that these assessments are done after the fact and are usually referred to as summative assessment, which means they measure the overall effectiveness of instruction once it has been completed (Morrison et al. 2011). "After" assessments can be used for either accountability or as a way for learners and instructors to gauge the effectiveness of the instruction. For example, closure exercises or reflections such as the minute paper (Angelo 1998; Angelo and Cross 1993) can be viewed as "after" assessments since they are done at the very end of a particular class. Paper or projects that learners produce using the skills they learned during the instruction are another example of an "after" assessment, as are any type of formal examination or test. Surveys/questionnaires, interviews, and so forth, that are used to gather qualitative information about the learners' instructional experience can also be viewed as examples of "after" assessments as well if they occur after instruction has been completed. In general, tests or examinations fall under the heading of accountability assessment, as they are usually associated with graded types of instruction. However, all other types can be used either for accountability or for learning and instructional effectiveness depending upon how the data collected is being used. Furthermore, while most "after" assessments occur fairly close to the end of the instruction itself, all these techniques can also be used in longitudinal studies to assess the effectiveness of the instruction over time (Grassian and Kaplowitz 2009; Kaplowitz 2012).

Instructors tend to use a mix of "before," "during," and "after" types of assessment. Regardless of which ones you use, remember that information gathered from these assessments can help you assist your learners attain instructional ELOs as well as provide information that will help you improve the effectiveness of the instruction for the future. If structured correctly, they can also be used for the accountability function of assessment. However, if accountability assessment is your goal, you will need to include a way to gather data from the assessment activities. Pretests, surveys/questionnaires, interviews, examinations, and so forth, all have built-in potential for data collection. However, you can also gather data from the "during" type of assessments by having learners turn in their worksheets after completing the activities. You can also collect the products of the closure activities from the end of a specific session. If you have access to the papers or projects that learners produce following their instruction experience, you can analyze them to see what if any impact your instruction had on the quality of these items. It helps to have some examples of similar work that was done by learners who did not have the instruction to serve as a baseline. Working with your instructional partners, especially in the K–20 environment, can be a particularly fruitful way to explore the impact of your instruction on the actual work learners are producing following instruction (Grassian and Kaplowitz 2009; Kaplowitz 2012).

Before we move on to a closer examination of the types of assessments available to you, take a moment to consider your ILI practice and look for places where you already include assessment—whether it is "before," "during," or "after" your instruction. Then complete the worksheet in figure 7.2 to give yourself a snapshot of your current assessment practices.

SELECTING YOUR ASSESSMENT

Deciding upon the type of assessment you will use and the timing of the assessment itself is dependent upon a number of factors. One way to help you make appropriate decisions is to ask yourself a series of questions about the purpose of your assessment. To assist you in the planning process, consider the questions that appear in figure 7.3. Your answers will help you select both when to assess and what type of assessment will be most appropriate for your needs (Grassian and Kaplowitz 2009).

WHAT TYPE OF BEHAVIOR DO YOU WANT TO MEASURE?

Having identified why you are doing the assessment and for whom you are doing it, you are ready to begin thinking about how to design your assessment. In the discussion of selecting learning activities in chapter 6, the point was made that it is important to match the activity with the level on Bloom's taxonomy that represents the ELO being addressed. A similar idea holds true for assessment. In general, assessments will address one of the following levels of assessment. In order to select the most appropriate type of assessment, you must first determine the type of behavior you are trying to measure. The characteristics of each of the four levels are summarized below (Booth 2011; Johnson and Dick 2012; Kaplowitz 2012; Kirkpatrick 2006).

Level 1: Reaction Assessments

These assessments answer the question "Did they like it?" In brief, instructors using reaction assessments are trying to find out if learners enjoyed the instruction, if they liked our presentation, and were comfortable with the way we interacted with them. These are often referred to as "happiness scales" and usually take the form of questionnaires or surveys. While they provide valuable information about how your learners feel about the instructional experience, they do not offer any data about their learning or the attainment of ELOs. While you might include a question or two about whether or not they felt they learned anything and/or if they might use any of the information shared with them in the future, you are only soliciting their opinions and are in no way measuring what they learned or might actually do with what they experienced during instruction.

Level 2: Learning

Learning assessments ask the question "Did they get it?" As such, they are attempting to gauge the learners' experience as it relates to the instructional ELOs. However, while they do include ways for learners to demonstrate what they have gained from the instruction, learning assessments are generally done under the strict control of the instructor. In other words, the instructor sets the parameters under which the learners will interact with the material. He or she selects the problem to be solved, identifies resources to be used, and gives the learners a set amount of time to do so. As such, learning assessments represent a somewhat artificial view into what has been learned and may not reflect what learners will do in real-life situations when they have to decide for themselves what resources to use and how to use them. So learning assessments only offer a picture of what learners might do once they leave

FIGURE 7.2

Before, During, and After Assessments

Think about your current ILI practice. See if you can identify assessments you are already doing that occur "before," "during," or "after" your ILI.

➤   Examples of assessments I do *before* my ILIs are:

➤   Examples of assessments I do *during* my ILIs are:

➤   Examples of assessments I do *after* my ILIs are:

FIGURE 7.3

What Is the Purpose of Your Assessment?

Deciding on the types of assessments to use depends on many factors. Complete this worksheet to help you determine what you need to assess and how best to do so.

Who wants to know?

➢   Things to Consider:

  ○   Once you determine "who wants to know" you can decide on how formal or informal your assessment needs to be.
  ○   Identifying "who wants to know" will also help you choose the type of assessment tool that will provide the most helpful data for your audience.

➢   Information Needed:

  ○   Who is the audience for your assessment?

  ○   Are you doing this for constructive feedback or for accountability?

What are you trying to find out?

➢   Things to Consider:

  ○   Different types of assessments result in different types of data.
  ○   Data can be in the form of numbers (quantitative) or narrative (qualitative).
  ○   Identifying the information you wish to gather from your assessment helps you select the type of assessment tool you need to use.

➢   Information Needed:

  ○   What is the aim of the assessment?

  ○   Are you trying to measure what learners have gained from instruction?

  ○   Are you trying to compare the effectiveness of different modes of instruction?

○ Are you interested in changes in your learners' attitudes toward ILI?

○ Are you examining the effectiveness of an individual ILI offering or looking at the entire program?

What are the ELOs you are trying to assess?

➤ Things to Consider:

    ○ The whole point of including assessment in your ILI is to provide ways for learners to demonstrate the attainment of ELOs.

    ○ Make sure that your learners have an opportunity to show they have attained each and every one of the ELOs.

    ○ You can measure overall instructional effectiveness by how well learners have attained all the ELOs set for your ILI.

➤ Information Needed:

    ○ What are the skills, knowledge, and abilities you expect learners to be able to exhibit following instruction?

    ○ How will you know that your learners have attained the ELOs set for your ILI?

What opportunities will you include in your instruction for your learners to demonstrate attainment of ELOs?

➤ Things to Consider:

    ○ Assessments can use specialized tools such as quizzes or surveys.

    ○ Assessment data can also be gathered by watching learners during instructional activities.

    ○ Planning what types of assessments you will use and where you will place them in your ILI (during or after) is a critical part of ID.

    ○ Therefore, you should select your assessments immediately after you have written your ELOs.

➢ Information Needed:

  ○ In what way will your learners exhibit attainment of each ELO?

  ○ When will the assessments take place, for example, during or after instruction?

How will the data you collect be used?

➢ Things to Consider:

  ○ This goes back to the first question—"Who wants to know?"
  ○ Assessment data can be used to help learners improve, to assist you in determining instructional effectiveness, or as a way to justify your instruction to others.
  ○ Who will be reviewing the results will often determine the type of data that needs to be collected.

➢ Information Needed:

  ○ Will the data you collect be used internally or will it be shared with a wider audience?

  ○ If you plan to share it with a larger audience, who will that audience be?

Will you be required to prepare and distribute a formal, written report on the data collected?

➢ Things to Consider:

  ○ If your assessment goal is to inform and influence your stakeholders you need to make sure you are summarizing and synthesizing the data into a format that will help you make your case.
  ○ If you are expected to provide grades to your learners, you need to make sure you are collecting appropriate forms of data to allow you to do so.
  ○ While more informal or formative assessments may not require written reports, noting the results of these assessments is important and will help you improve the instructional experience for your learners during the instruction itself, and may offer suggestions for revising it for the future.

➤   Information Needed:

  ○ Are your stakeholders asking for a formal report for accountability purposes?

  ○ If so, who will receive this formal report?

  ○ Is your assessment for grading purposes? If yes, the grades will be your report. What will you use as a basis for your learners' grades?

  ○ Is your assessment for constructive feedback? If yes, the results of this more informal type assessment will probably be shared only with those involved—the instructor and the learners. With whom will you share this information and how will you share it?

the instructional situation. However, these are often the only types of assessments available to you. So you try to use the data you gather in order to infer how your learners will (hopefully) act when they are called upon to address their information needs in the future.

Level 3: Behavioral

Level 3 assessments look at the how learners behave when dealing with real-life, authentic information needs. They answer the question "Can they do it?" Papers, projects, and the like are examples of this type of assessment. Learners must call upon what they learned in order to apply it to whatever question they are trying to answer. Behavioral assessments look at whether or not the ways in which learners solve a problem have changed as a result of participating in instruction. While these types of assessments provide valuable insight into learners' current capabilities, they do not provide data regarding what the learners actually did in the process. In other words, although behavioral assessments can demonstrate learners' abilities to solve a problem, they don't offer evidence about whether or not these abilities are a result of an instructional intervention. In working with behavioral assessment it is therefore helpful to have some baseline data with which to compare learners' work before and after instruction, or to examine any differences between learners who participated in instruction and those who did not. If learners who participated in instruction perform significantly better after instruction than before, or produce higher-quality work than those who did not, you can infer that the instruction had a beneficial result (Farmer 2011; Grassian and Kaplowitz 2009; Kaplowitz 2012).

Level 4: Results

Results assessments attempt to answer the question "Did it matter?" In other words, these assessments look at the overall and long-term impact instruction might have had on learners. These are often referred to as confirmative assessments and may involve longitudinal data collection (Morrison et al. 2011). While these types of assessment are critically important to demonstrating the importance and impact of ILI (and all types of instruction), they are difficult, often costly to do, and frequently require the assistance of people and groups beyond your institution. Unfortunately, this means that results assessments not are done very often (Grassian and Kaplowitz 2009).

Before we move on, take a moment to think about your ILI endeavors in terms of the four levels of assessment just described. Then complete the worksheet provided in figure 7.4 as a way to reflect on the questions you are trying to answer (reaction, learning, behavioral, results) and the types of assessments you might be using (or plan to use) to collect that information.

ASSESSMENT PARAMETERS

Tools and Techniques

Thinking about the questions you are trying to answer with your assessment helps you build a general picture of why you are assessing your specific instructional session or program. Once you have established the "why" you need to move on to the "how to" or the selection of the type of assessment tool that will provide the answers you need. In order to do so, you need to know a bit more about the various types of assessments. Assessments can be grouped into one of six overall categories. Table 7.1 provides a brief overview of each type of assessment as well as the advantages and drawbacks associated with each one (Grassian and Kaplowitz 2009; Kaplowitz 2012; Morrison et al. 2011).

FIGURE 7.4

What's the Level?

When including assessments in your ILIs, you need to make sure that the type of assessment you choose will answer the question you are asking. Complete this worksheet to help you identify the types of assessments you are using in your instructional offerings. Does the level match the question you are asking?

➤ Level 1—Reaction: Did they like it?

　○ I include the following *Level 1 (Reaction)* assessments in my ILIs:

➤ Level 2—Learning: Did they get it?

　○ I include the following *Level 2 (Learning)* assessments in my ILIs:

➤ Level 3—Behavioral: Can they do it?

　○ I include the following *Level 3 (Behavioral)* assessments in my ILIs:

➤ Level 4—Results: Did it matter?

　○ I include the following *Level 4 (Results)* assessments in my ILIs:

Table 7.1. Types of Assessment Tools

Type	Characteristics	Why Use it?	What to Look Out For
➢ Forced choice—multiple choice, true/false, matching, etc.	• Questions have only one right answer, which is determined by the test developer in advance.	• Easy to administer • Easy to grade • Easy to quantify • Provides a lot of data in a short period of time • Good for testing recall and recognition of presented material	• Requires learner to remember exactly what was presented • Expertise needed to design and analyze • Artificial situation. May not reflect what learners will do in real life • Not appropriate to measure higher levels of comprehension (e.g., analysis, synthesis, evaluation)
➢ Open-ended assessments—short answers or essays	• Allows more latitude for answering than forced choice since responses are in learners' own words, but there is still only one right answer, which is determined in advance	• Good for testing recall of presented material • Easy to administer • Learners can express ideas in their own words. • Can be used to assess higher levels of comprehension such as analysis, synthesis, and evaluation	• Grading can be time consuming and open to interpretation. • May be difficult to quantify • While offering more latitude in the ways that learners can respond, these assessments still do not provide complete insight into what learners would do in real life.
➢ Surveys/questionnaires—ranking or rating scales	• Often used to measure demographics, opinions, or attitudes	• Easy to administer and score • Easy to quantify • No right or wrong answer • Gives learners the opportunity to express attitudes or opinions by selecting how much they agree or disagree with a specific statement	• Only measures how learners feel about instruction, not what they gained from it • Good for measuring changes in affective behavior, but less appropriate for gauging other types of learning • Can be time consuming to develop • Requires specialized skills to develop and analyze • Learners may report what they think you want to hear rather than what they really think or feel.
➢ Interviews/focus groups	• Also used for measuring opinions or attitudes, but offers more latitude for discussion of responses • Interviews are done one-on-one. • Focus groups are interviews done in a group setting.	• Respondents can elaborate on answers and ask for clarification about the questions being asked. • Interviewers can ask follow-up questions to gather additional data. • Focus group interviewing allows for data collection from multiple participants at the same time.	• Can be very time consuming to administer • Requires skilled facilitator/interviewer • Verbal responses can be difficult to compile and synthesize. • Learners may feel uncomfortable expressing true opinions to someone directly involved. • Hiring an outside facilitator to gain more candid responses can increase the costs of using this approach. • Not a real measure of learning as learners are just describing what they think they would do rather than exhibiting attainment of ELOs
➢ Classroom assessment techniques—minute paper, empty outline, concept maps (Angelo 1998; Angelo and Cross 1993)	• Done during instruction itself • Usually takes the form of exercises and other classroom activities	• Allows learners to exhibit their progress toward attainment of ELOs • Promotes active learning • Useful for providing on-the-spot feedback to both learners and instructor on effectiveness of instruction as it happens • Allows instructor to monitor learners' progress and correct misconceptions and errors during the learning experience.	• Difficult to measure and quantify • Although learners are being given the opportunity to demonstrate what they have learned, they are doing so under the constraints imposed upon them by the instructor. • Data from CATs may or may not reflect how learners will behave when they have to apply what they have learned beyond the classroom setting.
➢ Authentic assessment—problem-based learning, case based learning	• Learners are given a real-world problem, issue, or question to solve. • Solutions are not specified in advance. • Learners have a great deal of latitude in deciding how to approach the task at hand. • Most effective if the examples used are based on real-life situations that are relevant to learners	• Learners can solve the problems in their own way. • Allows for diversity in approaches and solutions • Learners can demonstrate transfer of learning to novel situations. • Offers learners insight into the types of problems faced by people in real-life situations	• Well-designed problems/cases can be time consuming to create. • Solutions can be time consuming to grade/score. • Results can be difficult to quantify. • Scoring can be subjective and open to interpretation unless scoring rubrics are defined in advance. • Difficult to judge how learners solved the problem and/or if they received additional help

Control versus Relevance

Another thing to consider is that assessments tend to vary in two basic attributes—control (how much latitude learners are given in the ways they are allowed to respond) and relevance (how closely the assessment situation reflects real-life situations). Assessments high in control tend to be low in relevance and vice versa (Battersby and Learning Outcomes Network 1999; Grassian and Kaplowitz 2009). Assessments at the high-control end of the spectrum can also be viewed as more teacher-centric, while those at the other extreme tend to be more learner-centric.

Forced-choice and open-ended assessments are high in control since only specific answers are allowed, and the instructor determines these answers in advance. They are low in relevance since learners are only indicating what they think is the right answer and their answers may not reflect what they will do in real life (Marzano, Pickering, and McTighe 1993). Classroom assessment techniques (CATs) and authentic assessments are viewed as being fairly low in control since learners are given more latitude in how they work with the material. On the other hand, these types of assessments are regarded as being highly relevant since learners are working directly with material. Authentic assessments represent the most relevant assessment type as they are based on and often take place in real-life situations. CATs are slightly less relevant since learners are working with the material in the somewhat artificial constraints of the classroom. Surveys, questionnaires, interviews, and focus groups fall somewhere in the middle on the control and relevance scales. While they are somewhat under the control of the facilitator, respondents are fairly free to answer the questions in their own way. As for relevance, although the information being solicited could be very relevant to the respondents' real-life experience, the data being collected is only a description of what the respondents say they feel or would do, rather than a direct measure of their actual behavior (Barclay 1993; Colborn and Cordell 1998; Glitz 1998; Sonntag and Meulemans 2003).

Control and relevancy concerns are one more issue you need to keep in mind when you select your assessment methodology. If you want to gather a lot of data easily and in a short period of time, you may wish to go with assessments that are higher in control. However, when you make that decision, you must also acknowledge the artificiality of the situation and be careful regarding how you extrapolate your data to real-life situations. Most high-control assessments (forced choice, open ended, surveys/questionnaires, and interviews/focus groups) only provide information about what learners think they will do, but are not especially good measures of actual behavior. So if your goal is to measure attainment of ELOs, you may need to take a closer look at assessments that are higher in relevance (CATs and authentic assessments). You can also use a combination of assessment approaches to help you gain a more complete picture of what happened as a result of the instruction.

Quantitative versus Qualitative

One more aspect of assessment to consider is the nature of the data being collected. That is, will your data be quantitative (numeric) or qualitative (descriptive) in nature? Some assessments are obviously geared to easily gather quantitative data—for example, forced choice and surveys. But the more narrative-type information gathered from interviews and focus groups also can provide numeric data through response analysis and categorizing responses. Developing scoring rubrics for essays and authentic assessment responses can help you turn these more descriptive types of responses into quantifiable data. Rubrics are especially important if you are working in a for-credit course situation that requires you to provide grades for your learners (Cruickshank, Jenkins, and Metcalf 2009; Huba and Freed 2000; Wiggins 1998).

Deciding What to Assess: The Role of Professional Standards

As already noted, assessment is meant to help you determine how well your learners have attained the ELOs set for them. Determining those ELOs for ILI is dependent upon how information literacy is viewed in your particular environment. Check to see if your institution, region, or professional organization has developed any standards for information literacy. These can be used as the basis for your ELOs and will serve as the benchmarks against which you measure your learners' progress toward becoming information literate. For more on information literacy standards and ELOs, see chapter 5.

ASSESSMENT FOR CONSTRUCTIVE FEEDBACK VERSUS ASSESSMENT FOR ACCOUNTABILITY

While the six types of assessment techniques vary in their characteristics and methodologies used to collect information, all of them can be used to provide feedback to learners, as a way to monitor instructional effectiveness, and/ or for accountability purposes. It is not the type of tool you use to collect the data, or even the form in which you collect the data that determines the purpose of the assessment. It is how you implement the assessment, when you schedule the assessment to take place, how you record the data collected, and who ends up seeing this information that makes the assessment either an example of constructive feedback or of accountability. Take a look at table 7.2 to see how each type of assessment can be used for either constructive feedback or accountability.

Table 7.2. Using Tools for Feedback or Accountability

Assessment Tool	Constructive Feedback for Learners or Instructors	Accountability for Learners (Grades) or Stakeholders (Reports/Presentations)
➢ Forced choice	• Structured Q&A during instruction can be used for comprehension checks before moving on to a new topic. • These could be verbal exchanges or brief written quizzes. • The instructor determines the correct answer in advance, making it a type of forced-choice experience.	• Data collected from graded examinations occurring after instruction can be used to provide grades to students and/or for inclusion in reports or presentations for stakeholders to illustrate the effectiveness of instruction.
➢ Open ended	• Discussions or collaborative activities during instruction are usually kicked off by some kind of general question or problem and so could be viewed as open-ended types of assessments.	• Essay-type examinations as well as papers or projects fall in this category. • As in the case of forced-choice assessments, data collected can be used to provide grades to students and/or for inclusion in reports or presentations for stakeholders to illustrate the effectiveness of instruction.
➢ Surveys/questionnaires	• These can be used as preinstruction needs assessments tools, or placed at points during instruction when you are trying to assess changes in feelings, attitudes, or opinions.	• Survey/questionnaire data can be collected, analyzed, and synthesized into reports/presentations for stakeholders.
➢ Interviews/focus groups	• Information gathered from these assessments can be used internally to help improve specific instructional offerings or the program in general.	• As in the case of survey/questionnaire data, the information gathered from interviews/focus groups can be collected, analyzed, and synthesized into reports or presentations for stakeholders.
➢ Classroom assessment techniques (CATs)	• Assessment data gathered by observing learners interacting with material during instruction can be used to provide ongoing feedback to learners and to provide information for future review and revision of instruction.	• Although generally viewed as a constructive feedback technique, the worksheets and exercises that learners complete during instruction can be collected, reviewed, and analyzed in order to provide accountability reports/presentations for stakeholders.
➢ Authentic assessments	• Assessment data gathered by observing learners during collaborative group exercises based on real-life problems or issues can be used to provide feedback to learners during instruction, and as well as by the instructor for future review and revision of instruction.	• Papers, projects, or products that result from individual or collaborative activities can be collected and the data from these end products can be used to provide grades to students and/or for inclusion in reports or presentations to stakeholders to illustrate the effectiveness of instruction.

INCORPORATING ASSESSMENT INTO YOUR ILI

Clearly there is a lot to consider when you are deciding upon the types of assessments you will use for your ILI. As you make your decisions, try to keep in mind the relationship between ELOs, activities, and assessment. If you focus on these three Tripod elements, you might find it a bit easier to integrate assessment into your ILI practice. The worksheet in figure 7.5 can provide a template for incorporating appropriate assessments into your ILI.

PRACTICAL CONSIDERATIONS

As in all things in life, there is the ideal and then there is the reality. So please keep in mind that you need to weigh the value of the type of assessment you think would best serve your purposes against what you can actually accomplish given the resources available to you, and whatever constraints may exist in your particular situation. For example, is there anyone on your staff (yourself included) with the expertise to design, administer, and analyze the data gathered from your assessment? If not, will you be able to hire someone from the outside to help with this? Will there be costs involved and if so, do you have the budget to support the task? How much time do you have to develop your assessment tool? What are the logistics involved in administering the assessment to your learners? For example, will the assessment take place during the learning itself or at a later time? If assessment is taking place during instruction, you need to factor in the time needed for your learners to interact with whatever type of assessment you will be including. If you are planning to assess at a later time, how will you gain access to learners and/or their work after instruction has been completed? Will you need to partner with organizations or groups outside your library or even beyond your institution? If so, how will you develop these partnerships and gather the necessary data for your assessment?

Be realistic about what is possible and do the best you can. Sometimes the more informal, observational types of assessments are the only ones available to you. Remember, your goal is to help your learners gain something valuable from the instructional experience. So make sure that you include ways for your learners to exhibit that they have attained the ELOs set for the instruction and have moved another step closer to becoming information literate individuals. Informal, observational assessments are fine if you are only looking for constructive feedback data. But if your goal is to collect assessment data for accountability, you will need to develop more formal assessment approaches. Therefore, you will have to consider issues of expertise and budget in a bit more detail. Accountability assessments tend to require careful planning, can be quite time consuming, and come with built-in costs. It might be helpful to look into outside assistance in the design and analysis stage, as well as external funding sources to help support the cost of the project. In any case, accountability assessments take time to plan, design, and implement. So make sure you take this issue into consideration before embarking on any type of accountability assessment task (Grassian and Kaplowitz 2009; Kaplowitz 2012).

WRAP-UP

Assessment is a crucial part of your ILI endeavors. Without assessment you will never know what actually happened as a result of your learners working with the material you have shared with them. There is really no point in developing ELOs and designing learning activities to allow your learners to attain those ELOs without including some way to see if your instruction was effective. Assessment answers the overall question "What did learners get from the instructional experience?" The Teaching Tripod is incomplete without the inclusion of some type of assessment. The formal or informal nature of your assessment depends on your specific situation and what type of information you are trying to gather from the assessment. Remember, assessment data can be used for constructive feedback and/or for accountability purposes, and base your assessment decisions on what you are trying to learn about your ILI.

FIGURE 7.5

Putting It All Together

Think about some of your own ILIs. What type of assessments do you include? Indicate the level of each assessment (1–4), and why you choose that particular assessment activity. Don't forget that observing learning activities during instruction can be used as an assessment technique, if appropriate. Space is provided for five ELOs for a particular ILI endeavor.

➢ Outcome 1

    ○ Assessment:

    ○ Level of assessment (1–4):

    ○ Why did you select this assessment?

➢ Outcome 2

    ○ Assessment:

    ○ Level of assessment (1–4):

    ○ Why did you select this assessment?

➢ Outcome 3

    ○ Assessment:

    ○ Level of assessment (1–4):

    ○ Why did you select this assessment?

➤ Outcome 4

  ○ Assessment:

  ○ Level of assessment (1–4):

  ○ Why did you select this assessment?

➤ Outcome 5

  ○ Assessment:

  ○ Level of assessment (1–4):

  ○ Why did you select this assessment?

Given the nature of ILI and its dependence on stand-alone or one-shot types of sessions, instruction librarians tend to rely on the more informal types of approaches that occur either during instruction or at the very end of a particular ILI session. Of course, if you are teaching a full-length course, you will have to include more formal ways to assess for grading purposes. But don't forget the accountability aspect of assessment and its potential impact on your ILI endeavors. You need the support of your stakeholders to keep your ILI programs viable. Not only do stakeholders tend to hold the purse strings that fund your endeavors, they set policy and priorities for your institution. If your stakeholders do not value ILI, there is little chance your learners will, either. Accountability assessments can help you present your case that being information literate is crucial for everyone to succeed in the world today, regardless of the library environment (Farmer 2011). So as difficult as it may be, you need to engage in some kind of accountability assessment from time to time to sustain the ongoing support of your stakeholders and all those who matter in your environment.

WHAT STUCK?

Your feel your instruction librarians have really bought into the idea of writing ELOs for their instruction and selecting learning activities that will help their learners attain those ELOs. But you sense your librarians are still somewhat reluctant to tackle assessment as part of their ID. Since you feel very strongly that instruction without assessment is incomplete, you would like to help them become more comfortable with the concepts and methods associated with assessment. You decide to call them together one more time to discuss this crucial aspect of ID for ILI. Complete the worksheet in figure 7.6 to help you organize your thoughts and develop talking points and/or activities for this session.

Once you have answered these questions yourself, you can develop talking points and activities to help your colleagues become more knowledgeable about assessment. Develop a plan in which you facilitate interactive discussions on each of these seven points. You might begin by asking your colleagues what they already know about assessment, what types of assessments they may already include, and what concerns they may have about incorporating assessment into their ILI. Make sure to point out the various informal as well as formal approaches to assessment that are available to them and that they may already be using.

FIGURE 7.6

The Why and How-To of Assessment—A Brown-Bag Presentation

Take a moment to answer the questions listed below in order to develop "talking points" for a brown-bag presentation to help your colleagues learn more about the "whys" and "hows" of assessment.

➢ *Talking Points*

  ○ Why do you think librarians are so reluctant to include assessment in their ILI practice?

  ○ How would you address their concerns?

  ○ What reasons would you give them for the importance of assessment?

  ○ How would you describe the relationship between assessment and the other two elements of the Teaching Tripod?

  ○ What do you think are some important questions to consider when making assessment decisions? Include a discussion of both formal and informal ways to assess.

  ○ What are some assessment parameters instruction librarians need to take into account when selecting their assessment techniques? Include issues related to timing as well as the advantages and drawbacks of the various categories of assessment tools.

  ○ What are some logistical issues or constraints instruction librarians may need to consider when making their assessment decisions? That is, what would constitute a reality check regarding the types of assessment that are possible for a specific situation?

REFERENCES

Angelo, Thomas A. 1998. *Classroom Assessment and Research: An Update on Uses, Approaches and Research Findings.* Vol. 75 of *New Directions for Teaching and Learning.* San Francisco: Jossey-Bass.

Angelo, Thomas, and Patricia Cross. 1993. *Classroom Assessment Techniques: A Handbook for College Teachers.* San Francisco: Jossey-Bass.

Barclay, Donald A. 1993. "Evaluating Library Instruction: Doing the Best You Can with What You Have." *RQ* 33 (2): 195–203.

Battersby, Mark, and Learning Outcomes Network. 1999. *So What's a Learning Outcome Anyway?* ERIC Centre for Curriculum, Transfer and Technology. http://files.eric.ed.gov/fulltext/ED430611.pdf

Booth, Char. 2011. *Reflective Teaching, Effective Learning.* Chicago: American Library Association.

Cerro Coso Community College. 2011. "Online Student Skills Quiz." Cerro Coso Community College. Accessed May 29. http://www.cerrocoso.edu/studentservices/survey1.asp.

Colborn, Nancy Wooton, and Rosanne M. Cordell. 1998. "Moving from Subjective to Objective Assessments of Your Instruction Program." *Reference Services Review* 26 (3/4): 125–37.

Cruickshank, Donald R., Deborah Bainer Jenkins, and Kim K. Metcalf. 2009. *The Act of Teaching.* 5th ed. Boston: McGraw-Hill.

Farmer, Lesley S. J. 2011. *Instructional Design for Librarians and Information Professionals.* New York: Neal-Schuman.

Glitz, Beryl. 1998. *Focus Groups for Libraries and Librarians.* New York: Forbes.

Grassian, Esther, and Joan Kaplowitz. 2009. *Information Literacy Instruction: Theory and Practice.* 2nd ed. New York: Neal-Schuman.

Huba, Mary E., and Jann E. Freed. 2000. *Learner-Centered Assessment on College Campuses.* Boston: Allyn & Bacon.

Johnson, R. Burke, and Walter Dick. 2012. "Evaluation in Instructional Design: A Comparison of Evaluation Models." In *Trends and Issues in Instructional Design and Technology*, edited by Robert A. Reiser and John V. Dempsey, 96–104. Boston: Pearson.

Kaplowitz, Joan R. 2012. *Transforming Information Literacy Instruction Using Learner-Centered Teaching.* New York: Neal-Schuman.

Kirkpatrick, Donald. 2006. *Evaluating Training Programs: The Four Levels.* San Francisco: Berret-Koehler.

Kounin, Jacob S. 1970. *Discipline and Group Management in Classrooms.* New York: Holt, Rinehart & Winston.

Marzano, Robert J., Debra Pickering, and Jay McTighe. 1993. *Assessing Student Outcomes: Performance Assessment Using the Dimensions of Learning Model.* Alexandria, VA: Association for Supervision and Curriculum Development.

Miller, Marian I., and Barry D. Bratton. 1988. "Instructional Design: Increasing the Effectiveness of Bibliographic Instruction." *College and Research Libraries* 49 (6): 545–49.

MiraCosta College. 2011. "Test Your Potential as an Online Student." MiraCosta College. Accessed May 29. http://www.miracosta.cc.ca.us/Instruction/DistanceEducation/quiz.aspx

Morrison, Gary R., Steven M. Ross, Howard K. Kalman, and Jerrold E. Kemp. 2011. *Designing Effective Instruction.* 6th ed. Hoboken, NJ: Wiley.

Sierra College. 2011. "Online Student Readiness Quiz." Sierra College. Accessed May 29. http://lrc.sierra.cc.ca.us/dl/survey/OL-student-assess.html

Sonntag, Gabriela, and Yvonne Meulemans. 2003. "Planning for Assessment." In *Assessing Student Learning Outcomes for Information Literacy Instruction*, edited by Elizabeth Fuseler Avery, 6–21. Chigaco: American Library Association.

Wiggins, Grant. 1998. *Educational Assessment: Designing Assessments to Inform and Improve Student Performance.* San Francisco: Jossey-Bass.

Putting It All Together

Organizing and Sequencing Your ILI

I have completed the three elements of the Teaching Tripod and feel really good about the expected learning outcomes (ELOs) I have selected, and the activities and assessments I am going to include in my information literacy instruction (ILI), which will help my learners attain those ELOs. But I still feel like I am not quite ready to share this material with my learners. What else do I need to do to get my ILI ready for "prime time"?

Completing the elements in the Teaching Tripod ensures that you have all the pieces necessary for effective ILI. You have identified what learners need to know in order to address their knowledge gaps and selected your instructional goal(s) based on that information. You have composed measurable and observable ELOs to help your learners reach those instructional goal(s). You have chosen or created learning activities that will help your learners interact with the material in a productive manner. And you have included assessment opportunities (both during and after instruction) that will help you determine how well your learners have attained the ELOs set for the ILI.

The next step is to organize the material logically and systematically so that learners will be working through the material in a way that supports their learning. In other words, you need to address issues related to instructional sequencing, a.k.a. designing the instructional message (Booth 2011; Morrison et al. 2011). The attention you give to this aspect of instructional design (ID) can make or break your ILI. The order in which learners are asked to interact with the material they are trying to learn can either be supportive, with each component building on what came before, or it can be disjointed and confusing and thus act as a hindrance to learning. So let's look at how to sequence your ILI in an effective, well-organized, and supportive fashion.

QUESTIONS TO CONSIDER
➢ How does sequencing support instructional effectiveness?
➢ How is sequencing related to the elements in the Teaching Tripod?
➢ What are some approaches to sequencing?
➢ What elements are included in sequencing?
➢ How does sequencing address issues of attention and motivation?

ORGANIZING FOR EFFECTIVENESS

The sequence in which you organize your instructional material is of utmost importance if your learners are to attain the ELOs set for the instruction (Goodman 2009; Morrison et al. 2011). You want to make sure that learners are ready to tackle each aspect of the instruction as they encounter it, and that you are not asking them to do something for which they have no background or preparation. Your aim is to have learners feel successful rather than frustrated as they work on the material you have prepared for them. Furthermore, you want to ensure that they feel confident and comfortable with each aspect of the instruction before asking them to move on to something new. The following are some issues to consider as you make your sequencing decisions.

Sequencing and ELOs

One way to start thinking about how to sequence your ILI is to go back to your ELOs. As you look at your ELOs, perhaps a logical organization may suggest itself. Identify the ELO that needs to be attained first. In other words, which of the ELOs is so fundamental that learners must attain this one before they can tackle the rest? For example, knowing how and why to formulate an effective search strategy might be something useful to learn before introducing learners to the various database options open to them. Then identify the next ELO that needs to be attained and so on. Look at the task analysis you used to select the ELOs in the first place to help you decide on this logical order (Morrison et al. 2011). You can also think back to when you first encountered this material/resource yourself, and reflect on how you learned it. The steps you took to learn the material may also suggest a sequence for presenting this information to your learners.

Sequencing and Prior Knowledge

Another thing to consider is organizing the material so that learners can gain an appreciation of how the new material relates to what they already know. One way to do this is to start with what is already familiar to learners, and then help them see how the new information relates to that familiar material. Showing learners how what you will be teaching fits into the knowledge structure they already have can make it more meaningful to them, and help them create mental models that are personal and relevant to them (Ausubel 1977; Booth 2011; Morrison et al. 2011). Of course, the assumption here is that you know something about your learners' past experiences and their levels of expertise. This background information could be based on data you gathered in your needs assessment prior to instruction, or you could ask some investigative questions before you begin the current instruction. See chapter 4 for more on needs assessments and chapter 7 for suggestions regarding doing "before" assessments at the beginning of your ILI.

Here is an example of how you can help your learners make connections between what they already know and what you will be addressing in the current ILI. Let's say you are trying to teach how different databases cover different topics/subjects. You could ask your learners what types of music they like. Then point out that they wouldn't look for classical music on a radio station dedicated to jazz, or try to download a rock music track by browsing online under the heading "country music." Tie that idea to how databases specialize in particular types of information—by date, by subject matter, by material type, and so forth. Learners should find the concept of database scope and coverage a little more accessible when they realize they already use that idea in their everyday life.

Another way to build on prior knowledge is to start your instruction by asking your learners what types of information they have looked for in the previous week or so. Then find out how they looked for that information and how satisfied or dissatisfied they were with the approaches they used. Although many people may talk about Google or other online search tools, you can use this discussion to segue into selecting resources, searching techniques, and even evaluating results in other types of information resources. Show learners who use online search tools for their everyday information needs how the resources you will be sharing with them are similar to the ones they are already familiar with, as well as the merits of these more specialized resources. Having bridged the gap between "what they already know" and "what they need to know," you can now move on to sharing with them the best strategies for using these "new to them" resources.

Sequencing and Cognitive Load

Connecting new information to prior knowledge also helps learners deal with cognitive load issues. Remember that learning only happens when material in short-term memory is transferred to permanent long-term memory storage. Keep in mind that short-term memory has limitations. The way that you sequence your instruction can put a strain on this short-term memory capacity. Poor sequencing choices might result in learners struggling to process more information than they can handle at one time. The net result will be that less new information will be processed and transferred to long-term memory as learners try to sort through the material, identify key elements, and make some sense out of it all (Booth 2011; Grassian and Kaplowitz 2009; Morrison et al. 2011). Helping learners to see the relationship between what they are currently learning and what they already know and have stored in long-term memory eases some of the pressure on their short-term memory. Creating a logical order for your instruction and introducing each new topic by showing how it links to the previous ones addressed also helps to ease some of these cognitive load issues. For more on cognitive load see chapter 6.

Here's a good analogy: Let's say you are reading a book. If you are familiar with what all the words in the book mean, then you can read the book fairly easily and quickly. But if you are reading a book that is full of words you don't recognize you may have some trouble understanding the content. Furthermore, if you have to stop to look up the meaning of each unknown word, your progress through the book is slowed down considerably. The same is true for learning and cognitive load. If learners are ready for the new material—either because they can tie it to knowledge they have already learned before instruction or because they have successfully navigated through the instructional segments leading up to this material—they can more easily process the new material and incorporate it into their long-term memory stores (Booth 2011). They don't have to waste precious short-term memory processing space on what they already know and can concentrate on learning the "new to them" material.

Focusing on Concepts

Another way to reduce the strain on memory processing is to carefully select what you will be emphasizing in your instruction. Go for the bigger, broader concepts rather than the specific mechanics associated with using a particular resource. Emphasize transferrable skills rather than the "click here, click there" approach (Booth 2011; Grassian and Kaplowitz 2009). Empower your learners by teaching them how to explore new resources. Share with them what to look for in a resource's functionality, coverage, organization, and so forth, rather than concentrating on the features of individual ones. For example, when teaching database searching begin by teaching the overall basics of database searching. These could include concepts like author versus topic searching, controlled vocabulary versus keyword searching, limiting (perhaps by specifying time frame, geographic area, or language, or by adding other search terms using Boolean "and") and expanding search results (for example, by truncation or by incorporating synonyms into the search statement using Boolean "or"), and so on. You can then show how to explore a database that is unfamiliar to them by looking for how/if the new resource employs these concepts. Then trust that learners will be able to apply those ideas to any other database they encounter in the future. Rather than putting a strain on cognitive load and memory processing capacity, you have created an effective way for learners to transfer the current learning to their future information needs.

Chunking and Pace

Sequencing is also related to chunking, or the breaking down of material into manageable units. Again your goal as you "chunk" your material is to ensure that you are not overloading the learners' capability to process incoming information (Booth 2011; Farmer 2011). Each chunk should be designed to build on previous ones and to prepare the learners for the next one. That makes the segues between chunks really important as it is how you show learners the ways the chunks relate to each other. Furthermore, you can use these segues as comprehension checks and assessments ensuring that the learners have obtained what they need in order to tackle the next new chunk. The bottom line is, the way you organize your material matters. Arrange the chunks in a logical and coherent order. Show how the chunks interrelate. And make sure the pace of the presentation is supportive of learning by checking that learners are ready to take in new information before moving on.

Before looking at the next aspect of this topic, take a moment to complete the worksheet in figure 8.1 to reflect on your current ILI practice as it relates to sequencing.

HOW TO SEQUENCE INSTRUCTION

Clearly, the order in which you present your material contributes to the effectiveness of your instruction. So how do you determine the most effective organization for your instruction? Perhaps you have heard of the phrase "Tell them what you are going to tell them. Then tell them. And then tell them what you told them." While this is a good basic idea, if you have moved to a more learner-centered approach to teaching, you no longer want to just tell learners what you think they should know. Using a learner-centered approach means that you strive to create instruction that encourages learners to generate their own mental models by building on and connecting to prior knowledge. To encourage this to happen, you include various opportunities for learners to actively work with the material to be learned so they can attain the ELOs you set for the instruction. As your learners generate new mental models, they take ownership of the material, ultimately organizing and storing the newly acquired material in a way that is meaningful to them—in other words, making it their own (Morrison et al. 2011; Wittrock 1974). While there may be some "telling them what you will tell them" in the form of sharing goals and outcomes and/or helping learners see how what they already know relates to what they will be learning, the "tell them" portion becomes more a "guide them through the material." The emphasis in this approach is more on learners' actions and less on the instructor's delivery of information. And although you can certainly do the summing up yourself at the end ("the tell them what you told them" idea), a more effective approach is to have them do that review and reflection for themselves (American Psychological Association Work Group of the Board of Educational Affairs 1997; Kaplowitz 2012; McCombs and Miller 2007).

So what are some of the ways to organize and sequence instruction effectively? One possible approach comes from Gagne's nine events of instruction, was described in chapter 2 (Gagne et al. 2004). As you may recall, Gagne recommends starting with capturing learners' attention, sharing what they can expect to get from the instruction, and helping them tie the new material to what they already know. Once those initial events are completed, Gagne's events move into the learning activities segment (presenting material, providing guidance, allowing learners the opportunity to practice, and offering feedback). Gagne's sequence ends with assessing instruction, and encouraging retention and transfer of learning. Table 8.1 illustrates how this instructional approach can serve as a framework for sequencing instruction.

John Keller is another theorist who offers an approach to instruction that can serve as a framework for instruction. However, while Gagne's events are looking at the cognitive side of learning, Keller's ideas focus on attention and motivation. Keller, therefore, encourages instructors and designers to consider motivational aspects as they design their instruction. While Keller's approach is more an instructional theory than an ID methodology, Keller's ideas offer some valid advice about designing instruction. Keller's main idea is that unless learners are motivated to learn, even the best designed instruction will fail. So he urges instructors and designers to think about ways to make instruction appealing as they organize and develop the content. Basically, Keller posits that learners are motivated to learn when their curiosity has been aroused (*attention*), when they feel that the material to be learned is relevant to them (*relevance*), when they believe they can succeed (*confidence*), and when they experience a sense of satisfaction (*satisfaction*), or in Keller terminology, the ARCS approach to teaching (Keller 1987).

FIGURE 8.1

What Do You Do?

Think about something you already teach or are planning to teach. Then complete this worksheet to determine what you already do when you are organizing your instruction.

➢ ELOs

  ○ Look at some ELOs you have written for your instruction. You might wish to refer back to the ones you used in the worksheets in chapter 5 or examine those in some other ILI you teach. Then organize the ELOs for a specific ILI in a way that makes sense to you and list them here.

➢ Prior Knowledge

  ○ Give an example of how you would help learners tap into their current knowledge and relate it to the goals and outcomes of what you will be sharing with them.

➢ Cognitive Load

  ○ What are some of the ways you could organize and present the material in order to reduce overloading learners' ability to process information in their short-term or working memory?

➢ Focusing on Concepts

  ○ What are the concepts you are trying to teach?

  ○ Are you emphasizing concepts or mechanics in your instruction?

○ If mechanics, is there a way to increase the emphasis on concepts? Give an example of how working with mechanics can serve as a way to illustrate more overall concepts.

➤ Chunking and Pace

○ Review your instructional segments to determine if the "chunks" are reasonable in size. Think about how much you are attempting to teach in each segment in terms of cognitive load. Do you need to break up some of your chunks into smaller ones? Give an example of how you would do that.

○ Also, have you included comprehension checks or informal assessments to check mastery after each chunk before you allow learners to move on to the next one? Give an example of one or two comprehension checks or informal assessments you will be including in your ILI.

Table 8.1. Sequencing Using Gagne's Nine Events of Instruction

Gagne's Events	What Is It?	How to Use It
1. Gain attention	• Start with something that will capture learners' attention—sometimes referred to as a "hook," "sponge," or a "gotcha."	• Show a video of people being asked to define information literacy. • Have learners complete the sentence, "When I have to do library research I feel _____." • Ask learners to describe information they needed in the previous week. Did they find it? Was it hard to do so?
2. Describe instructional goal	• Explain how the ILI will be useful. In other words, answer learners' "What's in it for me?" questions.	• Give an overview of what will be addressed in the ILI. • Supply learners with a graphic organizer that illustrates the key points that will be covered. • Create a paper handout using PowerPoint or other presentation software that presents an outline of the material to be addressed.
3. Stimulate recall of prior knowledge	• Help learners connect what they already know to what they are about to learn.	• Ask learners for examples of ways they searched for information in the past month. • Have learners work in pairs to share techniques they use when searching for information. Then have the pairs share with the entire group. • Find a familiar example (searching for restaurants using Yelp or other social reviewing sites or searching for information using Google) and show how that type of searching relates to what you are about to share with them about using information resources. • Show learners a series of printed items (scholarly journals, popular magazines) and ask learners to sort into categories just by looking at them. Then ask what criteria they used to do this.
4. Present material to be learned	• Select the delivery mode (text, video, face-to-face, online) and organize the material into digestible segments or chunks to avoid overload.	• Use lecture/demo to present an overview of the material. • Insert active learning activities between lecture/demo segments. • Check for mastery before moving on to new topic. • See chapter 6 for more on selecting methods.
5. Provide guidance for learning	• Include scaffolding support as necessary.	• Provide guide sheets, step-by-step instructions, and other handouts to assist learners. • Create LibGuides for the material. • Stop to ask, "What questions do you have for me now?" and address these potential points of confusion and misconceptions before moving on to next topic.
6. Elicit performance (practice)	• Stop at intervals to allow learners to try out newly acquired skills, knowledge, and abilities either individually or in groups.	• Ask learners which of the previously explored resources could be used to address specific information needs. • Have learners try to solve some authentic problem using any resource they like from the ones just explored.
7. Provide informative feedback	• Review results of practice and let learners know what they did correctly, where they went astray, and how they could improve for the future.	• Include some way to monitor practice—either as it is going on or by some reporting mechanism after the exercise is completed. • Offer constructive feedback as needed. • Ask learners to offer suggestions to fellow learners about how to improve practice results.
8. Assess performance task	• Provide some kind of measure for attainment of the task. This could be a grade or score if appropriate, or just some more informal measure of success.	• Review papers or projects done after instruction and review the appropriateness of resources used. • Collect exercise/worksheets and review how well learners accomplished task. • For more on assessment, see chapter 7.
9. Enhance retention and transfer	• Make sure learners look beyond the current instruction to see how what they have learned can be applied to new situations. • Give learners the opportunity to review and reflect on what they have learned and how they may use it in the future.	• Ask learners to create problems or questions that could be addressed by using resources taught during the ILI. • Have each learner ask a partner for an example of how he or she would use something they learned from the ILI to address his or her own current or future information needs. • Use some kind of closure/reflection exercise to gauge what and how well learners attained the ELOs set for instruction.

In many ways, what Keller is suggesting is a parallel thought process that happens alongside, and enhances the regular design practice. As in all design methodologies, ARCS starts with audience analysis. In this case, the goal of the analysis is to uncover what would be motivating and relevant to the target learners. It then follows much of the traditional ID path starting with defining outcomes, followed by the development of instructional strategies, and ending with assessing learners' attainment of the outcomes. However, in the case of ARCS, the designer is tasked to add motivational elements to the content-related steps. So the designer who is using ARCS will be looking for ways to address issues of gaining and sustaining motivation throughout the instruction as well as opportunities for learners to gain a sense of confidence in their newly acquired skills and a feeling of satisfaction as they complete the instructional interaction (Keller and Deimann 2012; Keller 2010, 1987).

Keller's ideas are very reminiscent of concepts associated with humanist psychology such as self-efficacy and self-actualization (Bandura 1982; Grassian and Kaplowitz 2009; Maslow 1987). The ARCS method is not an alternative ID process. Rather, it is a complementary approach that asks the designer/instructor to consider the affective side of learning. ARCS-inspired instruction includes ways to pique interest through the use of novel, paradoxical, or thought-provoking illustrations; uses methods and materials that have relevance and value to the learner; offers a degree of personal control over how the learner interacts with the material; and includes praise and constructive feedback to help the learner build a sense of and confidence in newly acquired knowledge and skills, and a feeling of accomplishment or satisfaction in the instructional experience. The ultimate aim of motivational design is to have learners complete the instructional experience feeling good about themselves and the newly learned material (Keller and Deimann 2012; Shellnut 1998). The more we can capture and sustain learners' interest and demonstrate how what is being learned is relevant to their lives (the "What's in it for me?" quotient), the more they will participate in the instruction, retain the skills and knowledge being addressed, and be able to transfer that learning to new situations (Booth 2011; Goodman 2009; Kaplowitz 2012). Table 8.2 offers some suggestions about how you might use ARCS as a way to structure your instruction.

Both Gagne's events and Keller's ARCS contain useful ideas about how to organize and sequence instruction. And they can be used in combination in order to create instruction that is both logically organized and motivating for the learners. As you may recall, the discussion on various instructional methods included in chapter 6 suggested that you should strive to listen, engage, and inspire when you are working with your learners. Using a blend of Gagne's and Keller's approaches can provide you with a possible way to sequence your instruction so that you are listening, engaging, and inspiring. To do so you start with an attention-grabbing activity. Then move on to introducing what you will be sharing with your learners, emphasizing the "What's in it for me?" aspect of

Table 8.2.   Using ARCS to Sequence Your Instruction

Keller's Segments	What Is It?	How to Use It
➢ Attention	• Motivating learners by arousing their curiosity	• Begin instruction with something that captures their attention—an interesting quote, a provocative question, an illustrative video, etc.
➢ Relevance	• Sustaining attention by showing that the material to be learned will matter to them personally	• Incorporate ways to help learners see how what they will be learning will help them in their lives. • Using relevant examples for activities can help to make this point.
➢ Confidence	• Helping learners believe they can succeed	• Arrange instruction so that learners will be able to accomplish each task presented to them. • Don't move on to new tasks until learners have mastered previous ones. • Offer constructive feedback and instructional support (scaffolding) to help them master each task.
➢ Satisfaction	• Making sure that learners complete instruction with a feeling that they accomplished something of importance	• End instruction with some kind of closure exercise that allows learners to reflect on what they have just learned and how they might use it in to address information needs in the future.

the information, and how the new material relates to what your learners already know. Both of these instructional segments are designed using the information you gathered from listening to your learners via formal or informal types of needs assessment. Having helped learners to see that what you will be sharing with them will directly address their specific information needs, you then offer a series of engaging ways for learners to interact with the material, interspersed with various types of assessments and comprehension checks, once again illustrating your desire to listen to your learners and help them successfully engage with the material. End your instruction with a big finish, some kind of upbeat, active, and fun activity that encourages learners to summarize, review, and reflect on what they learned, what it means to them, and how they might apply what they learned in the future—leaving them feeling inspired to use their newly gained skills, knowledge, and abilities. Table 8.3 illustrates how this listen, engage, inspire idea lines up with both Gagne's and Keller's approaches to instruction.

Having reviewed the three frameworks for instructional sequencing, take a moment to apply these ideas to your own ILI practice. Think about something you teach or are planning to teach and complete the worksheet in figure 8.2.

Table 8.3.   A Comparison of Ideas for Instructional Sequencing

Instructional Segment	What Is It?	Gagne's Principle(s)	Keller's ARCS	What You Could Do
➢ Grab their attention	• Begin instruction with some activity or thought-provoking questions, statements, or media that is intended to capture learners' interest.	• Gain attention.	• Attention	• Start with hooks, gotcha, or sponge activities to capture learners' attention and increase their motivation to learn what you will be sharing with them.
➢ Answer their "What's in it for me?" questions	• Provide overview of instruction including goals and outcomes. • Help them relate what they already know to what will be addressed during the instruction. • Highlight relevance of instruction.	• Describe ILI goal(s). • Stimulate recall of prior knowledge.	• Relevance	• Share goals and outcomes to help learners see what they will gain from the instruction. • Do some kind of exercise to find out what learners already know as well as what they want to learn from the instruction. • Include some kind of activity that helps learners tap into what they already know about the material to be learned.
➢ Instructional interactions/activities	• Offer learners ways to interact with material to be learned. • Provide guidance, support, and constructive feedback in order to promote attainment of ELOs.	• Present material to be learned. • Provide guidance/ scaffolding for learning. • Elicit performance/ practice.	• Confidence	• Organize material into manageable chunks and arrange chunks into a logical order. • Allow learners to practice newly learned skills and knowledge to help them transfer material to long-term memory and enhance their feelings of self-esteem and confidence.
➢ Checks for comprehension	• Include formal or informal assessment both during and at the end of instruction.	• Assess task performance. • Provide informative feedback.	• Confidence	• Make sure learners exhibit mastery of material in each chunk before moving on to new material.
➢ Big finish	• End with closure activity that allows learners to review and reflect on material learned and to think about how they might apply this learning to their future information needs.	• Enhance retention and transfer.	• Satisfaction	• Use some version of the minute paper (written or verbal) asking learners to list 3–5 things they learned, and 2–3 things that are still unclear to them. • Ask learners for examples of how they will use newly learned material in the future so that they will know how to apply what they learned beyond the instructional setting.

FIGURE 8.2

Sequencing My ILI

Select a topic that will be the focus on an ILI offering. This could be something you already teach, or something you are considering teaching. Indicate the topic below and use the worksheet to describe what you plan to do for each of the five instructional segments described in table 8.3. Refer back to chapter 6 for ideas regarding instructional activities, methods, and techniques. Keep in mind activities are being defined broadly and include lecture/demo as well as more learner-centered activities.

OVERALL TOPIC BEING ADDRESSED

➢ Grab Their Attention

    ○ What will happen during this segment?

    ○ Why did you select these interactions/activities?

➢ Answering the "What's in It for Me?" Questions

    ○ What will happen during this segment?

    ○ Why did you select these interactions/activities?

➢ Instructional Interactions/Activities

    ○ What will happen during this segment?

    ○ Why did you select these interactions/activities?

- Comprehension Checks

  - What will happen during this segment?

  - Why did you select these interactions/activities?

- Big Finish

  - What will happen during this segment?

  - Why did you select these interactions/activities?

THE HEART OF THE MATTER—ORGANIZING LEARNING ACTIVITIES

As you can see, the three approaches described above have a great deal in common. All three suggest starting with some kind of attention grabber and an overall introduction to the material and ending with a closure activity that encourages retention and transfer. But you still have to determine how you are going to organize the material that lies between that attention-capturing opening and the "big finish" ending. In other words, how will you sequence the various learning activities that will allow your learners to attain instructional goal(s) and outcomes? Furthermore, how will you ensure that learners are moving successfully through the sequence you have devised?

There are many ways to organize that central instructional piece. Selecting which one to use depends on many factors, including learner characteristics and the structure of the subject matter itself. For example, working with inexperienced learners might suggest a different approach than when you are working with more sophisticated learners. Consider the concept of prior knowledge, which was discussed above, as you make these decisions. The more prior knowledge learners have, the less background you will have to supply. Experienced learners can start learning the new material at a more advanced level than inexperienced ones, will probably learn it faster since they have more ways to tie the new knowledge to that which they already have, and will be able to absorb more complex material with minimal assistance. Or say you were teaching something that was historical in nature. Then you would probably wish to address the topics in some kind of chronological order—from oldest to most current to show how the topics evolved over time, or from most current to oldest to illustrate how current ideas grew out of what preceded them. See table 8.4 for ways to organize your instructional activities based on learner characteristics, real-world appearances, and logical interrelationship (English and Reigeluth 1996; Morrison et al. 2011; Posner and Strike 1976; Reigeluth 1987; Reigeluth and Stein 1983).

Obviously how you organize your instructional interactions will be greatly dependent on the subject matter being taught. Try your hand at one or more of these organization schemes by completing the worksheet in figure 8.3.

Table 8.4.   Organizing Instructional Interactions/Activities

Sequence	What It's Based On	What It Looks Like

➢ Learner centered	• Organizes the material based on learner characteristics—expertise, background, prior knowledge, interests	• Start with material that is:
		  ○ Basic/foundational material
		  ○ Most familiar
		  ○ Easiest
		  ○ Of most interest

➢ Concept related	• Organizes the material so that the order of the information being shared is consistent with how people logically think about the content	• By complexity—arrange material from simple/concrete to complex/abstract concepts. • Top down—present concept and then examples. • Bottom up—present examples first and then concept. • Logical order—organize concepts in a hierarchical order so that each concept is building on preceding ones.
➢ Elaboration approach	• Organizes the material to illustrate how experts working in a subject or discipline area think about the material.	• Present material in the order that an expert would learn it or a researcher might have discovered it. • Begin with the simplest component of the task to be learned and then move on to more and more complex components until the overall task is learned successfully.

FIGURE 8.3

Organizing Instructional Activities for My ILI

Refer back to the topic you worked on in figure 8.2 or select another topic you teach or are thinking about teaching. Indicate the topic below and use this worksheet to describe how you plan to organize the instructional interactions/ activities segment of your ILI. Space is provided for multiple topics to be described.

➢ Topic 1

○ Organization scheme selected for this topic:

○ Interactions/activities in the order learners will interact with them:

○ Why this organization is relevant to the topic:

➢ Topic 2

○ Organization scheme selected for this topic:

○ Interactions/activities in the order learners will interact with them:

○ Why this organization is relevant to the topic:

➤ Topic 3

    ○ Organization scheme selected for this topic:

    ○ Interactions/activities in the order learners will interact with them:

    ○ Why this organization is relevant to the topic:

➤ Topic 4

    ○ Organization scheme selected for this topic:

    ○ Interactions/activities in the order learners will interact with them:

    ○ Why this organization is relevant to the topic:

THE BIG PICTURE AND THE INDIVIDUAL CHUNKS

There is one more thing to consider when you are thinking about how to organize and sequence your ILI. The three frameworks presented in tables 8.1, 8.2, and 8.3 represent a big-picture view of the overall instruction. However, when thinking about the instructional interactions segment, you may wish to engage in a sort of minisequence as you move from topic to topic. In other words, you might need to include more "attention grabbers," "What's in it for me?," and even something, although not quite a "big finish," that at least puts some closure on the experience before moving on to the next topic. You can use these mini closure activities as comprehension checks, as a way to review the segment just completed, and to help learners see how what they just learned leads into the next topic. Use the "between topics" segments carefully, and they will help learners move seamlessly through the instruction and also will offer them a way to build the new topic on what went before.

Sequence and organize your ILI so that the order in which learners encounter the "to be learned" material adds to rather than detracts from the learning experience. Making sure that your instruction follows a framework that is appropriate to the topic being taught, that captures and sustains learners' attention, is organized in a way that helps learners deal with cognitive load and memory storage issues, and provides learners with opportunities to reflect on what has been learned will increase the effectiveness of your instructional offerings. To make sure that you have addressed all the issues discussed in this chapter as you design your ILI, complete the checklist in figure 8.4.

WRAP-UP

Designing your instruction is a lot like cooking. First you decide what you want to make (your goals and outcomes). Then you gather up the necessary ingredients (your activities). But you can't just dump all the ingredients randomly into a bowl and expect it to come out as the dish you are trying to create. The order in which you add the ingredients/activities to the mix is also key to developing a successful product—be it a cake or a class. So make sure you spend some time thinking about the best way to sequence your instruction so that it supports learning, captures and sustains your learners' attention, and allows your learners to leave feeling confident about their newly learned skills, knowledge, and abilities, and satisfied with the instructional experience.

WHAT STUCK?

Your instruction colleagues are now very enthusiastic about using the Teaching Tripod approach to design their ILI. But they are asking you questions about how to actually present the material to their learners. Review the concepts addressed in this chapter by completing the worksheet in figure 8.5, and develop some "talking points" or supportive documentation to help answer your colleagues' questions and concerns about sequencing their ILI.

FIGURE 8.4

A Sequencing Checklist

Complete the following worksheet to see if you have included all the necessary segments in your ILI. If you decided to skip one or more of the segments, indicate your reasons for doing so.

➤   Are you planning to start with an attention grabber (hook/gotcha, sponge)?

   ○ If yes, give an example of your attention grabber.

   ○ If no, explain why you decided to skip this segment.

➤   Are you planning to include something that will tie the "to be learned" material to prior knowledge?

   ○ If yes, give an example of how you plan to do so.

   ○ If no, explain why you decided to skip this segment.

➤   Are you planning to address your learners' "What's in it for me?" questions?

   ○ If yes, give an example of how you plan to do so.

   ○ If no, explain why you decided to skip this segment.

➢ Did you select a specific organization for the topics/activities that was appropriate for the overall topic being taught?

○ If yes, why did you select that particular organization?

○ If no, explain how you decided to organize your ILI.

➢ Are you planning to include some kind of assessment/comprehension checks to ensure that learners have successfully completed the topic/activity before moving on to the next one?

○ If yes, give a few examples of how you plan to do so.

○ If no, explain why you decided not to include assessments/comprehension checks.

➢ Are you planning to end with a big finish?

○ If yes, how are you planning to close your ILI?

○ If no, explain why you decided to skip this segment.

FIGURE 8.5

Sequencing and Organizing ILI—A Review of Concepts

The way you sequence your instruction can either help or hinder your learners' abilities to attain the ELOs set for the instruction. Complete the worksheet below to review the topic of instructional sequencing. Use your responses to help you answer your colleagues' questions about instructional sequencing.

➤ What are some of the factors that you need to consider when thinking about how to sequence and organize your ILI?

➤ How does appropriate sequencing address these issues?

➤ What are some examples of overall instructional sequences?

➤ What are some examples of ways to order instructional interactions/activities within the overall sequence?

REFERENCES

American Psychological Association Work Group of the Board of Educational Affairs. 1997. *Learner-Centered Psychological Principles: A Framework for School Reform and Redesign.* Washington, DC: American Psychological Association.

Ausubel, David. 1977. "The Facilitation of Meaningful Verbal Learning for the Classroom." *Educational Psychologist* 12 (2): 162–78.

Bandura, Albert. 1982. "Self-Efficacy Mechanism in Human Agency." *American Psychologist* 37: 122–47.

Booth, Char. 2011. *Reflective Teaching, Effective Learning.* Chicago: American Library Association.

English, Robert F., and Charles M. Reigeluth. 1996. "Formative Evaluation Research on Sequencing Instruction with Elaboration Theory." *Educational Technology and Research Journal* 44 (1): 23–41.

Farmer, Lesley S. J. 2011. *Instructional Design for Librarians and Information Professionals.* New York: Neal-Schuman.

Gagne, Robert, Walter Wager, Katharine Golas, and John M. Keller. 2004. *Principles of Instructional Design.* 5th ed. Belmont, CA: Wadsworth/Thomson Learning.

Goodman, Valeda Dent. 2009. *Keeping the User in Mind: Instructional Design and the Modern Library.* Oxford: Chandos.

Grassian, Esther, and Joan Kaplowitz. 2009. *Information Literacy Instruction: Theory and Practice.* 2nd ed. New York: Neal-Schuman.

Kaplowitz, Joan R. 2012. *Transforming Information Literacy Instruction Using Learner-Centered Teaching.* New York: Neal-Schuman.

Keller, John M. 1987. "The Systematic Process of Motivational Design." *Performance & Instruction* 26 (9): 1–8.

———. 2010. *Motivational Design for Learning and Performance: The ARCS Model Approach.* New York: Springer.

Keller, John M., and Markus Deimann. 2012. "Motivation, Volition, and Performance." In *Trends and Issues in Instructional Design and Technology*, edited by Robert A. Reiser and John V. Dempsey, 84–94. Boston: Pearson.

Maslow, Abraham H. 1987. *Motivation and Personality.* 3rd ed. New York: Harper & Row.

McCombs, Barbara L., and Lynda Miller. 2007. *Learner-Centered Classroom Practices and Assessments: Maximizing Student Motivation, Learning, and Achievement.* Thousand Oaks, CA: Corwin.

Morrison, Gary R., Steven M. Ross, Howard K. Kalman, and Jerrold E. Kemp. 2011. *Designing Effective Instruction.* 6th ed. Hoboken, NJ: Wiley.

Posner, George J., and Kenneth A. Strike. 1976. "A Categorization Scheme for Principles of Sequencing Content." *Review of Educational Research* 46 (4): 665–90.

Reigeluth, Charles M. 1987. "Lesson Blueprints Based on the Elaboration Theory of Instruction." In *Instructional Theories in Action: Lessons Illustrating Selected Theories and Models*, edited by Charles M. Reigeluth, 245–88. Hillsdale, NJ: Erlbaum.

Reigeluth, Charles M., and Albert Stein. 1983. "The Elaboration Theory of Instruction." In *Instructional Design Theories and Models*, edited by Charles M. Reigeluth, 335–81. Hillsdale, NJ: Erlbaum.

Shellnut, Bonnie J. 1998. "John Keller: A Motivating Influence in the Field of Instructional Systems Design." PhD diss., Wayne State University, October 15. Accessed June 6, 2012. http://www.arcsmodel.com/pdf/Biographical%20Information.pdf

Wittrock, Merlin C. 1974. "Learning as a Generative Process." *Educational Psychologist* 19 (2): 87–96.

Getting Everything Ready

Implementing Your ILI

Having organized my information literacy instruction (ILI) in a logical and supportive way, I feel as though the time has come to actually take my show on the road so to speak—that is, to share the instruction with those for whom it is intended. What else should I consider before I make my ILI available to my learners?

The old expression, "The proof is in the pudding," seems very relevant at this point in your instructional design (ID) process. All the planning in the world means little until you try out your ideas with actual learners. Many an ILI has looked great on paper but floundered when put into practice, due not to the design itself, but rather to a lack of sufficient attention regarding details related to the implementation and delivery of the instructional product. These two aspects of the instructional design process include marketing your ILI product, preparing yourself and your materials, and logistics (scheduling, staff, space, furniture, equipment, technology, etc.). This chapter will address these topics.

> **QUESTIONS TO CONSIDER**
> ➤ How do I get key stakeholders to support my ILI plans?
> ➤ How do I get learners to participate in my ILI?
> ➤ What do I need to do to prepare myself for teaching in both the F2F and online environment?
> ➤ How do I prepare effective instructional materials in both the F2F and online environment?
> ➤ What do I need to consider regarding the learning space in both the F2F and online environment?

LETTING EVERYONE KNOW

There are several points in your ID process when you should be considering issues related to marketing your ILI. Some of this could be called the preplanning marketing phase—that is, what you need to do before you begin any design work in order to obtain approval for your ILI ideas. This type of marketing usually takes place once you have analyzed the data from your needs assessment and determined what type of instructional intervention you think will help your learners bridge the knowledge gap you have identified. Depending upon the scope of your proposed ILI project, you may only need approval from your immediate supervisor, or you may require the endorsement of those higher up in the administration. Once you have secured the "go-ahead" for your project, you also may wish to recruit collaborators from various parts of your institution or in your community at large to help you in the actual design work. Finally, after you have finished designing your ILI product you need to inform your intended audience about your proposed ILI, and convince them that your instruction will directly benefit them. In other words, you need to let them know what is in it for each of them (Bell and Shank 2007; Grassian and Kaplowitz 2005, 2009; Morrison et al. 2011).

As with all new ideas, your ILI must be sold to those members of your environment who can help make your vision a reality. In other words, you need to sell your ILI ideas to your stakeholders—those members of your institution whose support is crucial for your ILI to be launched successfully. In some cases, you will have to enlist approval and perhaps sponsorship from administrators, supervisors, and other institutional decision makers before you can start your ID process. You will need to convince these decision makers that your ideas have merit and are aligned with the institution's mission and goals in order to garner the necessary support. This is especially true when you are trying to develop some entirely new ILI offering or creating a new ILI program. You should have discovered the names of these key figures when doing your initial needs assessment (Farmer 2011, Grassian and Kaplowitz 2005, 2009, Morrison et al. 2011).

Recruiting appropriate institutional partners is also an important step in selling and launching your ILI. Again, these potential partners should have been identified in your needs assessment. Institutional partners can be found in your own department, within other departments in your library, as well as in your institution at large and/or the community in which your institution resides. Some of these partners can be enlisted to help you develop the content for your ILI. Others may only be called upon to help you persuade learners that your ILI is relevant and potentially useful to them. Sometimes your partners may serve in both capacities—as collaborators in the design process as well as "salespeople" for the final ILI product. Don't forget to consider your librarian colleagues and support staff within your library as potential collaborators. If your proposed project will impact their workload, it is a good idea to keep everyone who will be affected in the loop, and that you both solicit their input and pay attention to it. And of course, these coworkers may provide useful insight into the environment, your learners, and resources available as well as offer suggestions about how to design the instruction itself (Grassian and Kaplowitz 2009, 2005).

PLANNING YOUR MARKETING APPROACH

As with many things in life, it is usually better to have a plan than to just wing your marketing approach. Here are a couple of things to think about as you develop your plan.

Who Initiated the Instruction?

As already discussed in chapters 3 and 4, the reasons behind deciding that you need a new ILI project influence how you proceed in your planning. If the idea to develop a new ILI program, course, class, or workshop came from information gathered in some kind of formal or informal needs assessment (proactive mode), you will have to do quite a bit of marketing, especially to the decision makers in your environment in order to get initial approval and continuing support for your ideas. However, if someone in your institution or community requested the instruction (interactive mode), you already have the requester's support and so do not have to "sell" instruction to him or her. However, you may still need to negotiate with the requester about the content of the instruction, and may even wish to collaborate with him or her as you work on your ID. If you decided an instructional intervention was needed because of the pattern of problems and questions being presented to you by your learners during classes, at the reference desk, or perhaps in casual conversations (reactive mode), your marketing requirements will fall somewhere in between the above two extremes. These types of ILI endeavors tend to target specific resources, or perhaps are a response to changes in information technology. They are usually fast-tracked in order to address a pressing issue. Projects of this sort usually result in stand-alone (not attached to any particular course or institutional project) type workshops or online instructional aides. Therefore, you may only need to get approval from those in your immediate department to get the ball rolling. However, since attendance is generally voluntary in these sorts of

ILI, you will need some kind of marketing plan that will help you entice learners to participate in your instruction (Grassian and Kaplowitz 2009, 2005). Direct marketing to your learners will be addressed elsewhere in this chapter.

Institutional Climate and Culture

Another thing to consider as you plan how to market your ILI ideas is your institutional climate and culture—especially in terms of how your organization responds to and manages change. Would you classify your environment as an adaptable and risk-taking one, as a conservative/slow to change one, or somewhere in between? Are there people in your institution or community who are more open to new ideas than others? Will enlisting their support help you "sell" your ideas to others in your environment? Knowing how change happens in your organization and who needs to be convinced is vital to getting your ILI ideas endorsed and adopted. Identifying those who are most open to new ideas as well as those who can implement change will help you know how to frame your marketing message successfully and direct it to those who can be of the most help to you (Grassian and Kaplowitz 2005).

Creating an effective marketing plan, therefore, takes some careful thought and a thorough knowledge of your institution as well as your learners. Much of this information should be in your needs assessment. If you have not done a formal needs assessment, you can still find out a great deal from an examination of key institutional documents such as organizational charts and mission statements. And don't forget to talk to your colleagues. They probably are a gold mine of important information about who makes decisions, how those decisions are made, and the best ways to approach those from whom you need support.

Getting Your Learners to Participate

Once you have secured the necessary institutional support and have recruited your collaborators, you are ready to do your design work—that is, deciding on goals and outcomes, selecting learning activities and assessments, and sequencing your instruction. When the design work is completed, the next step is to develop a game plan for attracting your learners to your ILI. As stated above, your institutional partners can be a great deal of help here. But in many cases, you will need to create your own advertising campaign. How you approach this task will depend on a variety of factors such as your institutional climate and culture, who your potential learners are, the type of ILI you have designed, whether your delivery mode will be face-to-face (F2F) or in the synchronous or asynchronous online format, if attendance will be required or voluntary, and so on. A well-thought-out advertising campaign will only be effective if the message and delivery mode is appropriate to your specific situation. Once again, your needs assessment can provide invaluable information about how to reach your learners and what matters to them—the "What's in it for me?" factor. Find out where your learners "hang out" and approach them where they are. This could be online (Facebook, Twitter, your library's website, etc.) or physically (coffeehouses, computer labs, study spaces both in the library and in other areas within your environment). Knowing as much as you can about your learners is critical for the successful marketing of your ILI.

Keep marketing your product to your learners even after they arrive at your instructional space. Getting them there does not ensure that they will participate, or that they will be motivated to learn. Remember the ideas about getting and keeping your learners' attention that were discussed in chapter 8. Make sure you continue to emphasize how your ILI should matter to them. This is especially true in the K–20 environment when learners may have been told to attend your instruction rather than deciding to do so on their own. As a matter of fact, you may have to overcome some negative attitudes as a portion of these learners may feel that the "library tour" is unnecessary for them since they are such good Internet searchers.

Whether you end up delivering your sales pitch virtually through social media sites or via your library's or your institution's website, by meeting with them in person, via print flyers or posters, and/or by placing ads in the campus or local newspaper, make sure you are appealing to what matters to your learners. Point out the potential benefits of participation in your instruction. For example, show your learners how what they learn during your ILI can save them time when they are searching for information. It can help them find the most credible information for their academic/school or work projects and papers. And it can help them when they are trying to find information in their personal lives. The benefits of ILI are many—better grades, increased productivity, improved work projects, and/or more confident life decisions (Booth 2011; Grassian and Kaplowitz 2009; Morrison et al. 2011).

So that is a brief look at how to "sell" your ILI to the important people in your environment. Marketing takes thought, work, and time. But it should not be neglected. After all, if you cannot secure the necessary support, your ID is stopped before it begins. And if you can't entice learners to attend your instruction or to participate once they get there, your ILI will not succeed. The worksheet in figure 9.1 may help you formulate your thoughts as you consider how much and what kind of marketing needs to be done to implement your project.

The Elevator Speech

One final comment about marketing—you never know when you may run into someone who might be a potential supporter and/or collaborator. So be prepared and ever vigilant for the opportunity to "sell" ILI in general, as well as your specific ideas and proposed projects. One way to do this is to write is referred to in the business world as "the elevator speech" (Pagliarini 2013; Pincus 2007). The name comes from the idea that you should be able to deliver a persuasive message in the time it takes to ride in an elevator—anywhere from thirty seconds to a minute. When writing your speech think about why your ideas are important, how they support the institution, and how your ILI would be relevant and important to whomever you are speaking. You will probably want to arm yourself with several of these elevator speeches, each aimed at different types of people in your organization. Marketing may not be something that comes easily to you. But you can train yourself to be an advocate for your ILI products and ideas. You do this by knowing your environment, identifying the key players, preparing and practicing your elevator speeches, and being willing to put yourself out there a bit whenever you run into someone who might be able to help you advance your ideas. If you do not push yourself to move outside your comfort zone in this arena, your wonderful ideas may never become a reality.

GETTING YOURSELF READY—PREPARING YOURSELF TO TEACH

Congratulations on having successfully marketed your ILI ideas to the appropriate stakeholders in your environment, creating a plan for getting your learners to participate in your instruction, and developing ideas to gain and sustain their attention and motivation when they get there. Having completed these tasks, you went ahead and designed your ILI and are now ready to share it with your learners. Now is the time to identify any issues and/or potential pitfalls that should be considered before you can share your instruction with your learners.

Let's start with a bit of self-reflection to explore how you feel about the act of teaching. What goes through your mind as you prepare yourself to share your instruction with your learners? What emotions are you experiencing? Take a moment to complete the worksheet in figure 9.2 to explore your feelings honestly and candidly. Knowing how you really feel is the first step toward working out how to deal with those emotions—positive or not.

Teaching can be a scary undertaking. You are putting yourself on display. It is only natural to feel a bit vulnerable and concerned about how you present yourself and to question your skills as an effective teacher. Teaching is performing—whether you are facing your learners in a classroom setting, or virtually in either the synchronous or asynchronous format. And all good performers, whether they are actors, athletes, or teachers, want to do the best they can. And because they care, they all experience the anxiety and self-doubts about whether or not they can "pull

FIGURE 9.1

Marketing Your ILI—Who, What, and How

Even the best-designed ILI can fail if it is not marketed effectively to key members of your institution/community. Answer the following questions about your major categories of stakeholders—decision makers, partners/collaborators, and learners—to help you plan your marketing approaches.

➤ Who are they? In other words, who in your institution/community needs to be convinced? List specific names and job titles if appropriate, or just overall group characteristics.

  ○ Who are the decision makers in your institution/community?

  ○ Who are your potential partners/collaborators?

  ○ Who are your learners?

➤ What do these people care about? In other words, what matters to them? How would you appeal to the "What's in it for me?" factor?

  ○ What do your decision makers care about?

  ○ What do your potential partners/collaborators care about?

  ○ What do your learners care about?

➤ How would your proposed ILI support what they care about?

  ○ How will your ILI support what your decision makers care about?

    ○ How will your ILI support what your potential partners/collaborators care about?

    ○ How will your ILI support what your learners care about?

➢ What would be the best way to contact your stakeholders—in person, phone, mail, e-mail, print material, online/website, and so forth?

    ○ What is the best way to contact your decision makers?

    ○ What is the best way to contact your potential partners/collaborators?

    ○ What is the best way to contact your learners?

➢ What would you include in your message to convince them that your ILI is relevant and valuable to them?

    ○ What would you include in your message to your decision makers?

    ○ What would you include in your message to your potential partners/collaborators?

    ○ What would you include in your message to your learners?

FIGURE 9.2

A Reflection on My Feelings about Teaching

How do you really feel about teaching? Complete the following worksheet to help you explore your own views about being a teacher.

➢ List three to five words or phrases that would complete the following sentence: When I think about having to teach, I feel:

➢ On a scale from 1 to 5 with 1 being "not at all" and 5 being "extremely," how would you rate your level of nervousness when you are getting ready to teach? Circle the number that most reflects your feelings.

1   2   3   4   5

➢ What, if anything, do you currently do to deal with your preteaching nervousness, stress, and anxiety?

it off." Here are some ideas about how to get yourself ready to tackle your teaching tasks (Booth 2011; Grassian and Kaplowitz 2009; Morrison et al. 2011).

Learn to Relax—Dealing with Stage Fright

Whether you are a seasoned veteran or a novice when it comes to getting up in front of a group (either in person or virtually in some kind of synchronous online teaching situation), you will probably feel some degree of anxiety as you get yourself ready to "face" your learners. Some level of stage fright is not only natural, it can also be interpreted as a measure of your commitment to and concern about your instruction. You want your instruction to be effective, and so you care about how you come across to your learners. After all, you are responsible for helping them learn the material you will be sharing with them. Therefore, you want to be an engaging as well as an informative instructor.

There are a number of ways to deal with the symptoms of stage fright that can manifest themselves as sweaty palms, changes in respiration and heart rates, butterflies in the stomach, and so on. Understanding how and why the body is reacting the way it is can be one way to help you get over your trepidations. Basically all the signs of stage fright are indicators that your body is preparing itself for a stressful task. These reactions all stem from the body's so-called fight-or-flight response to physical danger. Interestingly enough, the body reacts in the same way to excitement as it does to fear. So when you experience these symptoms remember it is your body's way to prepare you for your upcoming exciting instructional encounter. You are sweating and shaking and feeling sick to your stomach because you want to do the best possible job you can do. Tell yourself that you are not terrified of facing your learners. You are just overcome with excitement (Grassian and Kaplowitz 2009; Roland 1997; Sapolsky 1998). Unfortunately, an excess of these feelings can lead to panic, which in turn can result in rushing through the material, forgetting vital aspects of the information being shared, and making it difficult to respond to your learners in an inclusive and supportive way. On the other extreme there is also such a thing as being too relaxed. In that case, you might come across as disinterested, indifferent, unconcerned, or just plain blasé about the instruction and your learners. So let yourself be a bit anxious, but learn to deal with your anxiety if you start to become overwhelmed by it. Find that perfect level of arousal that allows you to perform at your best (Bligh 2000; Grassian and Kaplowitz 2009).

So how do you deal with your particular level of stage fright? Basically, you need to develop some techniques that allow you to relax. Find out how breathing and relaxation exercises can help calm those nerves. Explore books and websites on acting, sports psychology, meditation, and yoga. You might even wish to take classes or attend workshops on relaxation, dealing with stage fright, or explore how performers and athletes get themselves psyched up to face their audiences (J. Kaplowitz 2012a, 2012c). Here are some brief ideas to get you started.

One way to deal with your stress is through your breath. Breathing comes naturally. You don't have to think about it. You just do it. But there are actually many different types of breathing—each with its own characteristics and benefits. See table 9.1 for examples of different types of breathing techniques. *Note:* It is best to try these exercises while seated in a comfortable position.

When you are nervous do you have the tendency to tense up or clench specific parts of your body? Do you scrunch up your face? Grit your teeth? Tighten your shoulders? Do you feel your tension in your neck, your shoulders, your lower back, or some other part of your body? Table 9.2 gives you some suggestions about how to relax your tight spots. All of the exercises described can be done standing or seated in a chair. *Note:* These exercises are intended to help you feel better. But everyone's body is different. Be kind to yourself. If something does not feel right or, worse, hurts, don't do it.

The material in these two tables offers a very brief look into yoga breathing and relaxation techniques. If you want to learn more about these topics, see the "Getting Ready" section in the "Moving On" reading list in the appendix of this book.

Table 9.1. Just Breathe

Description	How You Do It
➢ Focusing breaths	• As you are breathing naturally, start paying attention to the inhalations and exhalations. • Now begin to count your breaths—inhale on 1, exhale on 2, inhale on 3, exhale on 4. • Continue until you reach 10 and then start again at 1. Do three or four rounds of breathing in this fashion. • If you are still feeling anxious at the end of your last round, you might consider doing a few more until you start to feel a bit calmer.
➢ Balancing inhalation and exhalation	• Begin to focus on the lengths of your inhalations and exhalations. • Start by inhaling as you count to 4, and exhaling as you count to 4. • Once that count begins to feel comfortable, add one or two counts to each inhalation and exhalation. • Keep going until you reach an 8–10 count on each inhalation and exhalation.
➢ Three-part breathing	• Breathing should involve the entire body, but many people only breathe into one part—either the belly or the chest. • Start this exercise by placing your hands on your belly and breathe in so that your belly balloons out as you inhale, and hollows in as you exhale. • Once the belly breath feels natural, move your hands to your rib cage. Now try to expand your ribs out as you breathe in and move in as you breathe out. • Now try to put the belly and the ribs together. Start your inhale at the belly and move it up to the ribs. Reverse on your exhale—starting with ribs and then moving to belly. • Next add the third part—your chest. First just try practicing chest breathing. Place your hands on your chest. Try to feel your chest filling up and out as you inhale, and hollowing in as you exhale. • Once the chest breath is mastered, put all three pieces together. Breathe in starting with belly, then ribs, and then chest. Exhale starting with chest, then ribs, and then belly. • Your breathing should now be fuller and more satisfying.
➢ Alternate-nostril breathing	• Since this technique takes a bit of concentration, it is a great way to clear your mind as well as work on your breathing. • Take the thumb of your right hand and place it lightly on your right nostril. Take the pinkie and second fingers and place them lightly on the left nostril. The other two fingers can rest on the bridge of your nose or wherever it feels comfortable. • Use your fingers to close off the right nostril and breathe in through the left one. Then close off the left nostril and breathe out through the right. Keep left closed and breathe in through the right. Close off the right and open the left. Exhale through the left. That is one complete round. • Repeat for 10 rounds total and then breathe normally.

Know Your Stuff

Breathing and stretching are great ways to get your body primed for teaching. But another way to deal with stage fright is to make sure that you feel confident and comfortable about the material you will be sharing with your learners. In other words, it helps to know your stuff—not just the material itself, but also the way in which you plan to address it. So it is really important to go over your notes, outline, or speaking points thoroughly. Many instruction librarians advocate a full rehearsal especially if you are trying out something new. Rehearsing helps to smooth out your delivery, lets you check out timing, and often points out problems with flow or logistics. Trying out your instruction in front of a trusted colleague who will provide constructive feedback is an excellent way to build your confidence and to improve your presentation style. Rehearsals can also be used to test out your materials in advance with either colleagues or a representative sample of your learners (Grassian and Kaplowitz 2009). See the "Getting Your Stuff Ready" section below for more on this topic.

Stage Presence

Okay. You have conquered your nerves and are feeling pretty confident about your ability to deliver the material. But there is still more to getting yourself ready. Let's take a look at your teaching instrument—your body and your voice—as a means of getting and holding your learners' attention. Some pointers on how to get and hold your learners' attention using voice, body language, gestures, eye contact, and so forth, can be found in table 9.3.

Table 9.2. Stretch and Relax Away Your Tension

The Stretch	How You Do It
➤ Whole body	• Start in a standing or seated position. • Inhale. • Reach your arms over your head. • Stretch up as far as feels comfortable. You might imagine that you are reaching for something that you want. • You may even come up onto your toes as you stretch upward. • Exhale and release. • Repeat as often as you like.
➤ Side body	• Start in a standing or seated position. • Inhale and reach your arms over your head. • Stretch over to the right. • Exhale and release to center. • Repeat on the left. • Do two to three rounds.
➤ Neck—part 1	• Start in a standing or seated position. • Inhale and move your head so that you are looking toward your right shoulder. • Take a few breaths (in and out) in this position. • When you are done, exhale as you return your head to center. • Repeat on the left.
➤ Neck—part 2	• Start in a standing or seated position. • Inhale and move your right ear toward your right shoulder. • Take a few breaths (in and out) in this position. • When you are done, exhale as you return your head to center. • Repeat on the left.
➤ Shoulders	• You can do this standing or in a seated position. • Inhale and rotate your shoulders up and forward. • Exhale as you rotate your shoulders down and back. • Repeat three times. • Then reverse the direction of the shoulder roll—up and back on the inhale, and down and forward on the exhale. • Repeat reverse roll three times.
➤ Lower back	• You can do this standing or in a seated position. • Grasp your hands behind your back. • Inhale and lean forward as you exhale. Only go as far as feels comfortable. • Stay in the forward bend for two or three full breaths (inhale and exhale). • Rise up slowly on the last exhale.
➤ Neck and jaw	• You can do this standing or in a seated position. • Take a deep breath and then open your mouth as far as you can. • Exhale through the mouth with or without sound. • *Note:* Making some noise as you exhale is a great way to release some pent-up tension.
➤ Letting it all go	• You can do this standing or in a seated position. • Put on some favorite music. Choose something with a catchy, upbeat rhythm. • Close your eyes and start shaking your head in time to the music. • Add your shoulders to the shaking. • Work your way down the body—adding your arms, hands, torso, and legs. You may even consider jumping up and down if you are doing this in a standing position. • Continue for a minute or so and then stop. • Reflect on how you feel. Hopefully you are feeling nice and relaxed after shaking out all that tension.

Table 9.3. The Body and the Voice—Your Instructional Instrument

➢ *Verbal Pacing*	• If you speak too quickly, learners will not be able to keep up. If you speak too slowly, you run the risk of boring your learners. • Try to adopt a conversational tone and pace so your learners feel that you are talking with them, not to them.
➢ *Vocal Quality*	• Lower-pitched voices seem to carry further. If you have a naturally high-pitched voice, try to work at lowering it a bit. Do the best you can. Your pitch may come down over time as you train yourself to be more aware of how you sound. • Watch out for conversational fillers such as "Uh" or "Um." Including too many can become annoying or distracting to your listeners. • Fillers are usually used to buy time as you gather your thoughts. Try taking a breath instead. You will cut down on the fillers, buy yourself the needed time, and relax yourself as well.
➢ *Projection*	• This is somewhat related to pitch. Regardless of the pitch of your voice, you want to make sure you are reaching all your learners. You can compensate for a high-pitched voice by making sure you are loud enough to project to all parts of the room. • If possible, see if you can practice in your learning space. Have someone stand in different parts of the room to see if you can be heard in all areas of the space. • At the start of your instruction ask learners to let you know if they can hear you by raising their hands. Also, encourage them to let you know if they cannot hear you as the instruction goes along.
➢ *Pausing*	• Pausing is an excellent way to capture learners' attention. • Pauses can be used to emphasize important points, or as a way to call attention to the fact that you are moving on to a new topic. • Also make sure that you insert a pause after asking your learners a question. Give your learners time to respond. Count slowly to 10 before you say anything else. • If you answer your own questions too quickly, learners will become discouraged and will stop trying to answer your questions. Why should they respond if you are going to answer the questions for them? • Furthermore, if you don't wait for them to answer, it seems to indicate that you really don't carry about their ideas, thoughts, and answers.
➢ *Gestures*	• Gestures can be quite effective as ways to emphasize and/or illustrate important points. • However, don't overuse gestures. Too many and/or inappropriate gestures can end up being a distraction.
➢ *Movement*	• Try not to stay in one place in the room for the entire session. • Moving around the room helps to keep your learners interested and involved. • As you move to different parts of the space, you are also illustrating that you are interested in including all your learners in the instructional endeavor.
➢ *Approaching Learners*	• If you want to get particular learners' attention, try moving toward them. • Furthermore, reducing the space between you and your learners indicates you really care about what they have to say.
➢ *Eye Contact*	• Make sure you are moving your gaze to all points in the space. • Pay special attention to those in the far corners of the space. It is easy to look at the learners who are directly in front of you. Make sure you include those to the sides and in the back as you scan the room.
➢ *With-it-ness* (Kounin 1970)	• Keep a close eye on your learners in order to monitor their attention levels. • Watch for signs that you may have lost your learners—boredom (yawns, fidgeting), confusion (quizzical looks), or being overwhelmed (glazed eyes). • If your learners are no longer with you, this is your cue to change what you are doing in order to get them back. • Slow down if they seem overwhelmed by too much information. Move on to a new topic if they seem bored with the current one. • Ask yourself if you need to review the material, paraphrase it, or present it in a different way. • Maybe you need to offer more examples or you should introduce a new learning activity to help them understand the content. • Or your learners may just be trying to tell you they are done with the current topic and would like to learn about something else.

Warming Up Your Voice

In order to make sure your voice is ready to be effective, take some time to warm up your vocal cords before your instruction. Performers do a number of different things to get their voice ready—humming, singing, vocalizing, running scales, and so forth. Find something you are willing to do and then do it. A warmed-up voice will project further and sound better. And if you warm your voice up in advance, you reduce the likelihood that your voice will crack or break as you address your learners.

Get to Your Teaching Space Early

Another good idea to help with preteaching anxieties is to get to your teaching space (physical or online) a bit before your learners. That way you can make sure everything is the way you expected it to be. And you can greet your learners as they arrive in the room or at the online space. For example, if you are doing a synchronous online session, you can use some kind of chat feature to welcome each participant as they sign in.

Starting to interact with your learners even before the more formal instruction begins can go a long way to calm your own nerves, and helps you connect with your learners as well. By casually chatting with them, you begin to break down the barriers between you and your learners. You start to get to know them as people—not as members of a faceless, anonymous group. And they can begin to connect to you as well. It is much easier to interact with people you know—even if you've just met them—than it is to try to work with strangers.

You can do something similar in the asynchronous online course environment by identifying your learners in advance and sending them a welcoming e-mail, or creating an introductory animation or video. If your online instruction takes the form of an independent tutorial or website, you can still insert a welcoming piece that introduces yourself and the content, thus adding a friendly face to the somewhat impersonal nature of stand-alone, independent, online ILI material. Adding your contact information and inviting learners to contact you if they have further questions or concerns also makes your learners feel like someone is out there who cares about their issues and needs. While this may not do much for your own anxiety, it can certainly add a more personal touch to the somewhat impersonal mode of asynchronous online instruction. You can find tips on how to create brief videos using a webcam and YouTube elsewhere in this chapter.

So those are some things to consider as your prepare yourself to teach. Use the worksheet in figure 9.3 to help you review this material and to develop your own personal approach to getting yourself ready.

GETTING YOUR STUFF READY—PREPARING YOUR INSTRUCTIONAL MATERIALS

Tackling the task of preparing yourself—in mind and body—for your teaching experience is of course only part of your preinstructional preparation. You also have to consider a variety of issues related to preparing your instructional materials. Whether you are teaching in person or online, you need to make sure you will be able to present the material smoothly, coherently, and in an organized manner. You want both your print and your online content to be graphically appealing as well as informative, relevant, and easy to read and understand. So let's take a look at some of the factors that go into getting your stuff ready.

Outlining

If you are teaching in real time, either in a physical classroom or online, you need to make sure that you have the material you wish to present organized clearly and logically. Sequencing your content appropriately has already been discussed in chapter 8. But you also need to develop some kind of notes system that will help you make sure you are covering all the points you wish to share and are doing so in an orderly and coherent fashion. Some people write out their notes word for word. Others create lists of talking points or brief cue cards. As you become a more experienced

FIGURE 9.3

My "Getting Myself Ready" Checklist

How do you get yourself ready to teach? Answer the following questions in order to reflect on your preparation process.

➤   What are 4–5 things you currently do to prepare yourself for teaching?

➤   Having read the "Getting Yourself Ready" material, what are 2–3 things you are now considering adding to your preparations?

➤   What are 1–2 things you would like to know more about?

➤   What are your plans for finding out about these things?

teacher, you will find the approach that works best for you. No matter how you prepare your outline, remember that your notes are meant to help you stay on track and on topic. Never, never just read your notes to your learners. Not only is that boring for them (unless you are a very talented dramatic reader), it is sort of a waste of time for everyone. If you are merely going to talk at them and recite your notes, you could just let them read the notes themselves.

One idea is to start with an outline that includes pretty much everything you intend to say. This approach can help you organize your thoughts for the instruction and double-check that the material is being addressed in a logical and orderly fashion. Use these fully fleshed out set of notes for your initial rehearsals. As you begin to feel more comfortable with the flow, start highlighting key words and begin to only check your notes from time to time to remind you of "what comes next" in the session. Include timing notations to make sure that you are moving through the material as planned, and will not run out of time before you have shared everything with your learners. Once you begin to feel confident with this approach you might take it a step further and create an outline of your outline, which is fundamentally just a list of the highlighted cue words as well as the time allocated to each segment or chunk of instruction. Only do this when you feel confident enough to deliver the intended material based solely on these cue words or phrases. Rehearse to the point where you really know your stuff and the delivery is smooth and clear. But don't overrehearse, or you will begin to sound like an automated recording. We will return to rehearsal as a way of getting your stuff ready later on in this chapter.

New instruction librarians often wonder how they will know the amount of content to include in a particular time frame. As you gain experience as a teacher, you will begin to internalize a formula that allows you to make those timing decisions. But in the beginning, it is sometimes a very difficult matter. Beginning teachers (and even experienced ones) generally try to cram in more than they should for a given time frame. This is especially true for instruction librarians teaching in the one-shot mode. They have so much to share and so little time to do it. Plus, they often feel they may never get another chance to share their expertise with this particular group. So these instruction librarians tend to try and give their learners everything they will ever need to know in whatever time they have been allocated. However, remember the "less is more" rule of teaching. It is better to teach a few things well, than to try to teach a whole lot of stuff that will overwhelm your learners and that they will find impossible to absorb (Grassian and Kaplowitz 2009).

One way to deal with this issue is to create a three-tiered format for your outline or notes. This concept was already referred to in chapter 5 in the discussion of how to choose an appropriate number of expected learning outcomes for your instruction. As you may recall, the idea of the three-tiered approach is based on considering what your learners absolutely need to know (your core outcomes), what might be nice for them to know (your more advanced outcomes), and the additional bells and whistles material (the extras that only some learners may even be interested in).

If you apply this idea to your notes, you can create a full-blown outline that includes all the material for all three tiers, but with the idea that you will only move to the second- and third-tier information if time permits and/or if relevant questions arise. It might be helpful to color-code your notes so that each tier has its own color—yellow for tier one (need to know), orange for tier two (nice to know), and green for the extra bells and whistles of tier three. That way, you can concentrate on the tier one material but have the other stuff handy if needed (J. Kaplowitz 2012b; Grassian and Kaplowitz 2009). It is very useful to have this extra material already prepared as it allows you to easily deal with questions and comments related to tier two and three material if they come up. And on the rare occasion that a session ends earlier than you planned (perhaps because learners turned out to be more sophisticated than you had expected), you have some extra material to fill the gap. Of course, if you finish sooner than you anticipated, most learners won't complain about being allowed to leave early. However, for those who wish to hang around, you are completely prepared to continue the discussion at perhaps a higher level.

Rehearsing and Peer Coaching

Practicing your material out loud has already been touched upon in the "Getting Yourself Ready" section above. In that discussion, rehearsal was intended to help you feel more confident and comfortable with your delivery. Here, the rehearsing has a slightly different focus. You use the rehearsal to determine whether or not the material seems to flow in a logical and coherent fashion. Try practicing your notes out loud so you can hear how it sounds. Pay special attention to segue sections between chunks. These need to be smooth in order to help learners make connections between the various topics you are addressing. Also listen for clarity and basically try to pick up places where what you hear does not seem to be making complete sense, even though you wrote it and actually know what you are trying to say. Keep in mind that it is equally important to practice your material whether you are teaching in the classroom setting or online. Issues related to preparing online material such as welcoming videos and online lecture/demos will be addressed in the "Getting the Space Ready" section below.

Of course, getting a trusted colleague to listen to (and watch) you teach can be even more valuable as he or she can bring additional insight into the rehearsal process, and can help you improve your material as well as your delivery. An interesting approach to improving your teaching is to enter into a peer coaching relationship with a colleague. You each take turns acting as coach for the other person. That way you both benefit from the experience. And people who have used this technique often say they learn as much about teaching when they are the coach as when they are being coached. These instructors say that watching someone else teach often gives them great new ideas, helps them find out about different types of learning activities, and introduces them to new and different ways of approaching the material (Grassian and Kaplowitz 2005, 2009).

Field-Testing and Pilot Projects

Related to both rehearsal and peer coaching is the idea that you should set aside some preparation time to field-test your materials—especially your exercises, activities, and other support or supplementary print or online content. Just as rehearsing what you intend to say helps you check to see if your comments make sense, field-testing helps you ensure that exercises, activities, handouts, web pages, tutorials, videos, and so forth, are accomplishing what you intended them to do. Instructors often do initial field tests with colleagues, but in the end you really don't know if your materials will work with your learners until you test them out with those very learners. So see if you can find a small but representative sample of people from your target learning audience, and have them try out your stuff. Watch them as they interact with the material and encourage them to give you constructive feedback and critique. It is far better to fix potential problems before you put your material into actual practice than to try and recover from a crisis during the instruction itself. Field-testing can also be a valuable way to help you sell a large-scale instructional enterprise. In this case, you can try out a pilot project representing perhaps only a portion of your overall plan. Use what you learn from this pilot to help you revise and expand into the bigger endeavor. You can also use the success of the pilot (and the positive word of mouth it might generate) as a way to market and promote your bigger project, and to sell that project to your stakeholders (Grassian and Kaplowitz 2009).

Visual Appeal (Graphic Design, Layout, etc.)

Field-testing will also help you to determine if what you have prepared in terms of print or online support materials are well organized, visually appealing, clear, and communicating what you intended. Obviously, going into great detail on the art of graphic and web design is beyond the scope of this book. This is an area for which appealing to an expert may help you move a humdrum item to a dynamic and effective learning object. However, here are a few things to keep in mind when creating paper or online instructional items (Mayer 2009; Morrison et al. 2011).

Effective Use of White Space

You can create emphasis by leaving extra space between a topic heading and the subtopics related to that heading. White space can also be used to signal a change to a new topic. Make sure you are not trying to pack too much onto a page or screen. Your learners may become overwhelmed and confused by the quantity of information being provided, and find it difficult to focus on the most relevant items. Help them out by using spacing, indentation, and other text placement that attracts their eyes to what you are trying to communicate.

Typographical Variations

You can also create emphasis by varying typeface being used (boldface or italics, changing type size, etc.) to create a change in the visual pattern. The eye is drawn to this difference. Use this technique to highlight important words or new information. However, do not overdo it. Too many changes can actually be distracting. Furthermore, make sure you are consistent with your decisions. For example, if one major heading is twelve-point and in boldface, then all the major headings in the material should also be twelve-point and bolded. Finally, mixing of fonts is generally not recommended and requires some advanced knowledge regarding typography and graphic design.

Color

The use of color can also help to draw the learners' eye, create emphasis, and/or signal a change in topic. The same cautions related to typographical variations regarding consistency, overuse of the technique, and/or making too many changes hold true for color as well as for font variations.

Pictures and Graphics

The addition of relevant pictures and/or graphics can certainly enhance the visual appeal of both print and online material. They can help the learner put abstract concepts into concrete terms and illustrate examples of the information being shared. Here again, you should err on the cautious side. Make sure the pictures or graphics being added are relevant, and add to the learning rather than distract from it. While a small amount of decorative graphics may be fine to increase the visual appeal, keep in mind that any reasonably sized graphic or picture will take space away from the informative text you are sharing. The "less is more" rule may actually be a good one to consider when you are making any of these design decisions. Weigh the potential impact of the picture or graphic, and only use those that will give the most "bang" for the visual and instructional "buck."

Organization and Navigation

Whether you are working in the print or the online format, make sure that your material is easy to follow, well organized, clear, comprehensive, and readable. Pay special attention to issues of navigation in the online format. Consistency is a factor here as well. Make sure that links learners use to move through the material are placed in the same place on each page. For example, always put the "next" button at the bottom right of each page. Or create a navigational menu either in the left-hand column or along the top of each page to allow learners to move from topic to topic as needed. This allows learners to make their own way through the material rather than forcing them to follow the steps you have created. The actual location of the menu, link, or button is less important than the fact that the navigational tool can always be found in the same place on the screen.

Before moving on to "Getting the Space Ready," take a moment to review the ideas discussed in the "Getting Your Stuff Ready" section by completing the checklist in figure 9.4.

FIGURE 9.4

My "Getting My Stuff Ready" Checklist

What are some of the things you do to get your "stuff" ready? Answer the following questions to reflect on how you prepare your instructional materials.

➤   What are 4–5 things you currently do to prepare your instructional materials?

➤   Having read the "Getting Your Stuff Ready" section, what are 2–3 things you are now considering adding to your preparations?

➤   What are 1–2 things you would like to know more about?

➤   What are your plans for finding out about these things?

GETTING THE SPACE READY

When considering issues related to space, issues related to the physical classroom are probably foremost in your mind. But advances in instructional technology have provided instructors with a wide variety of ways to reach and teach learners. So when discussing space issues, let's broaden the conversation to include both asynchronous and synchronous teaching "space" as well as the traditional face-to-face (F2F) classroom setting (Farmer 2011; J. Kaplowitz 2012b). Although some of the same issues apply to all settings, teaching online classes or courses or combining F2F and online elements in a blended or hybrid format require some additional thought, preparation, and skills (Conrad and Donaldson 2004; Ko and Rossen 2010; Palloff and Pratt 2007).

F2F

Be sure to check out the physical space you will be using well in advance of the actual instructional experience. You want to become familiar with the room arrangement, lighting options, the equipment and technology available to you, and so on. Is seating fixed or movable? If fixed, how will you implement some of your collaborative group activities? One way to have learners form groups when in a lecture hall, auditorium setting, or any room where the seating is set into rows, is to have the every other row (starting with the first) turn around and work with those behind them.

If you have the luxury of working in a space with flexible seating, consider the best room arrangement for the activities you have planned. In some cases the inverted "U" shape works nicely, especially if your learners will be engaged in a lot of open discussions. In this setup, you are in the opening in the U and the learners are seated in the U's arms and back. The advantage of this arrangement is that learners are facing each other during the session, but can still break off into smaller groups as needed. However, the use of the inverted U is somewhat limited by the number of learners and the physical shape of the teaching room.

Another potential setup arranges tables and chairs into multiple pods around the room. This room arrangement facilitates small-group work, but learners can still interact and share with each other as a full group as needed. Pods can even facilitate shared exploration of online material, especially if instructional laptops are being used for the session.

In addition to basic furniture arrangement, also check out your lighting options. Can you dim the lights, be selective about which banks of lights are on or off, or are your only options totally on or totally off? And of course, make sure you are comfortable with any kind of equipment and/or technology you will be using. Nothing causes an instructor to lose credibility with his or her learners faster than having to fumble around trying to get the computer or projector turned on, or not being able to move the screen up or down as needed.

Issues related to scheduling and staffing also need to be considered when working in the F2F setting. Your needs assessment data should help you figure out the best time of day and/or day of the week that would be most convenient for your learners. However, the availability of the learning space, equipment, media, as well as that of any instructors involved may also factor into making scheduling decisions. Obviously, if you are the only one teaching, you will have taken your own schedule into consideration when planning when to offer the ILI. But when your instruction is going to be taught by multiple instructors, scheduling becomes more complicated. In this case, it is important to obtain input from everyone who is involved so that the final schedule is convenient and appropriate for all concerned.

Synchronous Online

Most synchronous online is associated with teaching long-term, for-credit courses. However, you could find yourself in a situation where you are teaching a one-shot via the web or some sort of video conferencing. In either case, it is crucial that you familiarize yourself with features of the course management system (CMS) being employed and/or any other software and hardware you will be using to deliver instruction. You don't want issues with the technology to interfere with your instructional message. So check out all the features available to you and use the ones that seem most supportive of your instructional goals and outcomes. You may wish to start with the most basic elements and only add the more advanced features as you become more comfortable teaching in the online space.

Remember that although you are not sharing the same physical space as your learners, many of the issues related to getting and keeping learners' attention that were discussed above are equally important here. However, there are other factors associated with presenting yourself on camera. For more on how to prepare yourself for your "close-ups," see the section below on creating an online lecture/demo video.

Asynchronous Online

Although some of your online teaching may take the form of synchronous delivery, much of what you do with your learners may involve asynchronous interactions. Again, this could be in relation to a full-term online course, or some kind of one-shot situation. As in both the situation of the physical space and the synchronous online environment, you need to develop a facility with the technological tools with which you will be teaching. Whatever you choose to use, do some preliminary exploration with the tools and technology and be sure to do an honest evaluation of any product you create to make sure it is good enough to share with your learners. If you don't feel you have the skill set necessary to produce a professional-looking product, you may wish to enlist the help of those in your environment who do have those skills. However, there are now many fairly simple technologies available that you can use without too much training or experience. Many of these products are extremely user friendly, and you can conquer their use in a very short period of time. For example, you can produce a simple video using your own computer's webcam and then mount the video on YouTube. See table 9.4 for some tips on how to make a simple video that can be used as a welcome message for your online class or course, as a way to add a face to your online tutorials, or create a brief online lecture/demo that addresses some of the class or course content (H. Kaplowitz 2012).

Table 9.4. Making Instructional Videos Using Webcam and YouTube

Steps	Tips and Techniques
➢ Writing the script	• Make a personal connection by stating your name and telling viewers something about yourself. • Describe content and ELOs. • Let them know how material is relevant. In other words, answer their "What's in it for me?" questions. • Adopt a friendly, conversational tone. • Keep it short in order to hold their interest, and to avoid overwhelming them and overloading their memory processing.
➢ Rehearsing	• Keep pace slow enough for people to take notes. • Use your body and voice to capture and maintain attention. • Monitor your timing and delivery. Listen to yourself and check for smoothness of delivery, pronunciation pitfalls, etc. • See more on this in the "Getting Yourself Ready" section.
➢ Setting the stage	• Keep the set simple. • Avoid clutter or anything that might distract from your message/content. • Dress appropriately for the situation and your audience. • Make sure speaker/action is well lit.
➢ Framing	• Frame video so it appears that you are looking at the viewer at eye level. To do so, place yourself so your eyes are about one-third of the way down the screen. • Avoid placing your nose directly in the center of the screen. • Don't allow too much of the ceiling to show.
➢ Shooting	• Make sure nothing else is running on your computer—for example, turn off programs such as mail or messaging to avoid having an incoming message signal interrupt your filming. • Sign into your YouTube account and select "upload and record from webcam" option. • Check your image in the preview window and make adjustments as needed. • Do a final rehearsal and check audio levels. • Select "start recording." Look at the camera and then count slowly to three before beginning to speak. • When done, look at the camera and then count slowly to three before selecting "stop recording" to end filming. • Preview and do an honest evaluation of your product. Reshoot if needed or, if product is acceptable, upload your video.
➢ Captioning	• Add closed captioning using the "captioning" feature and typing in your script. • This is a very important step not only to address accessibility issues, but also to help learners who are trying to view the video in a noisy environment, and/or for those who like to read as well as listen to the presented material.

Making sure you are comfortable in your instructional space is an important part of your instructional preparations. Whether you are teaching in a physical space or are working with your learners online, you need to be confident that your instruction can be delivered in the way you intended. The instructional space should support your learners' ability to obtain the ELOs set, not hinder it. If you are working in the online environment, be sure to consider the technology and accessibility issues addressed in chapter 6. Before you move on to the next section of this chapter, take a moment to complete the checklist in figure 9.5 to review how you will get your instructional space ready for teaching.

GETTING READY FOR THE NEXT TIME

Now that you know how to approach getting yourself, your stuff, and your space ready for your ILI, there is one more thing to consider. It may seem logical that once you have implemented and delivered your instruction, your design process is now over. While that may well be true for this particular endeavor, each time you teach is in reality just a dress rehearsal for the next time. The ID process is a never-ending cycle. As you work through your instructional material, you are gaining insight into the effectiveness of what you have developed (Booth 2011; Farmer 2011; Grassian and Kaplowitz 2009). So once your learners have completed the ILI you have designed, you should take some time to think about what happened during that instruction. Ask yourself a few simple questions: What went well? What could use improvement? And what would you change for the next time you delivered this material?

Good teachers never seem to be satisfied and are always looking for ways to improve the effectiveness of their material. What better way to do that than to use what you have learned during your interactions with your learners to update and improve your material for the next time? Not only will your learners benefit from your dedication to continuous improvement, you will as well. Teaching the same thing over and over again in exactly the same fashion is the road to burnout. You cannot help but become bored with the material after you have presented it time after time after time. Keep striving to make your ILI better. Try out new activities and ways of sharing the material—especially for segments in your instruction that did not seem to go over that well. Changing it up every so often helps you keep it fresh for your learners and for yourself as well. So remember that delivering your ILI is only the last step in the current cycle. It is also the first step in starting your ID process over again for the next time. And if you honestly review and reflect on what you just completed, your next attempt will be even better.

WRAP-UP

You learn something every time you teach. And you can use what you learn to help improve how you design your next attempt. Honest self-assessment and the desire to improve are the foundations of being a good teacher. You do the best you can each and every time you teach. Then you review what you accomplished with an eye to doing it even better in the future. That is what makes being a teacher so exciting and so much fun. It is a constantly evolving process. Good teachers are never completely satisfied with their efforts. As good as the current incarnation may be, there is always the possibility that something better might still be out there if we are only open to looking for it. So feel free to be a little critical of your own work. You are not being hard on yourself. You are looking for ways to update and improve both your teaching skills and your instructional methodology. As a result your instruction will continue to be engaging, effective, inspiring, and hopefully fun for everyone concerned, and you will continue to grow as a teacher.

FIGURE 9.5

My "Getting the Space Ready" Checklist

What are some of the ways you get your instructional space ready? Answer the following questions to reflect on how you prepare your F2F or online teaching space.

➢ What are 4–5 things you currently do to prepare your instructional space—either for F2F or online teaching?

➢ Having read the "Getting the Space Ready" section, what are 2–3 things you are now considering adding to your preparations?

➢ What are 1–2 things you would like to know more about?

➢ What are your plans for finding out about these things?

WHAT STUCK?

Now that you have shared the various pieces of the ID process with your colleagues, they are all excited about trying out their new skills in a real-life ILI experience. However, some are new to teaching and others feel as if they could use a refresher on how to implement and deliver their instruction. So you call them together for a final meeting on the ID process to discuss how they prepare themselves and their material for the actual implementation and delivery of their ILI.

Complete the worksheet in figure 9.6 to review the material from this chapter, and to create "talking points" to help you share this information with your colleagues.

FIGURE 9.6

The Final Pieces—Implementation and Delivery

Complete this worksheet to create "talking points" that will help you address your colleagues' questions and concerns about these aspects of ID.

➢ Marketing

  ○ Describe some ways in which you market your own ILI.

  ○ Then ask your colleagues to share any tips or techniques that they have to "sell" their ILI products and obtain the necessary support to implement their ideas. What do you think they will say?

  ○ What else do you think you and your colleagues might add to your marketing plans?

➢ Getting Yourself Ready

  ○ Prepare a list of issues that need to be considered when you are getting yourself ready to teach.

  ○ Then describe some ways to address those issues.

  ○ Ask your colleagues to add to your list of issues and solutions. What do you think they might suggest?

➢ Getting Your Materials Ready

  ○ Prepare a list of issues that need to be considered when getting your instructional materials ready.

  ○ Then describe some ways to address those issues.

  ○ Ask your colleagues to add to your list of issues and solutions. What do you think they might suggest?

➤ Getting Your Instructional Space Ready

  ○ Prepare a list of issues that need to be considered when getting your instructional space ready.

  ○ Then describe some ways to address those issues.

  ○ Ask your colleagues to add to your list of issues and solutions. What do you think they might suggest?

➤ Getting Ready for the Next Time

  ○ Describe what you do to review and reflect on your ILIs after you have shared them with your learners. How do you use what you learned from that self-reflection to inform your ID process for the next time you teach?

  ○ Ask your colleagues to comment on what, if any, self-reflection they currently do. What do you think might hold them back from engaging in this activity?

REFERENCES

Bell, Stephen, and John D. Shank. 2007. *Academic Librarianship by Design*. Chicago: American Library Association.

Bligh, Donald A. 2000. *What's the Use of Lectures?* San Francisco: Jossey-Bass.

Booth, Char. 2011. *Reflective Teaching, Effective Learning*. Chicago: American Library Association.

Conrad, Rita Marie, and J. Ana Donaldson. 2004. *Engaging the Online Learner*. San Francisco: Jossey-Bass.

Farmer, Lesley S. J. 2011. *Instructional Design for Librarians and Information Professionals*. New York: Neal-Schuman.

Grassian, Esther, and Joan Kaplowitz. 2005. *Learning to Lead and Manage Information Literacy Instruction*. New York: Neal-Schuman.

———. 2009. *Information Literacy Instruction: Theory and Practice*. 2nd ed. New York: Neal-Schuman.

Kaplowitz, Hillary. 2012. Course Welcome Video: Using Your Webcam and YouTube—Guide for Instructors. Personal communication.

Kaplowitz, Joan R. 2012a. "Practically Speaking: Teaching Tips for Information Literacy Instruction." Accessed July 27, 2013. http://joankaplowitz.com/tips/

———. 2012b. *Transforming Information Literacy Instruction Using Learner-Centered Teaching*. New York: Neal-Schuman.

———. 2012c. "Two-Minute Yoga." http://joankaplowitz.com/yoga/

Ko, Susan, and Steve Rossen. 2010. *Teaching Online: A Practical Guide*. 3rd ed. New York: Routledge.

Kounin, Jacob S. 1970. *Discipline and Group Management in Classrooms*. New York: Holt, Rinehart & Winston.

Mayer, Richard. 2009. *Multi-media Learning*. 2nd ed. Cambridge, UK: Cambridge University Press.

Morrison, Gary R., Steven M. Ross, Howard K. Kalman, and Jerrold E. Kemp. 2011. *Designing Effective Instruction*. 6th ed. Hoboken, NJ: Wiley.

Pagliarini, Robert. 2013. "How to Write an Elevator Speech." Business Know-How. Accessed July 22. http://www.businessknowhow.com/money/elevator.htm

Palloff, Rena M., and Keith Pratt. 2007. *Building Online Learning Communities: Effective Strategies for the Virtual Classroom*. 2nd ed. San Francisco: Jossey-Bass.

Pincus, Aileen. 2007. "The Perfect (Elevator) Pitch." *Bloomberg Businessweek*, June 18. Accessed July 22, 2013. http://www.businessweek.com/stories/2007-06-18/the-perfect-elevator-pitchbusinessweek-business-news-stock-market-and-financial-advice

Roland, David. 1997. *The Confident Performer*. Sydney, Australia: Currency Press.

Sapolsky, Robert M. 1998. *Why Zebras Don't Get Ulcers: An Updated Guide to Stress, Stress-Related Diseases, and Coping*. New York: Freeman.

10

An Ending or Beginning Again?

Now that I have finished reading this book, I feel ready to incorporate what I learned into my information literacy instruction (ILI) practice. But I also want to continue to develop myself both as a teacher and an instructional designer. So where do I go from here?

QUESTIONS TO CONSIDER
- ➤ How can I "put it all together" to develop my own personal approach to instructional design (ID) for ILI?
- ➤ How can I keep track of my ID process for each of my ILI endeavors?
- ➤ How can I continue to develop my teaching and design skills?
- ➤ How can I continue to explore the various topics addressed in this book?

Since the first forays into library instruction back in the 1960s, instruction librarians have dedicated themselves to the task of introducing their learners to the concepts associated with information literacy. These librarians have strived to help those with whom they work become empowered information users—people who can locate information effectively and efficiently, critically evaluate the appropriateness and merit of what they find, and use that information creatively and ethically. In short, they have aimed to help create an information literate society.

Most instruction librarians (myself included) learned how to teach on our own, often by the seat of our pants. We watched others teach, tried (and sometimes failed) to teach our own classes and courses, attended workshops and conferences, read books and articles, and so forth—all with the goal of improving our instructional skills. We often focused on the act of teaching itself—presentation skills, effective teaching and assessment techniques, and so on with very little attention paid to the systematic approach to designing instruction advocated by professional instructional designers.

While I always tried to prepare the best instruction that I could, I knew very little about the concepts associated with ID until very recently. Once I began to learn about ID, I got very excited about how adopting an ID practice could improve the quality of my ILI endeavors. And so the ideas that formed the basis for the Teaching Tripod began to evolve and grow, and ultimately led to the writing of the book you just finished. I hope that the ideas I have shared within its pages have inspired you to apply a more systematic approach to your own ILI planning and design. The worksheets included throughout the book can provide you with a framework for using the Teaching Tripod to design your own ILI. And the suggested activities in the "What Stuck?" sections at the end of each chapter can serve not only as a way for you to reflect on the material yourself, but also as an approach to sharing what you learned about ID with your colleagues. I hope you decide to do so and spread the word that as good as our current ILI may be, it can only get better if we start to apply the concepts and strategies advocated by our instructional designer colleagues.

REVIEW AND REFLECT

While each of the previous chapters offered you individual pieces of the ID process, this last chapter is your opportunity to review and reflect on what you have read, and then put it all together into a methodology you can adopt for your own practice. To help you do that I am providing a few more worksheets. First, for a final snapshot and review of the Teaching Tripod approach, see figure 10.1 This worksheet can assist you as you apply the ideas presented in this book to your own instructional design process.

TRACKING YOUR ID PROGRESS

Figure 10.1 provides you with a way to think about all the pieces involved in designing your ILI. Looking at the overall process in this way can cause anyone to feel a bit overwhelmed. This is often the point when many instructors decide they don't really need to be that systematic and/or methodical about their ID process. They can even offer a multitude of reasons (excuses) why they don't need to engage in such a formal planning/design process. However, as I have advocated over and over in this (and other) books, if your want your ILI to be effective, engaging, and inspiring, you need to put in the up-front effort and apply some of the ID principles presented in this book to your practice. While you may not need to complete every single aspect of ID for each specific ILI you design, you should at least consider why or why not you are incorporating each element in your process.

The three Teaching Tripod pieces—expected learning outcomes (ELOs), activities, and assessment—are at the heart of the ID for ILI process. Everything else informs and/or supports your work on those three ID elements. How much or how little you need to devote to needs assessments, marketing, implementation, delivery issues, and so forth, depends on the specific instruction you are planning, and your past experience with both your learners and the instructional environment in which you will be working. If you are planning something new, you will probably need to spend more time on these support pieces. But if you are revising something you have already taught, expanding a program to new audiences, and/or are extremely familiar with your learners and your institutional environment, you may be able to cut down on how much energy goes into these other components of your ID process.

However, what I am proposing in this book is that you always consider ELOs, activities, and assessment, and the relationships between them each and every time you are planning to teach. These are the three crucial pieces of your ID process if you wish to effectively work with your learners and be assured that they have attained the goals and ELOs you have set for the instruction. If you can develop these elements based on your own knowledge and experience, feel free to just concentrate on the Tripod pieces. However, as you start your planning, you may find you need to revisit some of the other components (briefly or more in depth) to help fill in the gaps. Remember that this is a dynamic process. You do not have to work on each piece in a particular order. And it is also perfectly fine to return to elements you have already completed if you feel that you need to make further adjustments. Do as much or as little of the pre-Tripod (needs assessments) and post-Tripod (implementation and delivery) pieces as needed to help you design your ILI and create a logical and useful instructional sequence. The choices are yours. You now have the necessary tools. So go ahead and apply them as you see fit when you are "building" your ILI courses, classes, workshops, and programs.

If the task does seem somewhat overwhelming, here's a suggestion for how to proceed. As in many things in life, it sometimes helps to break down a big project into smaller, more digestible pieces, to develop an overall timetable for completing these smaller pieces, and check off each piece as you complete it. Not only will this checklist

FIGURE 10.1

The Teaching Tripod in Review—A Worksheet for Designing ILI

As you work to complete this worksheet, keep in mind that the first few items (needs assessments, instructional goals, and expected learning outcomes [ELOs]) represent what you need to do in order to identify what you should be addressing in your instruction. The learning activities, assessment, sequencing, and implementation/delivery items are all based those initial steps.

➤ Needs Assessments and Results

  ○ These are the method(s) I used and why I selected them:

  ○ This is what I learned about the characteristics of my learners:

  ○ This is what I learned about my institutional climate and environment:

  ○ These are some potential restrictions/limitations/constraints that may impact my plans:

➤ Instructional Goal(s)

  ○ Based on what I learned from my needs assessments I decided that the overall goal(s) for this ILI would be:

➤ Expected Learning Outcomes (ELOs)

  ○ In order for my learners to reach the designated goal(s), I developed the following specific ELOs for my ILI:

➤ Learning Activities

  ○ To help my learners attain each of my ELOs, I decided on the following activities:

➤ Assessments

  ○ To make sure that my learners attain the desired ELOs, I included the following assessments in my overall ILI design:

➤ Sequencing

  ○ My ATTENTION-GETTING OPENING (hook/sponge/gotcha) is:

  ○ My INTRODUCTION (ties to prior knowledge, sharing of goals and ELOs, answers to the "What's in it for me?" questions) includes:

  ○ The order in which my learners will experience the LEARNING ACTIVITIES is:

○ I have inserted COMPREHENSION CHECKS AND ASSESSMENTS at the following points during or after instruction:

○ I plan to close the ILI with the following BIG FINISH closure/reflection activity:

➢ Implementation/Delivery Plans

○ I plan to market/promote my ILI by:

○ I will need to address the following implementation issues:

○ I will get myself ready to teach by doing the following:

○ I will get my "stuff" ready by doing the following:

○ I will get my "space" ready by doing the following:

Table 10.1. ID Progress Checklist

Element	My ID Process Will Include	Planning	In Progress	Completed
➢ Needs assessment				
➢ Written goal(s)				
➢ Written ELOs				
➢ Learning activities				
➢ Assessments				
➢ Sequencing				
➢ Marketing, promotion, outreach				
➢ Getting myself ready				
➢ Getting my stuff ready				
➢ Getting my learning space ready				
➢ Reflect, review, revise				

approach serve to guide you through the process, as you mark items as "Completed," you will develop a sense of accomplishment and the feeling that you really have a handle on designing your ILI. Start your ID process by deciding upon the overall goals and the specific ELOs for your ILI. Once you have done so, track your progress by checking off items on your list as you move from the planning to the completed stage in each element. When you have finished the checklist and the process, congratulate yourself on following a systematic and methodical approach to the design of your ILI. See table 10.1 for a sample checklist that can help you track your ID progress.

I hope that my Teaching Tripod approach provided an accessible entry into ID that is suitable for the ILI you practice in your professional life. Try any or all of it and then let me know how (if) it worked for you. E-mail me at joan@joankaplowitz.com with your comments, questions, concerns, or just to chat. I would love to continue our conversation long after you close the covers of this book.

If I have whetted your appetite about all this and you want to know more about the various topics addressed, check out the "Moving On" reading list in the appendix. I have endeavored to highlight some of the material that especially informed and inspired both my writing and my actual teaching practice. This is far from a comprehensive list, but I think it is a good jumping-off spot for your own explorations into ID for ILI.

Although you have reached the end of this book, finishing your reading should not really be the end of your ID explorations. In fact, this ending just marks the beginning of the next stage in your journey. Hopefully what you have read has inspired you to continue pursuing the material I shared, and to try your hand at applying what you learned to your own practice. In keeping with the cyclical nature of ID, be sure to reflect on your ILI whenever you teach. You will probably learn something from each of your endeavors—the successful and those that were not quite what you had in mind. As you think about your teaching experiences, look for ways to improve and enhance your ILI offers. Follow this type of reflective teaching practice and you will continue to grow and develop into an even better ILI librarian. Your learners will thank you for taking the time to ensure that your ILI is engaging, effective, and inspiring. And you can take pride in the knowledge that you are always striving to provide the best possible ILI experience every time you teach. While being a reflective teacher can take some effort on your part, I think you may find that you benefit as much as your learners from the approach. The result will be that your ILI practice remains fresh, interesting, lively, and fun for all.

WHAT STUCK?

Before you close the covers of this book, I would like to leave you with my "big finish." This final closure worksheet is your chance to summarize, review, and reflect on all the ideas I have shared with you. So take a moment to answer the questions in figure 10.2 as you think about your "take-aways" from *Designing Information Literacy Instruction: The Teaching Tripod Approach.*

FIGURE 10.2

The Big Finish—A Final Reflection

The reading is completed. You have worked your way through the entire book. Congratulations on your accomplishment. Now please take a moment to think about the following reflection questions to help you put what you have read into perspective, and to make the material your own.

➢ In fifty words or less, how would you describe the ideas presented in this book to a colleague? In other words, prepare an "elevator talk" about this material.

➢ What, if anything, surprised you about the material in this book?

➢ What were 3–5 ideas/concepts/approaches that were most interesting to you about the material in this book?

➢ How do you think you might apply these specific ideas/concepts/approaches to your own practice?

➢ What are 2–3 ways you plan to implement the ideas from this book?

➢ What are 1–2 changes you expect to make in the ways you plan for, design, implement, and deliver your instruction?

Appendix

MOVING ON—DEEPENING YOUR UNDERSTANDING OF INSTRUCTIONAL DESIGN FOR INFORMATION LITERACY INSTRUCTION

The following is a selected list of items that I personally found useful as I explored the topics addressed in this book. I have also included some of my previous works in which I began to explore the ideas being presented here. Each entry contains a brief annotation to help you understand why I chose each of the items I included. The list is in no way to be considered comprehensive. The literature on these topics is enormous, and new material is being produced and published every day. So start with these items, but keep an eye out for even more inspiring information that will help you continue to develop yourself as an instruction librarian.

GETTING STARTED

Teaching and Learning

Bain, Ken. 2004. *What the Best College Teachers Do*. Cambridge, MA: Harvard University Press.

   Bain provides an interesting snapshot of how effective teachers put theory into practice. The book includes many great examples of learner-centered teaching in action.

Bransford, John D., Ann L. Brown, Rodney R. Cocking, and National Research Council, eds. 2000. *How People Learn: Brain, Mind, Experience and School*. Washington, DC: National Academy Press.

   These authors provide a summary of the research on learning and behavior that is both comprehensive and accessible. This work will allow you to get a lot of background information quickly and easily. It provides research-validated support for active learning and learner-centered teaching approaches, and can help you make a case for this type of teaching to the stakeholders in your environment.

Cruickshank, Donald R., Deborah Bainer Jenkins, and Kim K. Metcalf. 2009. *The Act of Teaching*. 5th ed. Boston: McGraw-Hill.

   This is an excellent basic textbook containing discussions of various types of teaching methods as well as chapters on assessment, diversity, planning, and the psychology of learning. The authors offer practical advice about all aspects of teaching and present their ideas in a clear and understandable format.

Eggen, Paul, and Don Kauchak. 2010. *Educational Psychology: Windows on Classrooms*. Upper Saddle River, NJ: Merrill.

   Refer to this 2010 textbook for an overview of psychological and educational theories in teaching and learning. This book provides an excellent review of the theories that support effective teaching practices.

Elliott, Stephen N., Thomas R. Kratochwill, Joan Littlefield Cook, and John F. Travers. 2000. *Educational Psychology: Effective Teaching, Effective Learning*. 3rd ed. Boston: McGraw-Hill.

   This textbook offers a thorough overview of teaching and learning research and practice. Read this book to find out more about the theory behind the practice, and how to apply that theory to your own teaching.

Freiberg, H. Jerome, and Amy Driscoll. 2005. *Universal Teaching Strategies*. Boston: Allyn & Bacon.

  The advantages and drawbacks of many different teaching techniques are described in this excellent textbook. Written in a clear and accessible way, this book can introduce you to a variety of teaching ideas that can help you design more effective and engaging information literacy instruction.

Palmer, Parker. 1998. *The Courage to Teach: Exploring the Inner Landscape of a Teacher's Life*. San Francisco: Jossey-Bass.

  A classic in the field of teaching, this book can help you remember why you wanted to be a teacher in the first place. It is a must-read for the beginning teacher, and a good refresher for those who have been at it for a while and are suffering the beginnings of burnout.

Slavin, Robert E. 2011. *Educational Psychology: Theory into Practice*. 10th ed. Upper Saddle River, NJ: Prentice Hall.

  An excellent textbook that provides a good overview of the theories associated with the psychology of learning. Slavin not only reviews the theories, but also goes on to show how these theoretical constructs can be put into practice.

Vella, Jane. 2004. *Learning to Listen, Learning to Teach*. 2nd ed. San Francisco: Jossey-Bass.

  How much do you actually listen to your learners? In this book, Vella promotes the idea that active listening, both prior to and during instruction, is vital to providing effective instruction.

Learner-Centered Teaching

American Psychological Association Work Group of the Board of Educational Affairs. 1997. *Learner-Centered Psychological Principles: A Framework for School Reform and Redesign*. Washington, DC: American Psychological Association.

  This is the American Psychological Association's (APA) foundational document that integrated research and theory on teaching and learning from a variety of fields. APA's goal for this work was to define learner-centered teaching from a research-validated perspective.

Kaplowitz, Joan R. 2012. *Transforming Information Literacy Instruction Using Learner-Centered Teaching*. New York: Neal-Schuman.

  This book offers suggestions on how to apply learner-centered teaching principles to information literacy instruction. The author also discusses how to use these ideas in all delivery formats—face-to-face, online, and blended.

King, Alison. 1993. "From Sage on the Stage to Guide on the Side." *College Teaching* 41 (1): 30–35.

  Are you curious about where this idea came from? Read this article to find out more about the thinking behind this popular expression.

McCombs, Barbara. L., and Lynda Miller. 2003. "Defining Tools for Teacher Reflection: The Assessment of Learner-Centered Practices (ALCP)." Paper presented at the Annual Meeting of the American Educational Research Association, Chicago, April 21–25. ERIC (Education Resources Information Center).

  In this book, Dr. McCombs offers ways for you to reflect on and monitor your teaching practice. You can use the various checklists she provides to gauge how learner centered your teaching practices are and discover ways to increase the learner-centered aspects of your instruction.

——. 2007. *Learner-Centered Classroom Practices and Assessments: Maximizing Student Motivation, Learning, and Achievement*. Thousand Oaks, CA: Corwin.

  Coauthored by the former president of the American Psychological Association who helped create the 1997 "Learner-Centered Teaching Principles," this work offers practical advice about putting those principles into practice.

Weimer, Mary Ellen. 2002. *Learner-Centered Teaching: Five Key Changes to Practice*. San Francisco: Jossey-Bass.

  This book offers a detailed exploration of Weimer's views and is the basis for the 2003 article. It includes many practical suggestions about how to apply learner-centered teaching ideas to your own practice.

——. 2003. "Focus on Learning, Transform Teaching." *Change* 35 (5): 49–54.

  If you were only going to read one thing on this topic, this would be the article. Reading this article inspired me to rethink my own teaching practice.

Online Teaching

Association of College and Research Libraries. Instruction Section. 2013. "PRIMO: Peer-Reviewed Instructional Materials Online." American Library Association. http://www.ala.org/acrl/aboutacrl/directoryofleadership/sections/is/iswebsite/projpubs/primo

> This is an excellent source for quality online information literacy instruction materials that can be incorporated into your own instruction. Items may be used as independent, stand-alone tutorials or as supplementary material for your courses and classes.

Ko, Susan, and Steve Rossen. 2010. *Teaching Online: A Practical Guide*. 3rd ed. New York: Routledge.

> Now in its third edition, this book is viewed by many as the premier resource about online instruction, and is full of practical advice for developing online courses. Although meant for those teaching full-length courses, many of the tips and examples can be used in the stand-alone and/or one-shot types of instruction as well.

Palloff, Rena M., and Keith Pratt. 2007. *Building Online Learning Communities: Effective Strategies for the Virtual Classroom*. 2nd ed. San Francisco: Jossey-Bass.

> This book is another must-read for those interested in developing effective and engaging online instruction. The authors take a very learner-centered approach, and provide tips and advice that can be applied to all types of teaching endeavors—full-length courses and one-shots as well.

NOTE: You can also find useful videos and other online teaching resources by searching information literacy instruction on YouTube.

Information Literacy Instruction

Association of College and Research Libraries. 2006. "Information Literacy Competency Standards for Higher Education." American Library Association. http://www.ala.org/acrl/standards/informationliteracycompetency

> Another foundational document on information literacy, the *Standards* not only offer useful definitions and background information, they include performance indicators and outcomes for each specific standard. Under review in 2012–2013, this document may soon be updated and revised to better reflect current views on information literacy.

ALA Presidential Committee on Information Literacy. 1989. *Final Report*. Chicago: American Library Association.

> Check out this foundational document in which the American Library Association defined "information literacy" for the first time. This is still the most referred to definition of the term in use today.

Curzon, Susan, and Lynn Lampert, eds. 2007. *Proven Strategies for Building an Information Literacy Program*. New York: Neal-Schuman.

> This work covers all aspects of information literacy instruction from planning to assessment. While most of the book is aimed at the academic library environment, the book also provides chapters on the public and school library setting.

Grassian, Esther, and Joan Kaplowitz. 2009. *Information Literacy Instruction: Theory and Practice*. 2nd ed. New York: Neal-Schuman.

> This expanded and updated second edition provides a comprehensive introduction to information literacy instruction, and includes discussions of the history of the field, the theory behind the practice, as well as all aspects of instruction such as planning, active learning, diversity, learner-centered teaching, assessment, and incorporating technology into your practice.

Veldof, Jerilyn. 2006. *Creating the One-Shot Library Workshop: A Step-by-Step Guide*. Chicago: American Library Association.

> Using a workbook-type approach, Veldof guides you through a systematic approach to planning and implementing one-shop workshops. This is a very well-organized and easy-to-read work that can help any librarian design his or her information literacy instruction one-shots in all library settings—academic, public, school, and special.

Instructional Design

Morrison, Gary R., Steven M. Ross, Howard K. Kalman, and Jerrold E. Kemp. 2011. *Designing Effective Instruction*. 6th ed. Hoboken, NJ: Wiley.

   Viewed by many as the definitive textbook in the field of instructional design, this sixth edition covers all aspects of the field—both theoretical and practical. It is a must for every instructional designer's personal library.

Reiser, Robert A., and John V. Dempsey, eds. 2012. *Trends and Issues in Instructional Design and Technology*. 3rd ed. Boston: Pearson.

   Reiser and Dempsey have gathered together an impressive array of ID experts to discuss the state of the field. Covering both the history of the ID and the current state of the art, this is also a must-read for the instructional designer.

Spector, J. Michael, M. David Merrill, Jan Elen, and M. J. Bishop, eds. 2013. *Handbook of Research on Educational Communications and Technology*. 4th ed. New York: Springer.

   This work, now in its fourth edition, provides information on cutting edge research in the areas of educational technology and instructional design. Topics covered include instructional strategies, assessment, methodology, instruction design models, implementation, and instructional technology. Contributors offer an international perspective on issues in the field of educational communication and technology.

Instructional Design for Information Literacy Instruction

Bell, Stephen, and John D. Shank. 2007. *Academic Librarianship by Design*. Chicago: American Library Association.

   Noted for their advocacy for the blended librarian approach that combines expertise in teaching, instructional design, and instructional technology, Bell and Shank offer some clear suggestions about how to apply the principles of these three fields to your information literacy instruction planning and design process.

Booth, Char. 2011. *Reflective Teaching, Effective Learning: Instructional Literacy for Library Educators*. Chicago: American Library Association.

   Booth provides an excellent overview of the principles of effective teaching and offers a step-by-step approach to designing learner-centered information literacy instruction. This is a useful book for librarians working in all library settings—academic, public, school, and special.

Cottam, Keith M. and Connie V. Dowell. 1981. "A Conceptual Planning Method for Developing Bibliographic Instruction Programs." *Journal of Academic Librarianship* 7 (4): 22–28.

   This is one of the earliest discussions of the importance of systematic instructional design for information literacy instruction. While the authors refer to standard instructional design practices and do not present a new approach, it is interesting to note that the need for more thoughtful planning and instructional design for information literacy instruction was recognized over thirty years ago when teaching in the library field was still referred to as bibliographic instruction.

Farmer, Lesley S. J. 2011. *Instructional Design for Librarians and Information Professionals*. New York: Neal-Schuman.

   Farmer provides a comprehensive, practical guide to systematic instructional design, and shows how to apply the basic concepts and principles of that field to information literacy instruction. Includes lots of practical suggestions that can be applied to a broad range of situations, and that are applicable for both youth and adult learners. As such, it should appeal to librarians teaching in all types of library settings—academic, public, school, and special. The author also addresses both synchronous and asynchronous online instruction as well as teaching in the face-to-face environment.

Miller, Marian I., and Barry D. Bratton. 1988. "Instructional Design: Increasing the Effectiveness of Bibliographic Instruction." *College and Research Libraries* 49 (6): 545–49.

   These authors built on Cottam and Dowell's 1981 article to promote the use of instructional design methodologies to information literacy librarians. Their article provides an excellent review of the field, as well as a discussion of instructional design's relevance for instruction librarians.

USING THE TEACHING TRIPOD APPROACH

Outcomes

Anderson, Lorin W., and David R. Krathwohl. 2001. *A Taxonomy of Learning, Teaching and Assessing: A Revision of Bloom's Educational Objectives*. Boston: Allyn & Bacon.

> This updated version of Bloom's classic *Taxonomy of Educational Objectives* was intended to reflect more up-to-date views on instruction, and adds the idea of information creation to Bloom's original comprehension levels. As with the foundational work, the taxonomy not only describes the various levels, it also offers suggestions about terminology to describe objectives for each one.

Arizona State University. Teach Online. N.d. "Objectives Builder." Arizona State University. http://teachonline.asu.edu/objectives-builder/

> New to writing outcomes? Need some help getting started? Try this interactive online tool that leads you through the steps of creating useful learning outcomes. Note that the terminology on this tool uses the word "objectives" rather than outcomes, but the principles for writing both are very similar.

Battersby, Mark, and Learning Outcomes Network. 1999. *So What's a Learning Outcome Anyway?* ERIC Centre for Curriculum, Transfer and Technology. http://files.eric.ed.gov/fulltext/ED430611.pdf

> Battersby provides a great overview of the topic and makes an excellent case for why writing outcomes is crucial to instructional effectiveness. "How to write outcomes" tips are also included.

Bloom, Benjamin Samuel. 1984. *Taxonomy of Educational Objectives*. Boston: Allyn & Bacon.

> This classic document was first published in 1956 and continues to serve as a major resource in the area of educational objectives and outcomes. See also Anderson and Krathwohl's 2001 update to this material.

Mager, Robert Frank. 1997. *Preparing Instructional Outcomes: A Critical Tool in the Development of Effective Instruction*. 3rd ed. Atlanta: Center for Effecive Performance.

> Mager offers a very readable introduction to writing outcomes. He addresses the characteristics of outcomes, how to select appropriate ones for the task you wish to address, and how to write clear, observable, and measurable outcomes that match your instructional goals.

Wiggins, Grant, and Jay McTighe. 2006. *Understanding by Design*. Upper Saddle River, NJ: Prentice Hall.

> Wiggins presents an excellent argument for why you need to include assessment in your instruction as well as descriptions of authentic assessment techniques, and the value of providing feedback to your learners.

Activities

Barkley, Elizabeth F., Patricia Cross, and Claire Howell Major. 2004. *Collaborative Learning Techniques: A Handbook for College Faculty*. San Francisco: Jossey-Bass.

> Barkley and her coauthors offer lots of great suggestions on how to incorporate collaborative learning into your instruction. Although intended for an academic librarian audience, the ideas presented can be used by librarians in any library setting—academic, public, school, and special.

Burkhardt, Joanna M., Mary C. MacDonald, and Andree Rathemacher. 2010. *Teaching Information Literacy: 50 Standards-Based Exercises for College Students*. 2nd ed. Chicago: American Library Association.

> This updated second edition has been expanded to include fifty exercises on typical information literacy instruction topics such as using library catalogs, searching article databases, and locating and evaluating websites. The entry for each exercise includes its goal, a description, and tips on how to conduct it.

Conrad, Rita Marie, and J. Ana Donaldson. 2004. *Engaging the Online Learner*. San Francisco: Jossey-Bass.

> The authors' aim is to create instruction that involves and engages the learner. They offer suggestion about how to adapt face-to-face activities to the online setting, and provide suggestions on how to create activities that encourage individual participation and learner-to-learner collaboration.

Cooper, James L., and Pamela Robinson. 2000. "Getting Started: Informal Small Group Strategies for Large Classes." *New Directions for Teaching and Learning* 81: 17–24.

Do you avoid trying some active learning techniques because you teach in large, auditorium-type settings? These authors urge you to use small-group exercises in your large lecture-hall classes, and offers practical suggestions on how to do so.

Davis, Barbara Gross. 2009. *Tools for Teaching*. 2nd ed. San Francisco: Jossey-Bass.

This revised and updated edition contains hundreds of great ideas for teaching both in the face-to-face and online settings. Contains useful suggestions for librarians in all library settings—academic, public, school, and special.

Marlow, Bruce A., and Marilyn L. Page. 2005. *Creating the Constructivist Classroom*. Thousand Oaks, CA: Corwin.

Marlow and Page describe practical approaches on how to apply constructive psychology principles in the classroom. The ideas presented could be adapted for use in all library settings—academic, public, school, and special.

Sittler, Ryan L., and Douglas Cook. 2009. *The Library Instruction Cookbook*. Chicago: Neal-Schuman.

This collection of activities is suitable for inclusion in all types of information literacy instruction (one-shots, stand-alone workshops, and full-term courses). Information about each activity includes how it relates to specific ACRL Information Literacy Competency Standards for Higher Education, preparation steps, and any potential drawbacks or pitfalls associated with the technique. Although intended for use in the academic setting, many of the suggestions can be adapted for other library settings as well.

San Jose State University website. Dr. Martin Luther King Jr. Library. "Tools for LibGuides." http://libguides.sjsu.edu/tools

Want to incorporate some interactive online tools into your instruction? Check out the suggestions on this extremely informative web page created by the librarians at San Jose State University. One caveat, however—although the librarians try to keep this page updated and accurate, web resources are not always the most stable. So some of the suggestions may end up being "missing in action." If you hit a dead end, keep looking. You are bound to find something that suits your needs.

Smith, Karl A. 2000. "Going Deeper: Formal Small-Group Learning in Large Classes." *New Directions for Teaching and Learning* 81: 25–46.

Think you can't do small-group activities in a large lecture-hall setting? Think again. Smith offers some interesting suggestions about how to create small-group learning in even the largest of instructional settings.

Assessment

Angelo, Thomas A., and K. Patricia Cross. 1993. *Classroom Assessment Techniques: A Handbook for College Teachers*. The Jossey-Bass Higher and Adult Education Series. 2nd ed. San Francisco: Jossey-Bass.

This book started it all when it comes to classroom assessment techniques. Angelo and Cross offer a comprehensive collection of assessment techniques that can be incorporated into instruction as it happens. Many of the techniques described, such as the one-minute paper and the empty outline, have become instructional classics.

Driscoll, Amy, and Swarup Wood. 2007. *Developing Outcomes-Based Assessment for Learner-Centered Education*. Sterling, VA: Stylus.

This is another great book to help you make sure your outcomes are being assessed appropriately. The authors emphasize the connection between outcomes and assessment, and promote the idea that if you don't assess your outcomes, you have no way of telling if your instruction was useful to your learners.

Huba, Mary E., and Jann E. Freed. 2000. *Learner-Centered Assessment on College Campuses*. Boston: Allyn & Bacon.

Huba and Freed offer a comprehensive collection of assessment techniques that can be incorporated into your instruction. The relationship between outcomes and assessment is also covered. Although this book was intended for the academic librarian audience, the ideas presented can be adapted by librarians working in other library settings as well.

Kirkpatrick, Donald. 2006. *Evaluating Training Programs: The Four Levels.* San Francisco: Berrett-Koehler.

Read this book to find out how you can ensure that the assessment technique you are using is actually providing the data you need in order to determine if your learners have attained the outcomes you have set. Kirkpatrick introduces the idea that there are four levels of assessment (Reaction—Did they like it? Learning—Did they learn it? Behavior—Can they do it? Results—Did it matter?), and encourages the reader to make sure that the assessment used matches the question you wish to have answered about your learners.

Oakleaf, Megan. 2008. "Dangers and Opportunities: A Conceptual Map of Information Literacy Assessment Approaches." *portal: Libraries and the Academy.* 8 (3): 233–53.

Oakleaf's article presents a great discussion of various types of assessment techniques and the advantages and drawbacks associated with each one. The material she provides can help you make informed decisions when you are selecting assessment approaches for your information literacy instruction.

Radcliff, Carolyn J., Mary Lee Jensen, Joseph A. Salem Jr., Kenneth J. Burhanna, and Julie A. Gedeon. 2007. *A Practical Guide to Information Literacy Assessment for Academic Librarians.* Westport, CT: Libraries Unlimited.

This is an excellent and comprehensive collection of various assessment techniques. Each entry includes information on how much of an investment of time and money is required for each type of assessment, as well as potential drawbacks, and the level of expertise needed to use the technique. While this work was primarily written for the academic librarian audience, the ideas presented can be adapted to other library settings as well.

MAKING IT HAPPEN—IMPLEMENTATION AND DELIVERY

Sequencing

Gagne, Robert, Walter Wager, Katharine Golas, and John M. Keller. 2004. *Principles of Instructional Design.* 5th ed. Belmont, CA: Wadsworth/Thomson Learning.

One of the most influential voices in the field of instructional theory, Gagne's nine events of instruction offer a useful way to think about sequencing your teaching activities to create the most effective and engaging instructional endeavor. The ideas presented encourage you to make sure you get your learners to care about what you are teaching, provide ways for them to attain the outcomes you set for the instruction, and check that they are "getting it" throughout the instruction as well as when the instruction has been completed.

Keller, John M. 2010. *Motivational Design for Learning and Performance: The ARCS Model Approach.* New York: Springer.

Keller encourages you to think about capturing and maintaining your learners' attention as part of your instructional design process. The ARCS model (attention, relevance, confidence, satisfaction) is presented as a way to sequence and structure your instruction so that learners are not only attentive to your instruction and motivated to learn, but also leave your sessions with feelings of confidence and satisfaction.

Maier, Mark H., and Ted Panitz. 1996. "End on a High Note: Better Endings for Classes and Courses." *College Teaching* 44 (4): 145–48.

Use the philosophy promoted in this article to ensure that you end your information literacy instruction on a high note. What you do in the last few minutes of your instruction can shape how your learners feel about what they have just learned, about their own abilities, and it may even change their ideas about what libraries and librarians have to offer.

Oswald, Tina A., and Martha Turnage. 2000. "First Five Minutes." *Research Strategies* 17 (3): 347–51.

Most teachers will tell you that you can win or lose your learners based on what you do in the first five minutes of a class. So make sure you start off with some kind of thought-provoking, attention-getting activity that not only engages your learners from the very start, but also sets the tone for your learner-centered approach to teaching.

Ruhl, Kathy L., Charles A. Hughes, and Patrick J. Schloss. 1987. "Using the Pause Procedure to Enhance Lecture Recall." *Teacher Education and Special Education* 10 (1): 14–18.

Don't be put off by the date of this article. The authors offer some interesting suggestions about how to enhance the effectiveness of a lecture segment by strategically inserting simple pauses for reflection into your teaching.

Marketing

Elliott de Saez, Eileen. 2013. *Marketing Concepts for Libraries and Information Services.* 3rd ed. Chicago: American Library Association.

Now in its third edition, this best-selling textbook provides a comprehensive look at marketing concepts and techniques that can help you "sell" your information literacy instruction to your stakeholders and your learners. This updated edition also includes information on topics such as social media, marketing 3.0, interactive marketing, values-driven marketing, holistic marketing, and video marketing.

Grassian, Esther, and Joan Kaplowitz. 2005. *Learning to Lead and Manage Information Literacy Instruction.* New York: Neal-Schuman.

This book covers many topics related to marketing your information literacy instruction to your stakeholders and to your learners as well. The material included is intended to help you understand how to obtain the necessary support for your instructional projects such as institutional culture, how to initiate and manage change, and collaboration and team building. Aspects of marketing, publicity, and promotion are also discussed.

Technology and Accessibility

CAST. 2011. "Universal Design for Learning Guidelines—Version 2.0." National Center on Universal Design for Learning. Accessed May 29. http://www.udlcenter.org/aboutudl/udlguidelines

An excellent discussion of how to create instruction that is accessible to all learners. While its primary focus is teaching with technology, the ideas presented are actually applicable to all forms of instruction.

TLT Group website. Teaching, Learning and Technology. http://www.tltgroup.org/

Dedicated to improving teaching and learning with technology, this group provides support for incorporating technology into instruction without sacrificing best instructional practices. The site includes suggestions about low-cost, low-threshold resources that can easily be incorporated into your own practice even if you have little or no experience in technology or online teaching.

Getting Ready

Devi, Nischala Joy. 2000. *The Healing Path of Yoga.* New York: Three Rivers.

This is a good introduction to the benefits of yoga. It offers insights into relaxation techniques as well as basic yoga postures. Read this book to learn more about how yoga can improve your health and your life.

Iyengar, B. K. S. *Light on Pranayama.* New York: Crossroad, 2003.

Iyengar's book is a very informative work on the various types of yogic breathing techniques. Use these techniques as a way to calm your teaching jitters—both as you get ready to teach and during the actual teaching itself.

Kaplowitz, Joan R. 2012a. "Practically Speaking: Teaching Tips for Information Literacy Instruction." http://joankaplowitz. com/tips/

This web page includes a variety of ideas about how to get both yourself and your materials ready for your instructional endeavors. It includes tips on activities, instructional planning, motivating learners, and many other helpful hints about teaching.

——. 2012b. "Two-Minute Yoga." http://joankaplowitz.com/yoga

The technique is a quick stretching and breathing routine that can be used as a warm-up prior to teaching, and as a stretch break for your learners during long instructional sessions. It provides a simple way for you to deal with those preteaching jitters, and to introduce a different approach to the "midinstruction" break for your learners.

Rama, Swami, Rudolph Ballentine, and Alan Hymes. 2007. *Science of Breath.* Honesdale, PA: Himalayan Institute Press.

The Himalayan Institute's book offers another excellent introduction to yogic breathing techniques. The authors offer some interesting insights into how the body reacts to different types of breathing and shows why breathing techniques help calm both the body and the mind.

Roland, David. 1997. *The Confident Performer.* Sydney, Australia: Currency Press.

Roland helps you understand that being nervous before you teach is a natural part of getting yourself ready. He offers useful suggestions about how to make those jitters work for you rather than against you as a way to improve your presentations.

Smith, Terry. 1991. *Making Successful Presentations: A Self-Teaching Guide.* 2nd ed. New York: Wiley.

Although intended for those making presentations in the business world, Smith provides great advice about how to get both yourself and your materials ready, how to connect with your audience, and how to prepare for and deal with instructional/presentation emergencies. The book includes many useful tips on improving your delivery to increase the effectiveness of your instructional presentations.

Walker, Julian. 2013. *Awakened Heart, Embodied Mind: A Modern Yoga Philosophy Infused with Somatic Psychology & Neuroscience.* Kindle edition. http://www.amazon.com/Awakened-Heart-Embodied-Mind-ebook/dp/B00D1CA8GU/

Julian Walker is a longtime yoga instructor who has developed some interesting and useful approaches to yoga. His website includes short videos on yoga postures, breathing techniques, and the neuroscience and anatomy that support his ideas about how and why yoga can be of benefit to everyone.

Yoga Journal website. http://www.yogajournal.com

One of the major magazines in the field, this publication includes philosophical essays, useful yoga practice techniques, healthy recipes, and lots more. It is a useful resource for finding out what is going on in the yoga community today.

Index

About the Author

Joan R. Kaplowitz began her interest in teaching and learning when she was working toward her doctorate in psychology. It was only natural that when she became a librarian, her specialty would become information literacy instruction. Dr. Kaplowitz's focus on information literacy instruction manifested in a variety of ways—in her day-to day-work as an instruction librarian, her committee work on the local, state, and national level, her many professional presentations, and her research and publications. Dr. Kaplowitz has been passionate about information literacy instruction for her entire career. Although she retired from her librarian position at UCLA in 2007, she has stayed active in the profession through her publications, her professional development workshops for librarians, and by continuing to teach the graduate information literacy instruction course in the Information Studies department at UCLA.

During her years at UCLA, Dr. Kaplowitz taught several sections of UCLA's undergraduate course, "Library and Information Resources," and collaborated with her fellow UCLA librarian, Esther Grassian, to develop the UCLA graduate library program's course, "Information Literacy Instruction: Theory and Technique"—a course that has been part of the program since 1990. Dr. Kaplowitz was also a member of the faculty development team for the Association of College and Research Libraries' Institute for Information Literacy's Immersion Program, and taught in six of the programs between 1999 and 2004. Her many publications include *Transforming Information Literacy Instruction Using Learner-Centered Teaching*, the award-winning *Information Literacy Instruction: Theory and Practice*, (coauthored with Esther Grassian), and the "Information Literacy Instruction" section the *Encyclopedia of Library and Information Science* (also coauthored with Ms. Grassian).